Family in Contemporary Egypt

Family in Contemporary Egypt

Andrea B. Rugh

THE AMERICAN UNIVERSITY IN CAIRO PRESS

First published in Egypt in 1985 by
The American University in Cairo Press
113, Sharia Kasr el Aini
Cairo, Egypt
© Copyright 1984 by Syracuse University Press
Syracuse, New York, 13210, U.S.A.
ISBN 977 424 092 8
Dar el Kutub No. 3053/85

Printed and bound in Egypt
by the Printshop of the American University in Cairo Press

Contents

ANDREA B. RUGH received her Ph.D. from American University. Now an independent researcher and consultant, she has lived and worked in the Middle East for 15 years. She is the author of *Coping with Poverty in a Cairo Community* and of a number of articles on Egyptian family life. She is presently engaged in research on the socialization of children in a Syrian village.

Preface

E VERY BOOK written is inevitably the personal expression of an author who feels both that the topic is significant and that certain insights may develop a deeper understanding of the subject. This book is no exception. Eighteen years of personal involvement with the Middle East, including thirteen years' residence in the area, have led me to a growing uneasiness over our Western myopia regarding Middle Eastern social systems. Our tendency to fit isolated facts into complicated theoretical superstructures and to assume that the emerging implications are as true for Eastern systems as they are for Western ones is dangerous and leads to numerous erroneous conclusions.

One of the fallacies that is at the base of this kind of reasoning is our assumption that all societies fundamentally believe in and derive their social behaviors as we do from a deep-seated faith in the individual and individualism. This is such a natural belief to Americans that they find it difficult to conceive of another world view that places corporateness of certain kinds ahead of individual interests and rights. This book is intended to challenge that view, to force us to face indigenous rationales, and to examine the implications of a social system based on fundamentally different values than our own.

The approach taken is a structural-functionalist one that seeks understanding of social systems through study of their sets of internally consistent social rules and principles. The ultimate test of their utility is how effectively they help a cultural group cope with its particular social and physical environment. The task of this book is to discover these organizing rules and principles and to investigate how they serve the interests of the human beings that manipulate them. Focusing on family is a convenient way of limiting the field of investigation to a unit embodying many of the significant corporate aspects of Egyptian society. In actuality, however, as in most fields of activity, the study tends to spill out into neighboring spheres causing us to reject the image of a closed system. "Family" becomes a field to the extent that it provides the focus of activity where each player brings to the games the rules, conditions, constraints, and skills that are considered appropriate to that context. We are not so much interested here in each person's unique set of these attributes but rather in that shared set which has been commonly assigned the name "culture."

Since 1964 when I received my first taste of life in the Middle East, I have been watching the permutations of family in four countries of the area where I have lived for extended periods of time—Lebanon, Saudi Arabia, Egypt, and Syria. This book is about Egypt not because some of the generalizations do not hold true for other Arab countries. Some do, but many do not. Rather it is because of my personal conviction that anthropology and its common methodological instrument, participant observation, provide more important insights when directed at limited and more confined subject matter. A second reason is that given the state of Western knowledge about the Middle East at the present time, it seems more useful to provide in-depth material that emphasizes the very real areas of uniqueness each Arab country possesses.

Specifically I lived in Egypt during the Nasser period from 1965 to 1966 and during the Sadat period from 1976 to 1981. After 1981 I worked on projects that have brought me to the country every year for periods of weeks or months. Because of these lengthy stays I have been fortunate to have the time to develop personal relationships in a leisurely way so that some of my subjects have become also my acquaintances and friends. As a consequence my use of participant observation has stressed participation as much if not more than observation.

In the late 1970s I was engaged full-time in active research in a low-income community of Cairo—Bulaq. There I was interested in the way families coped with subsistence living, in women's work, in parental strategies for educating their children, in the importance of religious affiliation in daily life, and in the institutions that develop in such communities to relieve the difficulties people encounter. This book is an accumulation and expansion of these lower-class studies some of which have been published in specific detail elsewhere (see Bibliography). In addition I have included cases of rural, middle-class, and occasionally élite families to give a more general picture of contemporary family life in Egypt.

The main focus of this book, however, is on lower and middle-class urbanites and their adjustments to the contemporary conditions of cities.

It seems appropriate to examine these groups for several reasons. In the past few decades Egypt's cities have grown at such a rate that soon urbanites will constitute more than one-half the population. Further, lower- and middle-class populations of cities tend to reflect the contemporary trends of a society as much if not more than other elements. They make up the large majority of urban populations. The lower-class city dwellers have origins that are both rural and urban, providing some insight into the different worlds of countryside and town. And most of the growth in the burgeoning new middle classes — with their "modern" ways of organizing social life — comes from those members of the urban lower classes who are able to move up socially. The lower classes are still at a point where few can afford the middle classes' obligatory extended education, and as a consequence their decisions about how to obtain income and to expend household resources tend to be a sensitive barometer to economic and social changes going on in the society as a whole. The great social cleavage in Egypt in terms of style of life, expectations, and opportunities comes between the lower and middle urban classes. As a result it seems reasonable to focus the study of contemporary family in these two social groups.

Despite the emphasis on contemporary family patterns, this study is concerned less with radical forms of change and more with the factors that have permitted a particular concept of family to emerge and remain stable over so long a period. It differentiates between superficial behaviors of adjustment that come and go over short periods of time and simultaneously in different contexts and structural principles that provide long-term stability for cultural patterns. The study does not describe the "demise" or the "resurgence" of family patterns because social change is not a linear process with a directional flow that can be discerned. Rather this is a study of the surface rearrangements of behavior in response to new contingencies across time and sometimes across social space. Once a society, or a sub-group of a society, develops a wholeness or completeness in its conceptual frame, when the contradictions inherent in the human condition are resolved by accepted modes of expression, it becomes difficult for a society to make any major changes unless forced to do so by some radical interference. Even then, traces of that early coherence and its embracing value structures come back to haunt the development of new organizational structures.

I would like to thank the many friends and colleagues, too numerous to mention individually, who encouraged and supported me in the research and writing of this and other studies on Egypt. In particular I gratefully acknowledge the scholarly integrity and thoughtful insights of Dr. Geoffrey Burkhart. His comments invariably reverberated in my mind until months or even years later they emerged to clarify some problem.

I want to thank too the administrators and staff of the Bulaq Center who graciously suffered my presence over a five-year period. I hope they have felt compensated in some small way by the aid I gave in later years setting up a self-help project for women. Without the willing cooperation and generosity of the women of Bulaq the study would, of course, not have been possible. I have grown to appreciate the range of qualities these women possess—their ready generosity to me and their neighbors, their rough, rollicking humor, their crafty maneuvering and prevarication to extract the ultimate benefit from a situation, their genuine dignity—even nobility at times—and in particular their articulate manner of speech filled with extravagant phrases and apt similes. Dealing with them has always been a battle of wits—but usually a pleasant one. Now I would like to turn their phrases back on them to wish them a long life, to hope that God will never desert them and to wish that they and their children and children's children will see only good coming to them.

I reserve my very special thanks for Madame Ansaf Aziz who plays such a major role in these pages. There is no way to express adequately what it means to a researcher to find someone whose talents are such that entry into a community of study is made easy and untraumatic. Mme. Ansaf is such a person, with her fund of knowledge about the community, her well-established relationships among the members, and her keen sensitivity to the many facets of meaning. In personal terms, she opened her life to me and shared her family with me; we consoled each other in difficult times and celebrated the good times together. There has been nothing but the deepest warmth in our relationship despite the great demands I made on her working and her leisure hours. I can only thank her from the bottom of my heart and state quite honestly that without her full and enthusiastic support this study would never have been possible.

Thanks also are due to the middle-class families who just as generously opened their homes and their lives to me. As with the lower class *baladi* families, I have tried to honor their trust in me by protecting their privacy with fictitious names and sometimes superficial alteration of the details of their cases.

I cannot forget my own family who, like most of the families in this book, rallied around to support my needs when it was most important: William as discussant and main critical advisor, Doug as main typist, David and Nicholas for their forbearance, Harriette Rugh for the many large and small tasks she has relieved me of (making her in the terms of this book the most uncharacteristic of mothers-in-law), and Richard S. Bear, my father, who perhaps more than anyone has inspired me, by his own example, to persevere to the completion of this book.

Is it possible also to acknowledge the gratitude felt for a country that has many lessons for the receptive foreigner to learn? Outings in the streets of Egypt bring one as close to the elemental human condition as is possible anywhere in the world — an exposure to joy, sorrow, birth, death, pathos, insensitivity, directness, deceptiveness, frustration, and humaneness, all laid out in sharper detail than is usually the case. Not content just to experience deep emotions, Egyptians accompany them with critical and often highly sophisticated commentary. Egypt and the Egyptians cannot tolerate the passive or neutral bystander. Willy-nilly he or she is forced into the role of critic, lover, interpreter, or recipient of what Egypt offers in the ways of human intercourse. As a researcher and as a person I have learned much from this close association.

There is much that is instructive to any Westerner in an understanding of Egyptian culture. Although this culture is quite different from our own we see played out with systemic consistency some of our most cherished desires: closeness, group support, maternal nurturing and warmth, the safety of respected paternal authorities, the family haven that acts as reliable safety net in time of need. In our Western rush to individualization and separation, to equity and equality, many of the opportunities to indulge such basic human needs are lost and in many cases regretted. In the Egyptian family we see an institution based on a culture's desire for corporateness — to belong inextricably to a caring group — and we learn the implications of carrying out the associated values of corporateness in a way that gives a measure of consistency to the social life of a people.

Family in Contemporary Egypt

1

Influences

"Eat what pleases you; wear what pleases other people"
— Arab proverb

"FAMILY" is a concept that has held a special place in Egyptian hearts from the beginnings of recorded history to the present. It is as evident in the Pharaonic tomb painting of a smiling wife standing with hand laid gently on a husband's shoulder as it is in a speech by a modern Egyptian leader proudly calling himself the head of the Egyptian family.[1] To what does Egypt owe this long-term persistence and stability concerning the value of family, this glorification of an institution that goes far beyond what is necessitated by the natural biological needs of parents and children?

THE LAND

One feature of the Egyptian experience given credit for its formative effect on local social patterns is the long-term involvement of Egyptians with the land. Of Egypt's total land area of 386,000 square miles, only 10 percent is arable. Ninety-six percent of the population live on this narrowly defined strip of green close to the Nile and to its branches that fan out in lotus fashion through the Delta. The key formative factors in Egypt's agricultural setting are the clearly bounded fertile lands that, because they are difficult to expand, create a limited resource, a need for an unrestricted water source in a rain-scarce country, and the vulnerability of life tied to

1

land which can neither be easily defended nor easily abandoned for other options. Given these conditions, society tends to thrive on the cooperative efforts of small groups with relatively clearly defined rights, ones that mobilize quickly and appropriately to the scale required by the problem at hand.

Whatever the specific effects of the unique set of geographical and climatic conditions on Egyptian institutions and social personality, it is apparent that a fairly homogeneous economy exploited in stable ways has existed for an extremely long period in Egyptian history. The length of time in itself has provided every opportunity for the rough edges of social institutions—in particular, those directly concerned with exploitation of natural resources—to wear into a smoothly functioning relationship.

Several characteristics of the Egyptian family are directly compatible with an agricultural existence: well-defined and elaborated inheritance codes by which property and usufruct rights are passed to succeeding generations; small compact family work units and efficient sex-segregated work arrangements; sanctions and values which protect the membership of work groups from loss by marriage; naturally segmenting kinship units that divide in accordance with different degrees of commitment people feel to one another and whose extent of effective mobilization is pragmatically limited by physical distance. Although it is not possible to claim that these patterns emerged as a requirement of their environment only, it seems clear that they would not have survived if they had not helped local populations cope in some real way with the natural conditions of their environments.

One specific example—the important activity of present-day water distribution—may make the relationship between environment and family structure come clearer. Few Egyptian farmers have unrestricted access to water resources. If their lands are directly adjacent to the Nile they need mechanical means, often of draconian strength, to overcome the height of the silt-laden banks. Farmers who take water from small feeder canals also require lift mechanisms or must await their turn in a gravity-fed rotational system. They depend on others to keep the canals clean and flowing rapidly enough to deliver sufficient amounts of water to their lands. Those farthest away often rely on private pumps (for which they pay fees) to bring water with enough force to their more marginal fields. At the local level farmers find that certain kinds of national and regional control of water resources—such as the amount of water released from the Aswan Dam, the quantity permitted to flow over individual barrages, and the scheduling of rotational systems—tend to be a relatively fixed input that local residents can do little to affect. Expandability and exploitability of

The closeness of family bonds in Egypt was forged in agricultural settings like the one this rural family occupies.

water resources at the field level can only be affected positively by the co-operative efforts of small groups. Because of the way that the Egyptian inheritance system breaks down parcels of land for distribution in set ratios to kin, farmers with adjacent pieces of land (and therefore common interests in water distribution) tend to be related. As a result they become, as kin groups, the natural units to keep canals clear, to cooperate in amassing capital for mechanical improvements, and in other ways to improve the efficiency of the local distribution systems. On the one hand, irrigation needs require cooperative efforts on the part of those using the resources; on the other, they provide fertile ground for contention when people feel their vital interests are at stake. Both cases support the organization of small local groups with ties of commitment usually more than those of friendship. Kin are normally the most stable of these groupings with potential to mobilize for the requirements of the moment.

Egypt is by no means just a peasant culture, even though some kind of connection to agriculture, however tenuous, may historically have drawn the single unifying thread through a number of subpopulations in oases, urban areas, Upper and Lower Egypt, fishing communities, and semi-nomadic groups. But ever-increasing numbers of people are losing their close intimacy with the agricultural environment — an environment in which many indigenous social values developed over the centuries. Now even the élite landlords who used to spend a large part of the year residing on their country estates have shuttered their large houses and moved to the cities, bringing with them many of the classes of people who provided them with services. Coupled with others who perceive better work possibilities in cities, who are attracted by educational opportunities or see brighter vistas as a result of military service outside the village, they make up a mass exodus from countryside to town. Only now in the 1980s are there signs that the vast tide is abating as a result of scarce urban housing and improved educational and employment opportunities in smaller towns of the countryside.

Urban life has in recent decades become the model of the good life, and urban occupations, bureaucracies, and businesses have become the desired ends of the thousands who endure long years in the educational system. The common impression of city people (and even of many rural people) is of a rural social life that is "backward," "uncivilized," and dominated by an atmosphere of ignorance, filth, and disease. Despite their growing suspicions of one another, however, the majority of urban and rural Egyptians still share a common cultural base of understandings that provides them with a world view more similar than they would probably care to admit.

INTERLOPERS

In Egypt forces and events that might have weakened family institutions in another society where bonds were more fragile are commonly cited as contributing to the strengthening of those institutions. For example, Egypt's unique geographical position at the juncture of Africa and Asia with easy access by land and sea has brought the disruptive forces of numerous foreign occupations with their challenging modes of social organization. Social commentators[2] attribute the success of Egyptian resistance to foreign cultural traditions to a tendency toward accommodation that, rather than permitting the easy transfer of values, allows public conformity at superficial levels while strong private values are kept intact. Even when new value structures take hold in Egyptian society, people recast them to their own notion of what is right. Because they never wholly sever their relations with previous periods, the society evolves slowly and incompletely.[3]

Successive waves of foreign interlopers have left a firmly implanted mark on cities and towns if not always on rural communities. The most devastating impact in social terms on local institutions came with the successful Islamic invasion mounted in A.D. 640 and consolidated by A.D. 642. From that time and for many centuries, except for brief periods, Egypt was ruled from bases of power outside its boundaries — Baghdad, Damascus, and Constantinople.

For most of the period from 1517 until 1798, when Napoleon's forces invaded the country, Egypt was considered a province of the Ottoman Empire. The Ottoman system of rule divided Egypt into twelve provinces, each ruled by a Mamluk bey recruited from slaves converted to Islam. Collectively these beys emerged as the effective authorities rather than the rapid succession of foreign Turkish pashas imposed from the outside. The major towns of the provinces were controlled by deputies of the Mamluks whose main functions were to collect taxes, keep peasants productive, maintain order, and provide military recruits for campaigns. They were not concerned with transforming the social order or imposing the Turkish language on the indigenous people. Though the Ottomans were aliens, there was a coincidence of family patterns between Ottoman rulers and Egyptians as well as similar modes of subsistence in peasant-based economies that left each basically sympathetic to the world view of the other.

Private life was a sphere in which the rulers were not inclined to interfere during the Ottoman period. Both ruler and ruled adhered to the same Islamic faith that supported distinct domains of private and public life. So strong was this conviction that a policy of non-interference was extended to cover the private lives of non-Muslims. One can argue that this permissiveness in private matters eased the administrators' duties. To keep the peasants tied to the land, engaged in family activities, and left as undisturbed as possible was also to keep them engaged in the productive activities the rulers depended on for accumulating wealth.

Much the same pattern continued throughout the Ottoman period. The French also, later and for different reasons, showed themselves tolerant of the practices of Islam and went out of their way to see that no obstruction to the religious practices of the local people would come about as a result of their administration.

From the French invasion to the present is generally considered the modern era in Egyptian history — that is, from about the beginning of the nineteenth century. The period is primarily dominated by British occupation, with brief bright moments when the revival of national spirit brought an intellectual and political renaissance to the aspirations of Egyptians: Muhammad Ali's enlightened rule and his defiance of the *Sublime Porte*;

the nationalist movements of the 1920s and 30s; and finally the Revolution of 1952 which drove out the last remnants of the British army and eventually brought Gamal Abdul Nasser to power. In September of 1970 Nasser died, and was succeeded by the then vice-president, Anwar al-Sadat, who in turn was succeeded by Hosni Mubarak after Sadat's assassination in October of 1981. The events of this book take place primarily in the last half of the Sadat years and the early years of the Mubarak period. What has been significant in Egyptian history is the constant barrage of outside influences the country has sustained, not just from a single source. Typical of Egypt is the persistence with which its people have retained a characteristic social and cultural life that is peculiarly Egyptian. Egyptians have learned to choose selectively or ignore what does not fit well with their own view of the world.

RELIGION

Religions have been particularly significant in shaping the character of Egyptian social life. They have not only provided the skeletal frame for how that life should be carried out but have also provided the moral authority that helps give patterns of behavior such persistence. Christianity was clearly the model used by Egyptians in the early centuries after Christ. A foreign-derived but quickly accepted system of religious belief, Christianity met the indigenous need for a rallying force, owing much of its early strength to its opposition to alien Roman rulers in the port city of Alexandria. Its weakness as a philosophical and political system, however, did not appear clearly until brought into direct confrontation with the hard-nosed practicality of Islam. While Christians were lost in internal debates over esoteric issues, Islam appeared upon the scene with a compellingly simple formula for daily life built upon a system of legal principles that gave the pattern force. It is estimated that the Christian population at the time of the Islamic invasion in A.D. 640 may have been as high as 90 percent (Wakin 1963). Official estimates from the census of 1976 place the present population of Christians in Egypt at 6.3 percent.[4]

It is not completely clear how the Islamicization of Christian Egypt came about. There is no doubt that the payment of tribute provided an economic incentive for tolerated subject peoples such as Jews and Christians to turn to Islam. Those who willingly converted were relieved of their extra tax burden and were accepted, according to reports, with great tolerance into the mainstream Islamic community. In remote southern regions people held out longer. Today in the middle regions of Upper Egypt near Assiut, Minya, and Sohag large numbers of Christians still survive.

One might suspect the superficiality of conversions were it not for evidence that profound and fundamental changes occurred with the advent of Islam. One compelling piece of evidence is the rapidity with which the Arabic language replaced Coptic as the language of the ordinary population, so that by A.D. 706 Arabic was established as the language of official transaction, and somewhere between the tenth and the seventeenth centuries — authorities disagree[5] — Arabic became the dominant language of the country.

Nubia, in southern Egypt, provides a good example of the significant changes that can come about in family patterns as a result of the adoption of Islam. Nubia came late to Christianity, converting only in the sixth century when the Empress Theodora of Constantinople sent missionaries to convert local leaders. The Nubians remained staunchly Christian for at least seven centuries thereafter, even long after the Muslim ruler Abdullah ibn Sad conquered Nubia in the seventh century. He demanded that an annual tribute of 350 slaves be sent to Cairo. Upon being effectively cut off from their kin, these slaves presumably found it advantageous to become Muslims. In Nubia, a strong incentive to conversion was to avoid the impress of children into the slave trade. Muslims were forbidden from exacting slave tribute from fellow Muslims (Fernea 1973: 9).

Intermarriage was perhaps the most successful means of conversion in Nubia. Invading Arab tribes intermarried with members of the Nubian Kenuz tribes, leaving with them a patrilineal segmentary kinship system similar to nomadic groups elsewhere but quite unlike the more bilaterally organized kinship structure, with rights accruing from both maternal and paternal relatives, that is characteristic of the main body of Nubians, the Fedija. Nubians also customarily consolidated ties with powerful surrounding tribes by offering their sisters to chieftains who were generally Muslim. The children of these marriages not only became Muslim by the Islamic custom that children follow the religion of their father, but the Nubians also effectively gave up their property rights which at the time passed from sister's brother to sister's son (Fernea 1973: 9, 20).

Nubian social customs played a large part in their vulnerability to the encroachment of Muslim groups. But at the same time credit must be given to the pragmatic and ingenious nature of Islamic practices that close the Muslim community to the outside marriage of their own women while encouraging the assimilation of outsiders to the Islamic community.

Scholars may argue about the pervasiveness of the social revolution brought about by Islam, some calling it an incomplete overlay to already existing patterns, and others seeing it as compatible with, and therefore not requiring serious restructuring of, prevailing patterns. It is well known that in Egyptian villages today a number of pre-Islamic, even pre-Christian, beliefs and practices flourish in funeral ceremonies, spirit beliefs, superstitions, and myths. It is probably accurate to conclude that in the interstices of the skeletal framework Islam provides there is room for local customs to coexist.

LAW

What probably induced changes in family patterns most directly for the new converts to Islam was the eventual emergence and institutionalization of a full set of laws governing family life. After the Islamic invasion in the seventh century there was a period of time when adherence to Islam meant mainly acceptance of principles of proper behavior laid down and exemplified by the behavior of the Prophet Muhammad. Guidance was provided on all matter of activity, including rules about honesty in business, courtesy, generosity, harboring strangers, the protection and behavior of women, the responsibilities of household members to each other, the legal division of property, contractual arrangements of marriage and divorce, general rules of conduct that should pertain between respectable members of society, and the modes of political rule that were deemed most suitable.

During the first four centuries of Islam, a more strictly defined set of laws emerged, as did a religious court system that provided more systematic ways of enforcing laws. Later, during the Ottoman Empire, a more comprehensive codification took place that diverged considerably from the original form.

Al-sharia ("the clear straight path"), a term typically but not always accurately used to refer to Islamic law,[6] forms the basis upon which appropriate behavior is molded and, in serious cases of violation, prosecuted. Islamic law is made up of several components. The first is *al-nass,* the text, which includes the Koran, the words of God revealed to the Prophet, and *al-sunna,* the Tradition of the Prophet (his reported sayings and actions). They are permanent and cannot be changed, with the exception of certain provisions on mundane problems that arose during the life of the Prophet that can be modified if circumstances change.

During the period when Ottoman rule prevailed, one means of exerting administrative control over the populace was through a system of *millets* (religious communities) in which the inhabitants were permitted to live as undisturbed as possible as long as they conformed to the administrative and tribute demands of the rulers. The *millets* were organized around religious leaders, who were given the responsibility for representing the communities to the outside world. This system preserved the differences between certain groups by, in many cases, physically segregating them residentially and permitting them to use their own forms of religious law. Vestiges of this system remain in Egypt in the continued use of separate personal-status legal codes in the various religious communities. This system accords with the Islamic stand of viewing law as basically religious and the legal system as one that should be supervised by the designated religious authorities of the community. Until the middle of the nineteenth century a system of religious courts remained, with certain qualifications, the accepted courts of law and Islamic law the written source of reference.

It was therefore a major change in the legal system when authorities formalized aspects of the law that were slowly being encroached upon by secular civil authorities. The early changes represented additions to rather than changes in the formal body of Islamic law. The laws adopted were increasingly of alien origin very different from the religious laws. Muslim rulers themselves began the process of secular encroachment on Islamic law when they set up courts of special jurisdiction presided over by governors, military officers, and other public authorities. It was generally recognized that rulers should be permitted a broad degree of discretionary (if not arbitrary) power in administrating their territories.

The areas of jurisdiction that first felt the impact of the departure from the Islamic law are predictable given the concerns of ruling regimes. Criminal codes were some of the first to change, followed by the development of commercial laws compatible with those that existed in the West. By 1863 a new Ottoman code frankly based on French law was applied in Egypt, and though Egypt became administratively and financially independent of the Ottoman Empire in 1883 it still continued to be tied juridically to the Empire until World War I. Throughout this period it was only in the area of family law that Islamic law was preserved intact.

Similarly under British occupation after 1882 there was little hesitation in altering the legal system to conform more closely to British interests as an occupying power (Hill 1979: 158). But these interests, as under previous regimes, did not generally include the jurisdiction of personal-status family law. The codes of 1883, 1904, and 1937 specifically stated that any laws contained within them not be construed to detract from the personal status rights recognized by Islamic law.

By 1897 a new law of organization and procedure in Islamic law courts, and an amending law in 1910, limited their competence to personal status, family law, gifts and religious endowments. Muslim Egyptians themselves did not press for a return to stricter compliance with the tradition of Islamic law in other areas of jurisdiction either because as liberals they were Western oriented and reform-minded or because as religiously orthodox or conservative they recognized the importance of keeping the vulnerable parts of Islamic law intact, if not used, rather than cooperate in its dismemberment (Anderson 1968: 220).

The situation at the time can be summed up by noting the increasingly clear-cut dichotomy in courts and in law. On the one side, new courts, both mixed and national with lawyers trained in modern educational systems, applied a codified law of composite origin in which Western influence dominated. On the other side were Islamic law courts using the *Hanafi* school as a basis of interpretation with legal principles as yet uncodified and applied by judges trained in the traditional way (Anderson 1968: 221). Of lesser importance in terms of magnitude was a third system found in non-Muslim communities also using uncodified laws and administered by religious authorities. A final system was that involved in cases concerning foreigners.

Thus, civil and commercial law, the law by which authorities regulate common public transactions, was conceived through the lens of international standards and given over to secular jurisdictions. Criminal law, too, responding to international pressures was one of the first areas to feel the need for reform. Foreigners were given special status exempting them from the full force of the law. And finally all those aspects coming under the rubric of personal-status or family law, as it was commonly called, remained virtually intact, equated not with secular norms but with religious morality.

Fragmentation of the law accomplished three ends: (1) it separated and defined more distinctly the realms of private and public life; (2) it preserved the boundary between ethnic (religious) communities and between foreigners and native Egyptians by permitting, in the case of the ethnic groups, separate personal-status codes that tend to cover those areas of social life which distinguish communities — marriage, dissolution of marriage, and inheritance; and finally, (3) it provided a stable legal-moral foundation for family institutions that does not encourage profound or rapid transformation.

How did it happen that family law became the sole survivor, in practical terms, of classical Islamic law? It was certainly more than a case of simple disinterest on the part of ruling groups. It is likely that rulers also anticipated the possibility of local resistance to interference in family issues which over the centuries had become firmly fixed as moral issues. It was in their best interests to maintain a stable and productive population. Egyptian family institutions have proved a successful means of accomplishing these ends. Also, in the long period before and during Ottoman rule, Muslim governments controlled Egypt, and thus there was no philosophical disagreement over the patterns of behavior on which family institutions should be based. In large part acceptance of Islamic family institutions and their body of related laws proved the marker of entrance into the Muslim community. For Muslim rulers the numbers of those passing this threshold indicated the extent of their like-minded support.

As long as family law was well regulated and judiciously applied, communities could carry on their daily affairs and even accept the outrages perpetrated in other areas of administrative jurisdiction. For this reason the reforms made in family law were mainly refinements in definitions, clarification in jurisdiction, and development of a more smoothly functioning judicial organization rather than changes in substance within the laws themselves. A strong religious cadre presented problems for secular authorities who moved quickly to contain their power in areas of jurisdiction directly affecting local rule. The struggle was never a serious one; power was always on the side of ruling groups. But in the long run, the distinction between a "secular" law and a "moral" law served to distinguish between a law that could be molded and a law that was virtually untouchable without recasting the moral grounds on which it rested. In such an atmosphere family principles became cast in the permanence of moral concerns, not exactly immutable, but nevertheless requiring a great deal of soul-searching to change.

On all fronts Egypt provided a stable environment in which family institutions could flourish and survive in relatively stable form: as a land with a major single agricultural base that favored family exploitation; as a culture that after the Islamic social revolution adopted foreign traits selectively and incompletely and, finally, as a society with a strong moral base in Islam and family law that foreign occupiers left relatively undisturbed.

2

Urban Contexts

"Happiness is one's fate" — Arab proverb

BULAQ

IN BULAQ, a populous lower-class quarter of Cairo, the tempo of activity picks up gradually in the early hours of the morning. The nighttime quiet of the narrow shuttered alleyways is interrupted first by the stirrings of chickens and goats in pens on balconies and roof tops giving the awakening quarter a sound deceptively similar to a village. Later the noise of horn-blowing, tire-screeching traffic sweeping overhead on elevated causeways or through major arteries at the peripheries of Bulaq penetrates to evaporate the sense of pastoral calm.

Next, semi-domesticated cats and dogs stretch slowly and emerge from favorite resting places in the protective crevices of collapsed buildings and communal entryways. The first human stirring are generally those on the early shifts of factory work — hurrying singly or accompanied sometimes in the case of women as far as the bus stop by a husband or brother. These "professional" women, including also those who go to government offices a little later in the morning, pick their way gingerly over the potholed street insecure in their high-heeled *"moda"* shoes and self-conscious in their tight fitting polyester knit skirts, blouses, or dresses. They cling to these discomforts as visible reminders to the world of their achieved or aspiring membership in the middle-class society. Their recent escape from lower-class households — perhaps not yet complete if they still reside

13

in the homes of illiterate, unskilled worker parents — hangs on the thread of their ability to take advantage of longer educational experience or, through their work, to afford the accoutrements of middle-class life. Their self-consciousness in the new role is evidenced in a slightly too long or too short dress, the "wrong" arrangement of color and styles, or some form of modern headgear that chastely conceals the hair so as not to offend the mores of more conservatively dressed neighbors.

Mothers, of the more conventional Bulaq kind, begin the preparation of breakfast for working husbands and children on the early school shift. Pots rattle, kerosene stoves hiss, a shutter clatters open, and finally a quick splash of washing water hits the street below to signal the end of those activities. Small children flutter sleepily through the streets, unkempt cherubs in their floor-length gowns, commissioned to fill their enameled bowls with *foul* beans sold out of great round copper and brass pots that have simmered continuously througout the night. Accidents are common as children teeter home through the uneven dirt streets with the steaming bowls; wails of anticipation of the smacks that await them at home rise in the morning air to produce the first real cacophony of the day.

Men appear sleepily in doorways or lean on broad window sills wearing the familiar striped pajamas of urban leisure wear or rumpled *galabiya* gowns that are reminiscent of the rural areas many have only recently left. The men yawn and stretch out the stiffness of sleep while keeping an eye out for a pretty figure or a glimpse of a quarrel in the homes of neighbors only a few yards away. While they await the ministrations of their wives, the men call out greetings to passersby — *sabah il kheer,* morning of brightness, *sabah il ful,* morning of jasmine, *sabah il ishta,* morning of the thick cream that rises to the top of the milk. As the flowery phrases roll off their tongues, they show pleasure at finding exactly the appropriate one to express the mood of the moment. Jokes and banter, playful insults, signal that daily routine has commenced again after a night's rejuvenation — a toss in the bed with a spouse and a restful sleep. Conversation and human intercourse are life in Bulaq and as such are carried on seriously. Work fades in and out of the day's schedule more as background to the significant effort of keeping up human contacts.

The symphony is gathering now, no longer a soothing Brahms or a tentative Haydn winding up the clockwork spring of action. Now a strident chord jars the calm of the community as one resounding exchange after another draws the attention first here and then there. The coffee houses occupy center stage much of the time. There every greeting produces a brief flourish until the clients settle down and order, usually not coffee but tea. From their vantage point they can watch the altercation of a customer who feels shortchanged in the portion received from a street vendor or observe the exchange between a passerby and a merchant hosing down the dust in front of his shop. Never mind the fact that a thousand feet will stir the dust again almost immediately; he reserves his right to make the street a soggy morass that dirties the shoes and the clothes of the work-going inhabitants. The coffee shops at this time of day attract workers who want a bit of companionship and a last glass of tea before moving on to their jobs. Most are young men dressed in the uniform of their age group; shiny colored polyester-nylon shirts with collars, tight-fitting bell-bottomed pants that drag in the dust when new, obscuring the square high-heeled shoes that make their wearers feel taller and more commanding. As it is for their sisters who are moving upward socially, discomfort is worth the image the clothing presents. They sweat their way on and off crowded buses in all seasons of the year, their fingers tugging and poking at seams that irritate. The young men move off slowly, but they will soon be back to while away their afternoons and evenings in the coffee houses with friends discussing their problems of work, money, trying to find an apartment, and marriage, playing backgammon or dominoes, and watching television. The hard-core customers come a little later in the morning—old men with proud dark robes, high turbans, shawls, and walking sticks. They settle themselves with dignity on chairs along the front of the shop to watch the morning stream of people pass by. Each newcomer is greeted by rising and a vigorous shake of the hand, and then they settle each in his designated spot so that day after day they can be found like images in an art gallery, soothingly and predictably where one expects them to be. Together the old men shift their chairs from place to place—from one side of the street to another to catch the warm rays of sun in winter and the cool shade in summer. The commercial territory of a coffee shop extends as far as customers can shout or a waiter can conveniently carry his small round tray. Standard orders for the tailor, for the ironer, for the shopkeeper down the street periodically set tea-boys running off in different directions.

Next come the hawkers calling out their wares in rhythmic sing-song cadence—the melodies become familiar but the words blur from constant repetition. The men have been up from earliest morning bringing back produce from the wholesale market and other distribution points at the edge of Bulaq. Their wives have scrubbed vegetables, and children have helped load the carts. Some young boys accompany their fathers to weigh out the goods and skillfully wrap them in a scrap of paper or pour the vegetables directly into waiting baskets. There are also gaily colored *kushiri* carts selling rice or noodles with hot sauce. There are peddlers of vegetables, trinkets,

A mobile vendor of *kushiri* (rice, beans, or spaghetti and spicy sauce) caters to the lower classes' need for ready-made foods.

cloth, kerosene, and other goods. Many specialize — this one sells potatoes, this one onions and a few tomatoes, this one mainly cauliflower and a few soup greens. Men and women sitting on the ground behind wholesale boxes sell more expensive items — lemons, oranges, apples, mulberries — hoping to turn a profit quickly and go home.

The clank of rising metal shop doors marks the opening of serious commercial activities in Bulaq. Still maintaining the centuries-old pattern of placing small stores on the ground floor of residential buildings the inhabitants of Bulaq need not go far to buy the limited range of goods they want. The morning opening for business transforms the streets from blank-walled, reasonably spacious thoroughfares to alleyways of open-stalled, commodity-filled caverns, with goods spilling out into the street until it is difficult to miss giving them a quick scrutiny as one passes along. Many shops have as many goods outside as inside the walls. Oases of calm are the shops of shoemakers, pharmacists, tailors, and shirtmakers who chat quietly with customers occupying the extra seats in their shops. If the proprietors are so inclined, their establishments become centers where gossip of the area is exchanged. The "modern" industries — iron works, plumbing shops, machine and motor repair shops — are the most serious in terms of abuse to the senses with their ear-splitting noises and their oil-blackening pollution. Adolescent boys, apprenticed at low wages to learn a trade, their clothes and faces darkened with grease, climb in and out of cars which are in various states of dismemberment, straighten rods with deafening determination, and otherwise run the small errands of the master craftsman.

Lines form outside of bread stores two or three times a day to receive the hot flat *baladi* loaves or thin french loaves that while less nutritious show a more refined taste. The loaves come out of the ovens like tautly inflated balloons, then gasp and expire as they are removed to palm stalk racks to be piled in the arms of waiting customers after they cool a little. Men with full bread racks balanced on their heads careen off on bicycles to distribute more distant orders.

One of the first out in the morning is the "Heidi" of Bulaq, the mentally retarded — "silly" they call him — goat herder, picking up his flock from their respective homes and shepherding them off to graze on the luxuriant garbage heaps of the quarter. People who scavenge bits of paper to sell to shops as wrapping paper or to consume as fuel for baking ovens need to arrive earlier than the flocks at the heaps for when the goats have finished there is little left to recycle. The swarming goats and sheep and their leaping kids add the falsetto accents to the crescendo of morning that is rapidly developing.

The quarter settles down by nine or ten o'clock to the continuous activity of the household brigade. With the exception of the main thoroughfares Bulaq becomes virtually a community of women until two in the afternoon. These women are unlike the straggling workers of the morning. They are dressed conventionally for the quarter in the traditional costumes of their or their antecedents' mainly rural origins: long, full, usually black, yoked overdresses with full sleeves covering printed dresses of much the same type as those from near Cairo or the Northern Delta areas. Their heads are covered with small scarves, often covered again by long yards of the black lightweight *tarha* (veil), wrapped fetchingly around the face and falling down the back. The more conservative *Saidis* of southern (Upper) Egypt are incongruously dressed in a more shape-revealing dress drawn in at the waist and extending only to a little below the knee. Over their heads a heavy, fringed waist-length shawl covers an underscarf, giving them a madonna-like appearance. Most married and elderly women wear black outer garments when moving anywhere outside the vicinity of their thresholds. The streets as a result are landscapes of browns (from the buildings) and blacks (from the women) during the day with only the young girls in their pajama-like pants and thigh-length fitted tunics in bright prints on white backgrounds to enliven the color scheme. Little children too provide fast-moving bright spots in this generally monochromatic scene.

The household brigade is everywhere — women bringing water; women running errands; women baking bread in ovens beneath the stairways; women washing clothes and hanging them from balconies to drip on the passerby below; women preparing vegetables or picking through rice with keen-eyed inspection; women protecting chickens set free from their coops under the bed to scratch for a few minutes of freedom in the street below; women rocking babies and chatting with their neighbors between tasks. They shout across the alley addressing each other in the traditional way: "Um Ibrahim" (mother of the eldest son's name or the name of the current child the neighborhood knows best) or with somewhat more courtesy "Sitt Um Ibrahim" (Mrs. Mother of Ibrahim), or adding more deference and respect to an elderly woman "Khallt Zahiyya" (Aunt Zahiyya using the term that designates mother's sister), or for an unknown person, the complimentary "Ya Haga" (one who has made the pilgrimage). Other women, usually older ones, take up accustomed spots on street corners, sitting cross-legged to sell the products of their morning efforts: stuffed squash and cabbage, aromatic soups, fried fish, or eggplant. The hours pass in this way, shifting from time to time as quarrels break out, as accidents occur, as sewer pipes burst, as a child needs reprimanding. When women hear news of the death of someone, or a birth, or a marriage in trouble they flock to the scene dropping everything to offer condolence, to give help, and to dispense advice.

As the sun creeps higher in the sky the *muezzin* calls the midday prayer, one of the five calls of the day, and mosques fill up with men emerging from workshops, behind counters, and from the ranks of the hard-core coffee shop habituées. Despite their numbers there is no diminution of the bustle outside. The women retire about this time to fill the alleyways with the delicious smells of garlic and frying onions, the poor man's "caviar." Again the errand-running angels emerge with their enamelled bowls bringing back dishes to supplement the family fare or to provide the main dish for families too poor to cook. Their scurryings and the penetrating aromas build anticipation until two or three o'clock when the men return and the family consumes its biggest meal of the day. From then until late afternoon, the pace relaxes as dishes are slowly washed and several of the family members drift off to sleep.

While the adult world runs down, the child's world continues in ever-increasing activity as school children join in the soccer games or general rowdiness of those who stayed at home and now are released from their tasks of the morning. Flocks of young girls take on the more enjoyable task of trailing small sisters and brothers around outside where they do not disturb the naps of their parents. The parents, however, never escape the shouts and bickerings of street games only a few yards from their resting heads on the other side of open windows and not-quite-thick-enough walls.

Natural noise is not enough for the people of Bulaq. They add the raucous sounds of Arabic music courtesy of "transistors" pitched at a level where the surrounding neighborhood can share—no one complains. Blending with these electronic sounds are those of the regular prayer calls, amplified so that there will be no need to miss them. On most days somewhere in the quarter a loudspeaker sets up a continuous chanting of Koranic verses read by a *sheikh* in a colorful tent set up to receive condolences for whomever has passed away the previous day. Life and death coexist as easy partners in the area; death is passed over in much the same way as strangers step carefully over the mourners sitting cross-legged under the tents—with a pause and a word of concern and then on to the next activity. This is not to regard lightly the days of mourning and the rituals of death, but these are repeated so frequently for everyone that their performance becomes mechanical for all those not personally affected. Life can be a living death for some in Bulaq, and people recognize that death for those can be a release that promises much more than life. In practical terms, death brings another topic of conversation to the quarter and an excuse to intensify human contacts.

By late afternoon and evening activity picks up again for the mostly male coffee shop crowd. Women chat quietly in doorways and from the slower pace of their conversations and movements it is clear that the important events of their day are over. They slowly withdraw their children and their attention from the streets to the shuttered interiors of their homes. By ten or eleven the streets are again empty and grown wider as shopkeepers draw in their displays and close up for the night. There are no strict closing or opening hours in Bulaq shops, only general tendencies to open around nine, to close around two for lunch-dinner, to reopen when it gets a bit cooler in late afternoon and to close again in the evening whenever business slows down. There is no sharp distinction between business and leisure in the quarter; shopkeepers take their recreation in between business transactions conversing with customers or friends or joining the adjacent shopkeeper in a cup of tea. When they close down a significant part of the activity of the quarter also closes down. Finally housewives slam shut their wooden shutters after seeing that all the laundry is carefully pulled in from the lines. From the streets only a crack of light here and there indicates that activity still goes on in some of the houses. A person guided by the daytime details of surroundings becomes lost in this fully transformed place and disoriented by the uncharacteristic silence.

Move into one of the buildings that stand wall-to-wall on the narrow streets and you must step down in many places into a cool damp interior. The firmest step is the metal sewer cover that occupies a central place in the downstairs hallway. Centuries of build-up in the earthen streets sinks ground floor dwellings a foot or more below street level making them inconvenient but inevitable collectors for the occasional rainstorm or the more frequent sewage overflow of stopped-up pipes. Raised sewer lids give a small head start on such calamities. Darkness is the first adjustment a visitor accustoms himself to; the smell of poverty is the second — the combination of animal and human urine, the moldiness of damp habitations, the inadequate supply of soap and other cleaning materials to wash away the deeply ingrained dirt from cracked and worn floors and walls, the cooking oil grease that clings to ceilings, and the soot of kerosene lamps and stoves with their own penetrating odors.

The typical house pattern on every floor consists of a hallway with four or more rooms leading off, a stairwell, and usually a small room beneath the stairwell or on the landing with toilet hole and drainage pipe. The ground floor may also have, in addition, if the inhabitants are fortunate, a single water tap and wash basin and in some cases under a stairwell next to the toilet, a baking oven. Floors are of dirt on the ground level and of wood or tile in the upper stories; the walls are of stone in the oldest houses and of plastered over brick or construction block in newer ones. Ceilings normally are constructed of beams covered over with slat filler and then plastered to give a finished appearance. In the older houses these ceiling-floors are the vulnerable part of construction as the beams rot under the onslaught of floor washings or disintegrate from insect damage. Rooftops, once the place for summer sleeping and a storage area for the tenants downstairs, now bear the dilapidated dwellings that represent the last stage in urban crowding, banged-together wooden sheds composed of odd-shaped boards and roofed with corrugated tin roofing or flattened oil cans. The rooftop dwellers have to endure the heat of summer and the long climb of three to five floors, but all things considered they enjoy cleaner air, more open space, and usually an extra place to put their poultry or goats.

Urban people, like those anywhere, find their space constricted in Egyptian cities. What advantages they gain in increased availability of services and entertainment they lose in being reduced to small box-like dwellings. A so-called apartment in Bulaq varies from a single room, with hallway toilet shared with others (for the largest proportion of the poorest population) to, at the other extreme, an apartment of several rooms and private but tiny kitchen and toilet areas. Many dwellings have tiny balconies that serve for storing old household goods or penning poultry or goats and which provide access to laundry lines that hang over the streets or an air shaft. It is characteristic of the lower classes that they utilize each room of their dwelling, as do rural people, for a multitude of purposes. Furniture serves more to distinguish activity areas than does architectural space, though even here the generalization is not completely true; a bed used for sleeping during the night is used for seating guests during the day; a table that defines a cooking area becomes the desk of a schoolchild in late afternoon and evening. Furnishings are spare and functional: a brass or other metal four-poster bed resists the infestation of insects; a *canaba* (bench for sitting) of wooden frame and cushions, serves with the rearrangement of cushions as a bed; these items and a large wooden wardrobe are the standard pieces of every household that has sufficient resources to own furniture. Furniture provides another useful function as a banking device for the family group. The accumulation of extra resources is put into more furniture which can then be sold when need arises. A brisk trade in used furniture goes on in Bulaq and the inventory of any one household is likely to change dramatically to reflect the momentary financial state of the occupants. Only the basic furnishings which a wife brings to marriage remain constant — to sell those would be to sell her own private security.

Housing was not always so cramped in Bulaq. Elderly people remember a time when even the poor resided in more spacious apartments. Now though some are affluent by Bulaq standards, housing shortages have meant that they too live in apartments that have been broken down into a series of smaller dwellings. In most cases, it was children marrying that began the encroachment on their parents' living quarters both because it was desirable to be close to them and because their usual alternative was to seek housing far on the periphery of larger Cairo where commuting to inner-city jobs was difficult. As they accumulate the extra money to move into better neighborhoods, many are still reluctant to leave the neighborhoods where they have established businesses and where their friends and relatives live.

For a time there was a certain elasticity to Bulaq found in this tendency to subdivide apartments, to build in any remaining open areas, and to knock together rooftop shacks. There was a limit, however, to how long this could go on. The low (three-to-five story) physical structures appear deceptively strong, but over the years and at a particularly alarming rate recently buildings have succumbed to the destructive effects of water seepage and rotting timbers. It is a rare building that can support vertical expansion and, of course, there is no longer room for horizontal expansion. Increasing the pressure on the housing market are the landlords who remove apartments from rental consideration when they become free, using them instead for storage areas rather than accept the paltry rents (50 p. to 5 £E) that inflation has reduced to child's pocket money. The bother of collecting the money and dealing with tenants is more trouble than it is worth. (During the late 1970s when most of the data for this study were being collected, the parallel rate of the Egyptian pound stood at 1 £E = $1.40. For convenience this rate has been used throughout. Since that time the value of the pound has dropped against the dollar and rampant inflation, at times as high as 30 percent, has made some of the salaries reported here seem ludicrously low when compared with family needs in the 1980s.)

The effects of housing scarcity, to be discussed more fully in a later chapter, are multifold. For Bulaq, it means that neighborhoods have stabilized and fewer newcomers are encouraged to seek dwellings there unless they already have relatives in the area. Since the newcomers are frequently the poorest of rural farmers, their adjustment to city life — for a long time peripheral at best — increases the shared burden their good-hearted neighbors and relatives are forced to assume. Also housing scarcities force upon people *ad hoc* living arrangements in unusual accomodations — a one-time chicken coop, an opened-out oven, a downstairs hallway open to the view of neighbors climbing the stairs — and with unusual arrangements of people such as a mother-in-law sharing the single room of her married son, or a woman, her mother, and her children seeking the protection of a father-in-law and mother-in-law in a single room when their son deserted her. One other consequence, for better or for worse, is that lower-class families are forced into close contact with one another, enforcing on the one hand their capacity for exerting certain kinds of social control over each other and on the other bringing them to know as neighbors, the "affluent," the self-sufficient, and the abjectly poor, Muslim and Christian, Upper Egyptian and Lower Egyptian, those of rural and those of urban origin. This is a change from earlier periods when Cairo was more strictly segregated along these lines. What the people of Bulaq share as a common denominator is a style of life that varies little except in terms of expenditures for consumer goods, the quality of food, and the elaboration of life-cycle events such as engagements, marriages, circumcisions, births, feast days, and pilgrimages. Basically, however, the essential patterns and expectations remain the same.

Bulaq is doomed now in the 1980s as a neighborhood. The avoided move to the periphery of Cairo has now become a necessity. Bulaq's central location and obvious appearance as an eyesore has attracted the attention of the authorities. For years there were rumors of urban renewal to open the area to commercial and touristic ventures. In 1979 the first families were relocated from a small but notorious section on one edge of Bulaq, Esh il Turgoman, known for drug trafficking and prostitution. Family-oriented residents of Bulaq look with disfavor on the residents of Esh il Turgoman, and were not displeased to find them removed early from the area and their rat-infested shacks and infamous coffee houses torn down. These residents and successive waves of Bulaq residents were moved to new apartment blocks at the far edge of the city in two main locations, Ain Shams and Zowya il Hamra, the first over an hour's commuting distance one way from the central location of Bulaq. There were advantages to the move; though families were given the same basic number of rooms they had left behind, they were also given an additional hallway, small kitchen, and bathroom for their own private use. For those residents who came from spacious older houses this did not mean an actual increase in overall living area, but it did provide a way of distributing the functions carried out in the household. All homes were also equipped with electricity and running water. Though buildings included more stories, adequate space was left between buildings for children to play in light, porous, sandy soils rather than the damp, bacteria collecting clay soils of Bulaq. People complained that the poor construction of the buildings was responsible for the signs of deterioration which appeared shortly after their arrival, they disliked the distance from the central city where some were employed and most still found it necessary to go for some kinds of shopping, and they complained of the destruction of their neighborhood social groupings by the seemingly arbitrary assignment of families to different housing blocks or different areas of the city altogether.

The old area of Bulaq is not representative of all lower-class neighborhoods in Cairo, but it does share a number of characteristics with all others. It typifies more accurately those areas of the city that early on were the centers of small commercial enterprises, that felt the pressures of urbanization and population increases, and that eventually simply as a result of physical limitation reached a level where neighborhoods stabilized and residents grew to know each other over long periods of time. The constant infusions of rural naiveté were replaced by a growing sophistication concerning how to manipulate the possibilities of an urban environment.

SHUBRA

In a typically middle-class area of Cairo like Shubra, a little north of Bulaq, a different tempo and atmosphere exist. The crowds are still ever-present, and activity is continuous and varied, but the tone is different. It is more restrained, less jocular, more monochromatic, and more subdued. Voices are quieter, verbal exchanges less colorful and extravagant, and respectful neutrality the expected mode of human relations. Whereas people in Bulaq often appear defeated by immediate crises they have inadequate resources to overcome, one feels the people of Shubra are defeated by the routine of life—the daily grind of paying bills, keeping things repaired, keeping the children up to standard in behavior, visiting appropriate people at the right occasions, dispensing gifts of suitable value, wearing the right clothes at the right time, surviving the educational system, the transportation, and the bureaucratic structures.

It is the waves of workers—most of them modest government employees—that catch the attention first in the morning, streaming through the streets and massing at intervals like an audience at a colossal traffic accident. In reality, of course, they are massing at bus and trolley stops in numbers that even empty vehicles could not contain. The continuous stream of vehicles, however, comes already packed to overflowing, grudgingly accepts a few more passengers clinging to the outsides, and moves on. While waiting, prospective passengers watch a raceway of honking, screeching cars hurtling toward the inner city. The sight is eventful enough with narrow misses as cars careen past people and bicycles with little room for margin, but the audience stands blank-faced, unimpressed with the carnage that has become their daily fare. When a bus arrives, people rush to the doors; women warily estimate their chances before the bus stops and young men hop on before the bus has come to a complete stop or when it slows for a corner a block or so away. The crafty take the bus in the wrong direction to guarantee themselves a seat on the return trip but this, of course, is only practical when the person starts from near the originating point of a run. Poked, pinched, caressed in some cases, pressed together, inhaling exhaust fumes, squeezing their way off at destinations with all belongings intact if they are lucky, riders suffer almost indescribable indignities, especially when one considers the strong feelings people have about maintaining appropriate physical distance between the sexes. No subject arouses such strong reaction in Egyptian urban dwellers as that of transportation problems. Yet one is struck on buses by the kind gestures —seated passengers holding the packages of those standing, squeezing in an extra child on a bench, giving each other directions, or responding pleasantly to questions.

Employees arrive at their offices well done in by their commuting and ready for the soothing cups of tea, their daily newspapers, friendly conversations, and other relaxing activities to build their strength again for the return trip home. Then like a reel rewinding, the process reverses itself until the employees find themselves again at home after a working day that lasted from about nine until two with a great deal of leeway in both starting and closing times. Women employees, upon reaching home, return to their "real jobs" of housework, child care, and supervising the homework and men to their dinners and their naps and then to an evening of television. In many families, men use the afternoon and evening hours for second jobs to supplement the meager salaries of government employment. Others in small businesses return for evening hours. Teachers give extra tutorial lessons. Family production centers gear up to make goods that can be sold at local stores or at religious festivals. The difference between a bare existence and the ability to afford simple luxuries often hangs on the second job. These middle-class denizens of Shubra are perhaps more to be pitied than those of Bulaq. Caught in the treadmill of the middle-class life style they have little room left to maneuver. They have too much to lose in terms of their middle-class status to be anything but monotonously conventional.

The daily exodus of men, women, and children to their jobs or schooling occurs with less urgency in Shubra than in Bulaq—it is a routine pattern of going and coming that in its repetitiveness has become ritualized. There is no expectancy in what awaits at the other end—today is like tomorrow; an extra effort or assuming greater responsibility today provides no extra bonuses tomorrow in the bureaucratic restrictiveness of seniority and certificate level advancement.

School children also plod with little enthusiasm through their daily schedules from October to April. They wait until just before critical exams before putting on the steam. Even then it is often not so much what they learned in school or the long evenings of rote memorization of homework but rather the material their tutors drum into them that counts in the major exams at the end of elementary, intermediate, and secondary levels. The nervous period of exam times affects seemingly unrelated activities in the city—hospital admissions decline for all categories of non-emergency illness; absenteeism from work increases so that parents can "study" with their children; television stations show reruns and religious plays to avoid tempting students from their studies. When exam season is finally over, solicitous parents help the children rest up over the four months of the summer to prepare for the school year to come. The annual cycles continue in this way until the child surmounts all the obstacles that lead him or her to a guaranteed government job after completing the university degree. This coveted job promises security in an economy that cannot provide white collar jobs as rapidly as the ranks of the middle class are expanding. For this reason, education becomes everything for the middle-class family; first, it guarantees economic security of a minimum level, and, second, by way of entrance requirements to university faculties, it opens the way to even better opportunities. High scorers of secondary school exams go on to the status professions of medicine and engineering, the low scorers into agriculture and teaching. Interest has little to do with the degrees people take, and indeed the majority who find their way into the private sector choose jobs in fields other than those they were trained in. The engineer becomes a public relations person, the agricultural student a secretary.

The vast bulk of the people one sees on the way to work in Shubra in the morning are those workers who have accepted poorly paying jobs in the public sector: This means they have become tracked in the regular system of promotion, afraid of branching out into new areas of work where they might sacrifice the security of "tenured" jobs and eventual pensions for the uncertainties of private employment. They are aware that in the public employ they are underpaid and offices are overstaffed, and their attitudes reflect that knowledge. It is common to hear people say, "Well, the government gets what it pays for," and to find them working out systems where people cover for each other for a few hours or even for whole days at a time. The work and the system provide little incentive for independent motivation. Work is what one does to earn a living. All in all there is, therefore, monotony to the methodical comings and goings in the streets of Shubra.

The neighborhoods of Shubra, with the exception of the main thoroughfares and business areas, clear out more completely during the day than those of Bulaq. This is because virtually all children go to school, fathers are away at work, and a large number of women also work. It is also because those women who remain at home focus their attentions on the interiors of their homes after brief forays on shopping errands. Life is more private, and homelife does not spill out in the street as it does in Bulaq. Visiting, when it occurs at all, occurs in quick snatches of conversation on the street with friends or with a local tradesman, or, in more "formal" contexts, over a cup of tea behind the closed doors of neighbors' dwellings. The middle classes feel a moral disdain for the adult who lingers overly long on the street with no apparent reason. Similarly parents

A garden restaurant gives apartment dwellers of the middle and upper middle classes a chance to enjoy the fresh air on holidays.

feel an almost moral responsibility to keep their own children from the "bad" influences of children whose parents are the kind that let them play freely in public areas. Middle-class children, as a result, grow up in enclosed spaces — in apartments and in schools, restricted in physical activity by the long hours of routine school work demanded of them and by the nature of the main pleasure, television, available to them. The fortunate are ones whose fathers' jobs provide membership in sporting clubs or who have sufficient income to afford membership themselves. Then on weekends and summer holidays while the parents sit nearby consuming tea and soft drinks, the children have the opportunity to meet with friends, kick a ball around, or go for a swim. The usual weekday afternoon and evening, however, finds the children bent over their books, supervised by an adult, usually the mother, who has assumed the duties of parent-teacher. Only the older boys who can "take care of themselves" occasionally escape to play ball in the street with their friends.

The streets are not wholly devoid of activity during the day — the density of Cairo population is too great for that — but there is an atmosphere of calm and restraint that characterizes the middle-class neighborhood. Although women still interact with street activities, they do so in a way that puts a respectable "frame" around their actions. The observer's attention is drawn to window sills and balconies where women linger while shaking out carpets or hanging wash. Some sit there at greater length helping an infant or toddler to get a little sunlight or fresh air while watching events below. Or it may be urgent for a woman to keep an eye out for the occasional peddler of vegetables and fruits so she can let down her basket for his products. In this way a woman keeps her reputation spotless while feeling justified in piously condemning her neighbor who lounges for hours at a time, elbows propped on the window sill, observing with undisguised interest the comings and goings in the street below.

In Shubra people wear a uniform that is no less standard than that worn by most of the *baladi* people in Bulaq. It is the ubiquitous "foreign" dress of a double knit or other synthetic — calf-length dress or blouse and skirt for women and suits or pants and shirt for men. A more practical adaptation is a two-piece suit for men similar to a safari outfit worn by the British in the colonial period. This foreign dress does not make it any more comfortable for Shubra inhabitants enduring daily bus trips to work in steamy offices in summertime than it does for the few who wear it in Bulaq. It is suffered for its symbolic value; just as in Bulaq, such clothing is considered a marker of middle-class status that demonstrates that wearer's sophistication, his/her educational attainment, and an acquaintance (though usually vicarious) with the world at large and the international way of dressing. These symbolic meanings are echoed in the use of foreign words, as for example, in the titles *Madame, Madmoiselle,* and *Tante,* and words such as *pardon* and *merci* which are commonly used by the middle class. Furniture styles and other home accoutrements also clearly take their inspiration from baroque styles of European salons. Gold-painted wood and red velvet plush, curved carved backs and arm rests grace the living rooms of the lower middle and middle middle classes. The upper classes tend toward these tastes too but often with more restrained and costly renditions of the models.

Even in gross physical characteristics, middle-class districts differ from lower-class ones. The streets are broader, permitting the use of cars or small delivery trucks on most of them. These vehicles are not numerous in relation to the size of the population resident in the area. The middle class in most cases can ill afford the expense for purchase and maintenance of a personal vehicle. The condition of side streets, continuously torn up for street repairs, discourages casual use to transit areas. As in

Bulaq, inhabitants are never far from essential services and stores that sell products needed on a daily basis. Unlike Bulaq, however, commercial areas tend to be more segregated, their shops more substantial and with fewer *ad hoc* vendors, and the goods carried in the stores comprise a wider and more expensive selection. Many specialize in services essential to the working masses of Shubra: ladies' coiffeurs, pastry shops, tailors, and laundries. The same carts peddle goods to housewives who remain at home, many of them older women in their black widow's garb helping out with the child care and housework duties of their employed daughters and daughters-in-law.

Apartment buildings rise higher in Shubra, not always because there are more stories in the older buildings but rather because the ceilings are loftier. Buildings are substantial and in comparatively better repair. All dwellings have running water within the apartment, electricity, private kitchens, and baths. Shubra was once a well-to-do area of Cairo forty or fifty years ago, but as in many older sections new buildings have filled in the open spaces and once-spacious, even lavish, family homes have been subdivided. Incongruities result under such circumstances. Older couples may reside in large multi-roomed flats, while their more recently married children occupy dwellings with the same number of rooms of such a cramped size that it takes an effort to maneuver around the overstuffed furniture that is still *de rigueur*. The older couple normally pays a few pounds for their spacious dwelling while their children pay three or four times as much. Some compensation is found in the more modern plumbing of the newer buildings but perhaps not enough to make up for the difference in cost. A rough estimate of rental costs for the middle class would show a range of between three pounds and fifteen pounds or higher for the most recently occupied dwellings. The middle-class expectation is to live in a flat of several rooms, each containing its own specialized furniture and each designated for a more or less specialized function. At a minimum such an apartment would include living room, kitchen, bath, and bedroom; a better apartment would include also a dining room and more bedrooms.

Differences in life style between the lower classes and middle classes in urban Egypt are more striking than those found in most Western cities. At the core of the differences are contrasting sets of expectations about the minimal standards that lead to the good life. Although those standards include much greater expenditure for the middle classes, the irony of modern-day Egypt is that the income of the middle classes is often not much more and sometimes even a great deal less than that of many in the lower classes. The second difference between the classes which has major repercussions on their life styles is their contrasting educational experience. The middle classes sustain a long-term involvement in formal educational institutions that develop in them or reinforce pre-existing patterns of middle-class expectations.

The lower classes frequent such institutions only for short periods, tending instead to find alternate forms of training such as apprenticeships and parental guidance within the home more useful. Families of both classes, as socializing agencies, pass on the values of class to their younger members; as the primary locus of decision-making activity, they determine in effect what the class membership of future generations will be.

3

Family as Social Group

"Can a cat eat its own kittens?" — Arab proverb

SOCIAL GROUP IN EGYPT

The young sheikh of a Sufi order, dressed in the blue striped brocaded robes passed down to him by his father, sat in a large tent in Tanta receiving a number of his 10,000 followers at the yearly *moulid*[1] of Seyyid Bedawi. On either side of him in seats of honor sat two foreign visitors. "What in fact do you do as leader of a Sufi clan?" one of the foreigners asked. "On weekends I visit villages to sit with my followers and listen to their concerns, and once a year at this *moulid* I receive them and provide food and a gathering place for them."

Foreigner: "But what is the purpose of the association? Do you collect donations? Do you build clinics or provide any services to your followers? Is there a political function — do they support you in negotiations with political leaders? Or is the purpose mainly religious?"

Sheikh: "It is really none of these. I accept donations from my followers, but it costs me so much money to conduct the meetings of the order that I only come out about even. I certainly don't make any extra. I also don't use the position for political purposes nor is there an especially strong religious aspect to our association, though we do take part in religious rhythmic rituals (*zikrs*) and we pray together at appropriate times. If there is a real purpose, it is social; we like to be together; my followers are strongly loyal to me and I act as the symbolic head of the group."

The foreigner again pointed out the possibilities that existed to

31

use his position in economic and political ways, but he remained adamant in claiming that the social advantages were by far the most significant for his followers.

THE POINT HERE is not to analyze whether or not there are manifest or even latent political, economic, or religious functions to such a Sufi order. The illustration stands rather as an example of how Egyptians appreciate social cohesiveness in a like-minded group as a good in itself and how they are willing to articulate this appreciation without hesitation or embarassment. Westerners with their strong sense of individualism conceive of most gatherings as places where the participants accomplish economic or political ends and leaders as people who take advantage of their positions to do the same. Social ends, regarded as secondary and somewhat frivolous, are, therefore, segregated into time periods labeled "leisure."

The Egyptian views the gathering together of certain kinds of people as a valid way to satisfy social needs. And he sees a need for social ease and trust between people before the other economic or political ends can be met. These other ends may never develop, or they may remain covert and implied, the social group simply preparing the field where they can materialize. When people are well connected in supportive groups, they feel a sense of security about being able to realize their present and future needs. But it would be a mistake to view them as joining social groups simply to guarantee these needs. Such a view would underestimate the high value placed on conviviality and togetherness in Egyptian society at all levels.

It is important in understanding how Egyptians view their family life to develop an appreciation of their emotional reactions to social corporateness and to distinguish between this view and the very different view of groups as social collectivities that is held by North Americans.

GROUPS AS CORPORATIONS AND COLLECTIVITIES

Corporateness is used here to define that sense the Egyptian has of the inviolability of his social groups, of their indivisible unity that persists regardless of the constituent members. The term is contrasted with the concept of collectivity which is meant to refer to the Western perception of groups as collections of individuals joining to achieve the common interests of the individual members. Within the collectivity individual rights supercede group rights and are only restricted where they may conflict with the rights of other individuals. It is the exception to discern in the collectivity any supra-individual rights that might devolve on the larger group. The individual is generally protected by legal rule or social custom from too great a tyranny of the group.

In a corporation, the group comes first and the individuals are expected to sacrifice their own needs for the greater good of the group. The personal status of individual members is defined by the group and not more than incidentally by individual achievement. Individual behaviors are evaluated primarily by how they reflect on the group, the group taking the blame or the rewards for these behaviors. Personal lapses in behavior, if kept secret, are of little consequence; it is only their public acknowledgement and association with the lowering of group status that causes an individual a sense of shame and personal guilt.

The collective view, by contrast, considers the individual on his own merits. He can excel or not live up to the expectations of his group without reflecting more than marginally on that group. The individual draws on the group for support in achieving his own status level. He can personally overcome the deficiencies of his group, and the world will recognize his achievements. Society, as a result, holds him responsible for developing his own potentialities and only in special cases of disadvantage accepts the view that his group might hinder this effort.

A person holding a corporate view or a collective view organizes his life quite differently from one holding the opposing view. Each view is so deeply engrained in the cultural consciousness of a people that it is difficult for people to stand outside their own cultural perspective and project themselves into the consciousness of those holding the opposing view. People conceive of their own world view as representing logic, common sense, and other valued characteristics, and, indeed, given the whole social system within which the world view functions, it *is* the view with the best "fit" to provide coherence for the society as a whole.

The following illustration demonstrates the conflict in world view that occurs when members of a society that is corporate-based are asked to comment on the principles of a collectively based society:

An American literature class in an Egyptian University had just finished Thoreau's *Walden*. The American professor had explained all the pertinent points of Thoreau's return to nature, his attempt at realizing self-sufficiency, his strong sense of individualism. The class was clearly uncomfortable with what they had been reading and were having difficulty in putting the book into some sort of familiar perspective.

"How do you feel about Thoreau, the man, and do you think

that a life style like his would be appropriate in the Egyptian context?" the professor asked. Hands flew up and a number of answers came at once:

"He is a miser — he lacks generosity." The student based his comments on the lengthy accounting Thoreau made of all the materials he had bought to sustain himself in the woods. "What is the purpose of going off and living alone? What kind of life is that?" "Doesn't he have any family? He doesn't speak about them. How can he leave all his responsibilities behind like that?"

The consensus of the class was that Thoreau was not accomplishing anything useful by his anti-social behavior; he had abrogated his role as a social being. He should in fact be considered "crazy" and would be so considered if he should try to live in this way in the Egyptian context. The concept of self-realization and self-reliance were totally lost on the students.

Individualism has little positive value in Egyptian society, and often is equated with a number of negative outcomes. As one student later commented: "Individualism leads to sexual license and social chaos since everyone is seeking his own ends." Consider the words of one scholar describing human rights under Islam:

The concept of freedom in Islam implies a conscious rejection of a purely liberal and individualistic philosophy of "doing one's own thing" as the meaning of life, or as the goal of society. The goal of freedom is human creativity. Freedom is defined as belonging to the community and participating with the people in cultural creation. This egalitarian, community-oriented approach denies some of the asserted Western liberal characteristics of freedom. (Said 1979:74)

and later:

The West places more emphasis on rights while Islam values obligations. The Western tradition posits freedom in order to avoid the outcome of a despotic system while Islam emphasizes virtue as a goal to perpetuate traditions of society which often support a coercive system. The West emphasizes individual interests while Islam values collective good. (Said 1979:77)

One implication of belief in the value of corporate good is an inability in certain contexts for people to develop an individual sense of identity — an activity that Americans have been deeply preoccupied with in the last decades. Egyptians tend to see themselves in relation to others, as members of groups, or in the context of their structural roles. They rarely think of themselves as individuals with unique potentials to develop or unique needs to satisfy.

> A foreign television group was interviewing an employed middle-class woman for a documentary on Egyptian women. The foreigner phrased a question which was then translated into Arabic by a young blue-jeaned upper-class Egyptian. The subject of the interview had no trouble in answering questions about her work, her daily routines, her feelings about women working, and about the changes that had taken place in women's lives in Egypt. Then came the final question phrased by the foreigner as follows:
> "Do you feel you have been able to realize your own identity within the modern context or if not how might you change your life to better realize that identity?" The translator, educated at the American University in Cairo, understood the question and put it to the woman in the best equivalent she was capable of. The subject answered:
> "I am a mother, a wife, a grandmother, and a daughter to my mother who is still alive. I have no trouble being any of those things though there were times when my children were younger that it was hard for me to work and care for them properly." After several rephrasings of the question that emphasized her own needs as an individual, it became clear that she had difficulty in separating herself from her roles.
> "But that is what I am," she insisted, "a mother, wife. . . ." She could express a momentary need for food, for drink, for a new dress but not for a long-term personal psychological or emotional need. The television people were disappointed by her answer. As they expressed it,
> "Why isn't such a modern, articulate woman able to see beyond her position in the household?"

In a later chapter we shall see the status implications for a woman of her position in the household. For now this illustration serves as an example of the value placed on membership in certain groups.

PRIVACY AND SOCIAL SPACE

A world view that stresses togetherness has implications that permeate all of social life. An Egyptian delivering a talk on human relations in Egyptian business comments:

In Egypt where the family is the absolute center of life the daily pattern leaves very little room for the Westerner's highly prized concept of privacy. Egyptians are constantly moving in and out of each other's lives as they intermingle in a constant interweaving flow. When the Egyptian "adopts" an American, his attempts to make the American feel at home extend to the smallest details of his personal life. It is not an invasion of privacy but a sincere desire to be helpful that rises from the basic instinct that prompts the Egyptian to invade the loneness, the isolation, the alienation of the foreigner and make him one of them. (Boctor 1981)

A long-time resident of Cairo from the lower classes describing the changes in the city in recent years exclaimed how much more lively and exciting the city had become now that there were more people moving into its boundaries. What the Egyptian middle and upper classes and foreigners see as extreme overcrowding she finds pleasant. She has grown up constantly surrounded by friends and relatives, probably sleeping in a bed as a child with several other people. Privacy and absence of other human beings to her represents boredom and deprivation—even a state close to terror as in the following case.

Leila, fifteen, was the daughter of an elderly and poor kerosene dealer who had become incapacitated with age. Though Leila's mother took over the sale of kerosene, she was unable to earn enough money to feed all of the five children still at home. An elderly woman, living alone, offered to take Leila as a live-in servant with a good salary that would have enabled the family to meet their needs. Leila went to visit the woman to find out the terms of her employment. It was explained to her that she would be responsible for the cleaning of the house and that she would be asked to watch over the house when the old woman went out. The woman generously offered Leila a room by herself with simple but adequate furnishings and told her that all her clothing would be provided. Leila agreed to report to work the following day. But when the time came she did not return. Privately she confessed she would be glad to do the work, but when she had begun to think about being sometimes left alone in the house, and living in a room all by herself she became terrified by the idea. "I have always lived with my parents and brothers and sisters around me—at night in the same bed. I wouldn't know what to do alone."

Even the desperate plight of her family could not relieve Leila of her fears. The elderly woman, wealthy from her birth and accustomed to living in spacious quarters, had difficulty understanding Leila's rejection of the opportunities she had offered her. Her sense of social corporateness was expressed in other ways — in her desire to be visited frequently by relatives and friends, for example.

Hall (1959) and others have commented on the different sense of space that Westerners and Easterners entertain. Easterners tend to stand closer when they speak with each other, are less disturbed by crowded areas, indulge to a much greater extent in physical contact. Westerners on the other hand carry with them a spatial cocoon that they do not like to see violated. A Westerner in an empty theater feels resentful of the person who comes and sits down next to him or her even though the place is unoccupied. Westerners fill up theaters, beaches, buses — all public places in fact — by a system of keeping reasonable distances between themselves and others, modified only by such considerations as where they can see best, nearness to the sea, to exits, etc.

An Egyptian beach fills up by "clumps," people deliberately choosing places near each other and even near food stands or exits where they are likely to be trampled by people moving back and forth. They enjoy the movement around them of other people and like to watch and interact with their neighbors. Westerners forced to sit near each other effect privacy by not speaking to those around them; Egyptians by contrast, even strangers, initiate contact by "watching clothes," returning balls, shouting comments. A person in the street readily initiates contact to give information or do a favor. Usually no rewards are expected other than the pleasant sense of social contact itself. Only by some kind of exchange, material or verbal, is the Egyptian able to place himself in contact with others and assess what is the critical aspect for him — the content of his social relationship with others. As an individual he is insignificant; as a social being he has significance.

The Westerner's desire for privacy becomes strongest during illness. Then his or her need to retreat and "sleep it off" dominates the social context. Egyptians, as might be expected, feel quite differently. When they feel most vulnerable, they want the support of others. The Westerner wants to hide his vulnerability, fearing that it detracts from his overall image of strength and personal infallibility. The Egyptian shows his vulnerability to gain support and at the same time to affirm the nature of his relationships with others (see Chapter 6). He is not held personally responsible for his vulnerability — vulnerability is a natural consequence of the human condition.

> The American, affected by a stomach disorder, had somehow stoically survived the morning inspecting a development project near a provincial town. Now he was feeling much worse and wanting only to return

to his own bed and medicine. The head of the village council brought out a surprise picnic lunch for the twenty or so people congregated in the palm grove. The American sat dejectedly on the side unable to eat, becoming increasingly annoyed by the long dragged-out luncheon. There was a steady stream of jokes passing back and forth between Egyptians (all politely translated into English) and every few minutes the American was included in the joking—"Do you find our women beautiful? . . . Better than American women," they teased his wife. The banter was excruciating torture for the American.

"I feel sick," he finally said "and want to go home."

"Oh no, we will take you to our house, make some chicken broth for you and sit with you until you are better. We can't leave you alone." The American lost all patience and demanded to be taken back to the place in town where he was temporarily staying.

"Wait," his hosts said. "We are sending to the next town for some cola for you. It will make you feel better."

The American construed the encounter as a total lack of consideration for his need—to go home and sleep alone. The Egyptians felt they were doing everything they could to divert the American from his misery. They supported him with banter and good company giving up whatever else they might have had to do to stay with him.

FORMATION OF GROUPS

Once we recognize the high value Egyptians place on group membership and support, and we acknowledge that people abstractly perceive themselves most of the time as members of groups rather than as independent entities, it then becomes significant to look at what kinds of groups form and on the basis of what criteria.

Sociability is not so strong that social groups form randomly. For the most part, membership in groups, whether latent or manifest, is based on specified characteristics of individuals. In many cases, membership is ascribed (as in kinship); in others it may be based on association with particular institutions or through voluntary participation in informal groups. Depending upon the nature of the group where potential links exist, there is a more or less strong expectation that a member has rights of support and assistance he can call on from members of the group and that he will be willing to honor the obligations he owes to them in return.

Groups most commonly form in three ways: (1) around the latent mu-

tual interests (or mutual discontents) of potential members, (2) around the
overt mutual characteristics developed during the lifetime and, (3) around
ascribed mutual characteristics. The list roughly approximates a graded
scale from least to most permanent, from weakest to strongest definition
of obligation, from most to least specificity of goal orientation.

The first kind of group forms spontaneously in defense of a mutual
interest or in reaction to a mutual discontent. It reveals corporateness by
implication when all the group members suddenly find themselves with
a sense of identification over a particular issue. Such groups may form
publicly and rapidly as for example in cases where an accident occurs or
where general displeasure over government pricing policy overflows into
street riots.

> A Mercedes was moving slowly through the crowded streets of a lower-
> class neighborhood in Giza when a child darted out into the street
> and was knocked to the side by the car. As is common in such cases,
> an ominous group of bystanders from the neighborhood formed. How-
> ever, before they had time to act, the driver sprang from the car beat-
> ing his cheeks with his hands in the traditional mode women use to
> show their bereavement. This gesture of the driver coupled with the
> fact that the child was not seriously hurt turned the tide of the crowd's
> anger, and some began to reassure the driver.

The persisting discontent of the lower classes with the "fatcats" who
"don't care about us" lies dormant and volatile until an episode like the
one above serves as a catalyst for coalescing the discontent. A sense of
commonality develops almost instantaneously even among strangers who
have never met each other. The reaction is predictably different from that
of a Westerner whose tendency would normally be to remain aloof from
a problem that was not his own personal one. In this example the driver
was able successfully to turn the tide of anger directed at him by expressing his own grief, thereby establishing his own identification with the
crowd's concern.

Other mutual interest groups form on a more permanent basis. Examples are found at the most informal level in the circles through which
people raise small sums of money for personal use to, at the more formal
level, political parties, associations of people for special purposes such as
charities or the preservation of trees and parks, associations for achieving
certain religious goals such as are found in the variety of quasi-political,
quasi-religious associations of Islamic conservatives. The membership of
such groups almost always consists of people who have in common other

qualities besides their mutual interest; they may be long-time friends or relatives or have developed the kinds of achieved characteristics discussed below. Groups in Egypt derive their strength and durability from these kinds of overlapping, multiplex links.

The second type of group is similar to the first in that it develops around the mutual interests of the members. But in this case the interests develop slowly over a long period of time with more emotional and affective involvement of the participants. The interests are of a more personal nature rather than directed at impersonal goals. Such groups most commonly form on the basis of friendship, of common educational experience, or of mutual occupational interest.[2]

These three are recognized groups whose members are expected to have common ties and interests. Of the three, although friendship circles appear to have the most potential for individual definition, in practice their members are usually defined by a long-term connection of one kind or another: childhood acquaintance, neighborhood friendships, extended professional connections that develop into personal relationships, and even in a number of cases long-term incarceration in political prisons during the Nasser period.

Membership in all three groups presupposes certain obligations and rights depending on how seriously the participants identify with the group. At the very least all members expect all other members to give special consideration when they seek favors. An example of one common association of this kind is the *dufa,* those who graduate from the same institution or class:

> The Arab League, because of political disagreements with Egypt, was about to transfer its headquarters to Tunis. Egyptians not wanting to transfer were told by the League they would lose their jobs. The Egyptian government, however, assured their citizens that they would help relocate them in jobs within Egypt. A woman who had spent her entire career working with the League came seeking my help with the relocation promised by the government. For some reason her more obscure office had been exempted from the order for relocation. When I apologized for not being able to help, she commented, "Well, there is nothing to do but go to Mme. Sadat."
>
> "Do you know her?," I asked.
>
> "No, but I will remind her that we were in the same school together so she will feel obligated to help me."

Even the most tenuous of connections, like this *dufa* link, carries with it the potential for assistance. People's networks comprise a number of such potential links, but individuals vary in the extent to which they activate them or not, or whether they cultivate them continuously or only sporadically. These kinds of links leave a great deal to the discretion of the actors concerned.

The more intimate but still discretionary groupings such as *shilla,* friendship circles, carry with them a stronger sense of obligation once an individual has publicly evidenced an intention to participate. It is not uncommon to see members piggybacking their friends into higher political position and in return when opportunities arise finding themselves carried upward also. In this way whole cliques of individuals may gain control over government bureaucracies or other organizations. What is notable is that persons are not brought forward necessarily because of individual merit but rather because of their closeness of acquaintance with the right people.[3] It is enough that they belong to the right *shilla.*

> One evening we joined a *shilla* that regularly met once a week at alternating houses. The original participants had first become friends as young colleagues in a faculty of one of the universities. Now through their mutual efforts several had become prominent in the government. Two were in fact top Ministers, several were well-to-do businessmen, some consultants and some still in academic institutions. Discussion among the men revolved around national economic policies with the members urging the Ministers to adopt modifications in proposed tax plans for businesses. The women discussed the summer vacation that a number of couples in the *shilla* had enjoyed together in Europe. One wife confessed to me that she found the weekly meetings of the *shilla* very boring but she and her husband came because if anyone was absent frequently from the group the rest would withdraw their support and "be angry" with him.

It is perhaps clear from the examples that groups built on mutual interests developed in people's lifetimes are more likely to gather together in formalized gatherings of people of the middle and upper classes. These classes have greater opportunities to develop relevant educational and professional backgrounds; they have more reason to use the connections; and they have the resources to keep up the continuous round of visits and presents that some of the groups require.

The third type of group is formed on the basis of ascribed characteristics. The most intense of these groups is, of course, the kinship group. Theoretically, no person of any social class ever loses instrumental membership in his kinship group except through social ostracism or death, the two possibilities for cutting off an offending member. Elsewhere there exists more detailed description about the mutual obligations of kin group membership and of how marriage provides the opportunity to intensify ties or graft on more extensive membership. Here it should be noted that because kinship is ascribed and thus publicly known and recognized, kin members feel a strong sense of responsibility for keeping their public deeds exemplary to reflect well on the reputation of the whole group Where other groups can easily exclude members who do not meet their standards, it is much more difficult and more traumatic for kin groups to do so.

Religious affiliation and socioeconomic class to a large extent also provide membership in social groups by ascription. These characteristics can be, but are not often, modified during a lifetime. Membership in these large cross-cutting grouping provides a means for social identification rather than for developing a set of very effective or utilitarian obligations to other members. The Sufi sheikh's comments at the beginning of this chapter provide illustration of the more diffuse social and symbolic nature of this kind of identification. For the majority, the effective potential of membership in economic class or religious group generally lies dormant, providing a framework and guide for social behavior and style of life but not measurably affecting under normal circumstances the pool of those who provide effective support. One exception to this generalization is found in the special favors minority groups, like Christians, expect from their co-religionists — favors like help in finding jobs, in lowered prices in Christian shops and other special considerations. It is perhaps the Christian sense of themselves as a weaker group within a more dominant group that develops their special sense of obligation to each other.

Though religious affiliation usually lies dormant it nevertheless is a powerful force to be wielded by its members under certain circumstances. In particular, numerous instances can be cited where a dispute of another nature — a quarrel over land or a personal disagreement for example — has been transformed by the persons involved into a religious conflict, both as a means of calling in reinforcements and as a way of asserting the moral superiority of both sides' arguments. This is, of course, only possible when individuals of different sects are involved. As a result, any incidents which may have the potential for religious confrontation can be serious whether the initial issue involved religion or not. This last type of group formation has many of the earmarks of the spontaneously forming type of group in the first illustration of this discussion. It demonstrates the analytical difficulty in distinguishing too rigidly between the social groups that form in Egypt. Perhaps better than any other evidence it supports the contention that groups become more potent the more overlapping the mutual interests — ascribed, achieved, and spontaneous — of their members.

FAMILY AS IDIOM

Family as the most intense social group in Egyptian society with the strongest set of mutual obligations becomes the ideal by which other social groupings are measured. The idioms that are peculiar to its organization are used to reinforce other social, political, or economic relationships. It is common, for example, to hear the terms of kinship—sister (*ukhti* or the more formal *abla*), brother (*akhi*), uncle (*ammi*), aunt (*khalti*), daughter (*binti*), and son (*ibni*)—among the lower classes or the corresponding French substitutions in some cases among the middle classes used in other than their strictly appropriate sense to address kin members. A person may address friends or even a stranger in the street by these terms, selecting the appropriate one by the sex and the age of the person to whom he or she is speaking. In this way an Egyptian manipulates social space by extending the warmth of his personal network temporarily to include others, thereby co-opting their support and the quality of their response. The world takes on a warmer and more personal atmosphere.

Where other relationships can be constructed on the model of the family, the result is considered ideal:

Mostafa was explaining how he had set up his small business of about thirty-five employees who manufacture products used in the construction industry. "I have consistently chosen people from the village where my father owned land. Many had worked for our family before, so I knew them well. New ones I take by the recommendations of the older workers and usually from their families so most of the workers are related in some way or another. In one case the uncle of one who had been brought to me urged me not to take the boy because he was not a good one, but I persisted and with a great deal of fatherly guidance from me he has now become a good worker. I like to have this personal contact with my workers, encouraging them and supporting them when they have problems. It is not unusual for them to come to me in the middle of the night with their problems of illness, marriage, or whatever, and I solve their problems. To some I have given 200 £E just so they can marry a daughter, and I wouldn't ask to have it back again. In fact I would prefer to pay a worker 3 £E a day rather than 5 £E so that I can afford to offer them help when they need it. Some get better offers from other companies, but none of them would leave me because they feel such loyalty to me. We are more like a family than a workplace. When I have extra orders, sometimes they come to me and volunteer to work overtime just to meet our deadlines. Sometimes I am tempted to enlarge the business, which I could easily do, but if I did so I would lose the personal touch with my workers I enjoy, and we would all start working for the firm rather than letting the firm work for us.

Mostafa enjoys playing the role of father to his workers. It enhances the identity he conceives for himself. There is no doubt also that his workers, even those older than he, look up to him as one who carries their interests "in his eyes." Everyone is satisfied with the re-creation of family relationships in the factory setting.

One sees this phenomenon in offices, religious groups, universities, and other institutions and organizations as well.[4] Chiefs, bosses, sponsors all are expected to play fatherly roles that go far beyond what is required by the dry routine of office work. They provide mediation services, loan money, provide advice, listen to problems. On their side, employees perform small services for their bosses that go beyond their bureaucratic duties: buying groceries, seeing to small repairs, dealing with personal matters such as paying the electric bill or negotiating paper work in government offices. The employee assumes the role of son, dutifully performing menial tasks, and when necessary seeking the intervention of the powerful father-figure who usually has the means to resolve his small problems.

The family image permeates upward and outward even into the larger, more embracing institutions of the society, personalizing them in a way that is rarely found in the West. Nowhere is this more in evidence than in the public statements made by the late President Sadat. A common refrain in his speeches says, in effect, that Egypt is a great family and Sadat is its father. When he spoke of the neighboring country of the Sudan, he consistently spoke of its people and leaders as his brothers.

The image of a head of state who sees himself as a father figure is not a positive one to the Western audience. It calls forth associations with authoritarianism (which restricts individual freedom) and paternalism (which undervalues the individual's ability and right to choose for himself). To the average Egyptian, however, the image is a positive one. All but the most cynical respond with a warm sense of solidarity and a feeling that the president is acting "in the best interests of his family." There are no limits on the positive value equated with family cohesiveness.

Egyptian television serials continually make this point in a negative way when they portray the ultimate family tragedy — a father making marriage choices for his daughter or son, in what he thinks to be their best interests, but which in the end prove tragic because of a misjudgment of some kind or because a real love existed toward someone else. The tragedy is every bit as real for the father, whose intentions were of the best kind, as it is for the child who put obedience to parents above self-interest in choice of partners. Both behaved correctly, and the tragedy, beyond the capability of either to prevent, was not in fact supposed to have occurred.

The family model provides guidelines to other institutions in Egyptian society. It can be argued that where relationships are based as they are in the family on unequal reciprocities characterized by age differences, different expectations of the sexes, and different expectations of specific roles (see Chapter 5) patterns based on this model generally do not develop on the one hand the characteristics of egalitarianism or on the other of individual competitiveness. The complementarity of roles holds the fabric of the society together and not the static tension between equal entities of the same thing. Given that this model, socialized in children from their early years, creates certain expectations and tendencies, it becomes easier to see why Egypt's experiments in democracy in recent years have not been completely successful. The social institutions that provide the base for a democratic state have not developed the proper training ground.[5] Moreover the special character of social institutions like the family in Egypt tends to promote an authoritarian rather than a democratic style of leadership, with a policy that acquiesces to rather than challenges that leadership. The leaders as father-figures in any case tend to take it as a personal offense when their "children" become unruly and unwilling to submit to the authority of their elders.

In many ways, socialism comes closer to sparking the enthusiasm of Egypt's masses than democracy. There is a compatibility in socialist philosophy at the theoretical level with the value of corporateness found in Egyptian family institutions. The failure of Egypt's experiment with socialism, however, has partly been due to the inability to build on the sense of corporate obligation to include entities of more extensive membership than those where corporateness has a strong hold now: family groups, small face-to-face communities, and small industrial establishments. As long as the sense of obligation to small groups of this kind remains so strong, there will be difficulty in establishing a sense of allegiance to more embracing institutions that are seen as competing with the primary groups for resources of time and energy.

Another implication of extending the corporate family model to other social institutions develops out of the belief in the complementarity of roles within the family. No two members of the family enjoy structural parity in role function. Extending this model to social life as a whole, people in general do not occupy positions of equality in society either, though their positions may be regarded as complementary. Their positions are always relative ones determined by their structural relationships with others.

Two strangers meeting on the street, for example, begin immediately assessing each other's positions so that they can correctly determine the appropriate terms of address, manner of speech, level of service, or demand for service that should be extended to the other. People act as though they believe (and some articulate this belief) that people are born to certain roles — some to lead and manage, others to do physical labor and provide services for the élites. Both are essential to society, but both are not expected and do not receive the same proportion of the rewards the society has to offer.

This view of the complementarity of roles in society differs from that seen in the family mainly in terms of a greater fluidity in the family roles. Family members throughout their lifetime may remain in essentially the same structural relationship to one another in their family of birth, but somewhere along the line they, as individuals, move into the authority positions of parenthood as they move off into families of their own. In this way individuals in their lifetimes theoretically can experience the whole range of family roles limited only by what their sex and the actual realities of the situation allow. There is much more limitation in what people of a society are expected to experience in the way of social roles. They generally remain in a fairly fixed position within the social hierarchy.

This chapter has attempted to convey a sense of what corporateness means in the context of Egyptian family life, of how group preservation and happiness as they are perceived take precedence over individual desires and independent action outside of the group. It is not surprising to find in Egyptian society other parallels to this pattern of corporate activity. Here the family model is assigned primacy in establishing the pattern elsewhere in society, mainly because it is within the family that patterns first become learned and invested with their value connotations of "rightness" and "wrongness." There is no attempt here to determine whether corporateness over the long term has developed as an effective means of adjusting to a particular set of ecological or economic conditions or whether it has arisen as a cooperative resistance to a history of foreign domination. All these factors are undoubtedly involved. What is more important is that it works under all these conditions and provides a prevailing world view that colors behavior at all levels of the society.

4

Definitions

"If your father is an onion and your mother garlic, from where do you expect to get a good smell?"—Arab proverb

BULAQ—FOUR FAMILIES

U m Ilyas lives alone in a small room on the ground floor of a building that is overcrowded and structurally unsound. "Where can I go?," she remarks when we caution her against the sagging timbers of her room and the moisture that drips from the walls. At noon when the sun shines brilliantly on her rooftop neighbors, Um Ilyas lights a kerosene lamp in order to have light enough to see. Um Ilyas is grateful to her neighbors who are especially friendly to one another, partly as a result of their close proximity in the dead-end street that serves as a courtyard for the residents' activities and partly because of the many years and crises that they have endured together. Um Ilyas has become even closer to some of them in the year since Abu Ilyas died. They were a support to her in the months he lay dying in their single four-poster bed, and now she tries to help them out by walking children to school or running small errands. If you pause to talk with Um Ilyas for a little the subject almost always turns to her three daughters, two of whom live a stiff walk away and, therefore, do not see her very often. They are in any case occupied with their own husbands and children. The third daughter was burned to death a few months ago while trying to light a kerosene stove. She left seven children, including a young baby, all of whom the father now wants

Shopping for food in the bazaar is an important part of a lower-middle-class woman's activities.

to place in an orphanage because he cannot care for them. Um Ilyas is concerned for the children and feels unable to help because of her small room and limited resources—a small pension and supplementary welfare payment. It would be inappropriate for her to move in with her son-in-law, and "anyway he will be looking for a new wife who of course won't want to take care of the children." If Um Ilyas is asked who the members of her family are, she responds, "Just me and my two daughters now." Why doesn't she live with the daughters? "It would be shameful to ask a daughter for help and, living with her, I might cause her problems with her husband."

     Um Ali, by some definitions, is a fortunate woman with her four sons. She looks forward to the future when she hopes they will support her royally. Abu Ali, her husband, is a man crippled by palsy, a serious disadvantage in his profession as a barber. In order to continue his work he sits outside the local school and gives haircuts for 10 or 15 p. to the children who, for that price, are not so particular about the way their hair looks. Um Ali scurries around picking up jobs where she can, washing clothes here, carrying water there, scrubbing floors or cooking in a nearby school. None of her jobs are regular ones that she can depend upon so she must be continually on the lookout for new possibilities. Even handouts from a local welfare center are worth her time and attendance at required functions. While she is away from home, she normally takes only the smallest boy; her other children remain with her crippled sister-in-law, Fawziyya, who lives with them. Fawziyya cannot move from her bed, but she can talk to the older children or call out to neighbors if she needs help with the younger ones. Fawziyya has always lived with Um Ali and her husband. She is part of their family, and no decision would be made without considering what the effects would be on her. In the past they have spent money taking her to doctors but to no avail. Now though family members must give her a great deal of physical care, they also benefit from her presence in the house, caring for the children.

Um Amal lives in one small room with her husband and five children, the eldest of whom is a girl of eleven. Abu Amal sells tomatoes, barely making enough in a day to support the needs of his family. Recently he was put in prison for selling tomatoes at a price higher than that fixed by the government, a practice common among fruit and vegetable sellers in Bulaq. To gain his release from prison Um Amal borrowed 50 £E from neighbors. The rest of his 100 £E fine he can pay in installments. Um Amal is learning to crochet and now is beginning to bring in some income for the family. In the past she used her spare time to sew clothes for her children out of scraps from old clothes she had been given, but with so many children there is little time left in the day for extra work. Their small room rents for 3 £E a month; it has no electricity, and the woman on their floor who has the water tap in her room refuses to let the others use it. The daughter, Amal, carries water from the house of another neighbor down the street who charges 25 to 30 p. a month. The only other alternative is for Amal to walk a much longer distance to the crowded public tap. Even as a small child Amal has had to shoulder so much work in the family that it has never been possible to send her to school. In any case the family prefers to use its scarce resources on books and clothes required for the education of their boys. Once Amal's parents thought they could hire her out to a tailor, but she was young and the tailor was not satisfied with her work so he fired her.

Um Jamiil sits like a rotund Buddha on her front door step. Every morning finds her sitting there shucking peas, talking with the women or bouncing a grandchild on her knee. Um Jamiil's clan occupies the whole bottom floor of a building, four rooms in all. Until a few months ago, her husband ran a small "hole-in-the-wall" store on a main thoroughfare just around the corner from their house. He earned enough for them to be considered "rich" by Bulaq standards. Then suddenly one day he died, and the store was closed. Two married sons occupying two of the family's four rooms with their wives and children already hold good jobs with pensions and tenure guaranteed and are not anxious to run the store. A third son is studying at the university and has higher hopes for his future than running a cigarette and candy kiosk. The only daughter, divorced and living at home, was not greatly occupied during the day, but the family decided against allowing her to run the shop. For one thing she didn't know anything about managing a business, and for another it would give people the impression that the family was in dire financial straits if they sent their women out to work. They all agreed that the working men had sufficient income to support all the non-working members of the household. This large extended family eats together, watches television in the room of the mother together, and during the day keeps all their doors open to shout back and forth to one another. Anything that affects one, affects all of them.

SHUBRA — FOUR FAMILIES

Mme. Samia lives in an old but spacious building a block away from a street that is lined with stores of all kinds. On her way home from work Mme. Samia stops in to purchase the few needs of herself and her husband. She pays more for many items of food this way because she is not willing to stand in the long lines of cooperative stores to get government subsidized prices. "And you can't always ask your neighbor to buy for you." This is the price she pays for convenience. Her husband complains occasionally that she doesn't need to go out to work, that their income is sufficient now that their four children have finished university and are happily

Three young professional women enjoying an outing reflect the influences of Western fashions.

married. But her patterns were formed in the days when she began working to supplement the family income. Then it was difficult to juggle all her activities, but now she has few responsibilities and works simply to have something to do and because she likes her work. She has a two-day holiday every week — one day she cleans her own house and prepares any food for the week that is necessary. The other day she goes to visit one of her two daughters who lives nearby and cooks for her, or she prepares a big meal and receives other members of her family at her own home. These family gatherings may include her mother, her son's family, her sister's family, her brother's family, her daughters' families and other physically distant relatives passing through Cairo. Only rarely does she have dinner guests not of her immediate relatives, and almost always these are people sent to her by her son who works in a foreign Arab country or people she has met through her work. Her husband, Ustaz Tewfik, works mornings in a secondary school where he receives a modest government salary. A great deal more of his income comes from private lessons he gives in the afternoons, evenings, and on weekends. He is a scholarly man and enjoys a life mainly involved with books and learning. Both husband and wife enjoy an hour or two of television in the evening before retiring.

Mme. Nafisa and her husband Seyyid Anwar live in a flat with their two boys, now teenagers. The flat is relatively new and for that reason has modern plumbing and small rooms and costs more than some of the older, more spacious flats. The parents have a bedroom; the children share another; one small room crowded with furniture serves as a living room and a final room is devoted to the second job of Seyyid Anwar. Mornings he works in a school, and afternoons he runs a photography studio where people come to have pictures taken of special events like engagements or weddings. Mme. Nafisa colors in the portraits at home to give them an old-fashioned painted quality. By their industriousness they have been able to acquire a car and, back in the days when it was cheaper, bought an apartment in a new area of Alexandria, a bus ride away from the beach. They spend their short summer holiday there when they can manage to be away from the store for a while.

Ahmed Bey is the director of an office in one of the numberless departments of the government. His salary is good for a government employee, but he still needs to supplement his income in the afternoons by helping his brother out with the accounts in his small business. When his two daughters were teenagers their mother died leaving him grief stricken. Some of his relatives urged him to marry someone else as quickly as possible to take over the household and help him bring up his daughters. Others warned him against marrying, for the sake of his daughters whom they felt would be unhappy living with a stepmother. The girls encouraged this last view and maintained to their father that they could handle the household themselves. He finally decided to accept their advice. Both girls went to secondary school; one continued on to college and began working as an employee in the government. Eventually the elder one married and left her father's home. The younger daughter, less interested in school, did not continue on to university. She took over most of the household responsibilities and declared her intention not to marry but to remain with her father to take care of him. A kindly neighbor has helped the girls over the rough spots, standing in whenever a mother was needed. For example, at the elder daughter's engagement party, the neighbor helped prepare food and opened her own rooms to seat all the guests. She advised the girls on their clothes and listened to their problems in school.

Mme. Sara is a lively energetic person with a twinkle in her eye. She likes her house to be filled with activity. People come and go with such frequency that it would be difficult to determine who lives permanently under her roof. Her mother, for example, lives a great deal of time at Mme. Sara's house, but from time to time she rotates around to the houses of her numerous other sons and daughters to stay a week or two. One university age son of Mme. Sara comes and goes, off to visit relatives in another city or on a trip with his classmates. Her eldest daughter is married and living in the same building. She works during the mornings, and while she is gone from home her two young children are cared for by Mme. Sara. To save her the housework when she comes home, Mme. Sara cooks for both families. A younger daughter has recently finished university and has become engaged. The household is full of half-sewn dresses and other preparations for the wedding. Mme. Sara also keeps up a frequent correspondence with an unmarried son working in the Gulf States. The household clearly revolves around Mme. Sara. Her husband, Seyyid Khalid, owns and manages a small shop selling yard goods in the local bazaar area. He opens his shop about nine in the morning; he returns home briefly between about two and four for dinner and a short nap and then returns to the shop until eight or nine. He is, therefore, away from home most of the day, and when he does return home his presence is hardly noticed, except as a signal to commence the main meal. He is generally content to sit back quietly amidst the activity of the household. Mme. Sara notes that she often asks his permission when she wants to do something or spend money, "to let him feel he is the boss of the family," but his permission is obviously *pro forma;* she runs the household.

FAMILY DEFINITIONS

"Family" is a generic term in all societies, much in the same way that a word like "tree" is. Each person's momentary image of tree differs in certain particulars from what the next person imagines. Yet they all know essentially what they mean by the term. With a set of more specific descriptors, such as evergreen and a particular variety of tree name, they may be able eventually to form closely identical images.

The Egyptian term "family" has the same quality of including a broad variety of images at once, as the family vignettes above demonstrate. It is only when the term "family" is qualified and limited to a certain context that more precise definitions are possible. If, for example, one asks about the membership of a person's family, the response may include anywhere from one to literally thousands of people. A man asking another man how his family is may receive the answer, "She is fine!" if it is assumed that the questioner is using a delicate way of asking after his wife's health. A canvasser asking about the number of family members in a home he has just entered normally receives an answer based on residence. A person asking about the origins of a village may be told that everyone from the village comes from the same family. Other definitions are evoked in the context of operational, functional, religious, and other frameworks.

As a result it is difficult to define what family is to Egyptians, what it is composed of and what its characteristics are, in a way that is both concrete enough to be useful and broad enough to encompass the large variety of its manifestations. Severely limited definitions such as those characterized by residential factors or blood relationship are useful for certain purposes. Broadly dynamic definitions such as Piaget's "family is a creative tension" alert us to the fragile nature of each manifestation of family, but fail to show us what is lasting in the institution. Both kinds of definitions are important for an understanding of how Egyptians view and manipulate the components of family.

Arabic Terms for Family

The Arabic words that Egyptians use to designate family are ambiguous and leave a great deal of room for individual meaning. In general, the terms emphasize the quality of the relationship between the people concerned rather than precisely delimiting the kinds of people that should be included within a particular definition. When people consider whom they will include within a family circle, their answers are generally affected by such factors as financial commitment, complementarity of roles, physical residential arrangement, emotional commitment, and in a general way nearness of blood or marriage relationship. The most common answer to "Who comprises your family?" is without doubt an answer that includes all these factors in their most intense form—in what is generally called the nuclear family of mother, father, and children living under the same roof. But to accept this definition as the Egyptian family is to miss the subtle manipulations that give life to the institution.

The smallest family unit specified by Egyptian terminology is the word *bait* which means literally "house." The meaning includes a strong sense of residential place. It can be used, however, either to specify the place where the family lives or to designate the cluster of people who live most of the time under the same roof. Though the term generally refers, therefore, to the nuclear family unit of husband, wife, and children living together, it may also include children temporarily living away from home, a spinster aunt that lives with the family, a widowed parent, or broadly an extended family group of father, mother, unmarried daughters, and married sons and their families when all those people live under the same roof or in the same general compound. In a more abstract sense, as in *"bait* Mohammad Mahmoud," the term may extend to mean "those living under the authority of a male elder, Mohammad Mahmoud." It is interesting to note in this respect that the idiom, using the plural of *bait, ahl il buyutat* (literally people of houses), means people of good respectable families. The term implies that a more substantial presence is created by the inclusion of a number of residential family units.

The term *aila,* family, can similarly be used to refer to a nuclear or extended group of kin depending on the context. The phrase, *il aila il kabeera* (literally, the large family) specifies the use of the term in its broader sense. Some anthropologists equate this usage with the anthropological term "lineage" (see Fakhouri 1972:55). Commonly, however, the term is much more ambiguously used (as Fakhouri also notes). Rather than containing the residential overtones of the term *bait,* however, the subtle connotation underlying the relationship of those included in *aila* is one of mutual obligation. Arab words for bread winner, family provider, to be responsible, household — those depending on one's support — and dependents derive from the same roots and all carry the same sense of obligation to support. In the narrow sense of household, the support may be economic; in the broader sense of commitment to larger circles of kin, the obligation may be construed as a general one that supports the concerns of all those included as relatives.

Ahl is another general term for family which has a range of levels of inclusivity in its meanings — from immediate family to much larger groups of kin. The term emphasizes the qualifications for membership that come as a result of birth or contract (as through marriage). In an even broader sense, *ahl* means followers and those possessing the qualities required for membership in a particular group. For example, in the term *ahl il khibra,* people of experience, "membership" is based on the attribute of experience.

The final term commonly used to refer to a pool of kin is the term *qarayib,* (*garayib* in colloquial Egyptian) meaning relatives. Again the term is expandable to several levels of inclusivity. It emphasizes nearness, closeness of relationship in the sense of blood connection, contractual relation, or simply a sense of emotional attachment rather than closeness in the physical spatial sense. The *qarayib* would be the people with whom one feels a fairly strong sense of connection, the people upon whom one has no hesitation to call if there is a need.

The fact that Egyptian terms are ambiguous and flexible in defining who should be included specifically within different categories of kin is significant. Bedouin tribes of Saudi Arabia, for example, tend to define the segmental units of their tribal lineages much more precisely and their conceptual sense of kinship is characterized by much greater depth and specificity of genealogy than that of the Egyptians. The characteristics Saudis assign to matrilineal and patrilineal branches of the family similarly are much more sharply demarcated.

The Egyptian vagueness about kinship boundaries does not necessarily mean a casualness about kin relationships in general; rather it may serve pragmatic ends by allowing the social institution of family to be manipulated in more flexible ways. Within each definition of family, the Egyptian specifies his sense of what are the essential ingredients of family relationships: coinciding residence, mutual obligation, the attributes of membership, and the closeness of people in a structural and emotional sense. As we will see later, Egyptians tend to draw on family relationships in an *ad hoc* way, making do with the conditions and arrangements of people that exist and flexibly adjusting relationships to suit what seems appropriate in the given context. Saudis by contrast are much more likely to follow the prescribed relationships with kin and actively to structure spatial arrangements of people in order to bring about the ideals they value. To a certain extent the Saudi history of nomadism and their present affluence better provide them with the conditions and resources to effect these kinds of physical rearrangements.

Subjective Definitions of Family

If Saudi genealogies could be graphically represented as tall, branching trees emphasizing patrilineal relatives, then Egyptian genealogies in the same idiom would be seen as fat, squat bushes. A Saudi ignores many of the collateral relatives to focus on his long line of descent. The Egyptian places himself somewhere near the center of his genealogical bush with, if he is in middle age, considerably more young shoots overhead than stems underneath. The Saudi knows the overall tribal group to which he belongs. The Egyptian, with the exception of the well-to-do or the foreign-inspired, has no overarching name to refer to his larger family or even to his own specific family group.

An Arab proverb says that "the vein reaches back to the seventh grandfather" but few Egyptians, other than those with illustrious ancestors, would be capable of naming their seventh grandfather. A spontaneously recited Egyptian genealogy, including all the names an individual can remember, typically does not extend backwards beyond the grandfather's father and is more likely to stop at the grandfather's generation, with a few great uncles and aunts included in the scheme. If pressed the person may be able to name more distant relatives, but he may not know the whole name or may only know an outstanding detail of the person. What is often astonishing, however, is the almost total recall of the members of mother's and father's generation and their descendants until the present time, often as many as one hundred or more people in all. A person usually remembers not only their names but their precise relationship to himself or herself and their relationships to one another, which in the case of intermarriage, may require several terms of relationship for each person involved.

The average person does not consciously sit down and think XYZ are my family or ABC characteristics need to be present for a person to qualify as a relative. Rather the individual Ego finds himself or herself born into the middle of complex networks of people he learns to call kin. Very early he begins to distinguish levels of relationship based on consanguinity and mutual obligation, and he learns the subtle expectations that accompany certain kinds of relationships. With marriage he grafts on a whole new set of expectations and commitments.

In their simplest graphic form family relationships, from the perspective of an Egyptian, might appear as a series of overlapping circles of varying diameter. The tighter the circle around Ego the stronger the obligation related persons are expected to feel for one another. Kin have to help each other because they are kin.

A television drama demonstrates these levels of commitment in a shorthand way:

> A family pressed economically by inflation, the husband's retirement, and their rising material expectations decide to rent their apartment furnished to a foreigner for the magnificent sum of 600 £E a month. The dilemma is to find a place where the husband and wife and their two university age children can live.

"Simple," says the wife to her husband. "We will move in with your sister. She has a large apartment and lives all alone. She is very fond of our daughter and will be delighted to have us."

The sister has not seen them for a long time and is surprised to find them at her doorstep, their arms loaded with presents. Before presenting their case, they find out that the sister's son, his wife and two children are about to return from abroad and commence living in the apartment with her. They leave quickly taking their presents with them.

"What shall we do now?" asks the embarrassed husband. The wife thinks awhile and then remembers her mother's brother whom she hasn't seen in years. They go to his small, dingy, poorly furnished apartment with their gifts. He asks about their children whose names he doesn't know. It soon becomes clear to husband and wife that this apartment also is not suitable. Their next stop is the door keeper-janitor who has access to a small apartment on the roof of their building. He agrees to let them have the apartment after they meet his conditions. Eventually the family realizes that they will be giving up more than they gain by the move and remain in their original apartment.

The family in this drama reviews its circles of people who have a structural commitment to help, even though their contacts have been few and far between in the case of the relatives. They start with a sister who occupies a kin position of strong obligation, next move to a relative of somewhat less commitment, and finally turn to a non-relative acquaintance whose commitment is the weakest of all. The assumption in the plot is that the sister would have helped if she could. The uncle let it be known that he wanted certain returns, and the janitor-door keeper set even more stringent conditions.

A two-dimensional diagram of concentric but ever expanding circles with Ego at the center only approximates a sense of the structural relationship an individual feels toward other kin. These relationships may remain dormant temporarily or indefinitely but always retain the potential for activation. To such a diagram needs to be added structural ties of affection and ties of jural obligation (see Chapter 6). The diagram is also unable to show how Ego actually makes use of his familial relations or how his concept of family changes through his life time as he moves from childhood, through adolescence, to marriage, to parenthood, and eventually perhaps to widow or widowerhood. At each stage the immediacy of family relationships changes along with, in many cases, the persons who are included within the circle of effective kin.

Despite the inadequacies of diagrams to represent the many-layered nature of kinship, some aspects of family come clear. Such a diagram would be certain to reveal the pivotal position of children at the juncture of both parents' circles of blood relations. Ego counts the spouse's circle as a weakly related type of network because the bonds are fragile and subject ultimately to the contractual agreement of marriage remaining in force. The children strengthen the link between mother's and father's relations by creating a permanent bond even in the event that the marriage itself is dissolved. A parent would be loathe in such a case to keep children from their natural grandparents.

People feel strongly that it is children that give permanence to the marriage relationship. Before the children arrive, a young couple's interests are still invested to a large extent in their families of birth. Many people feel a couple only becomes a family after they have had children. The importance of children is symbolized in the new names that all lower-class and a large number of middle-class parents assume upon the birth of a child. These names are the familiar *Abu Foulan* and *Um Foulan,* father and mother of So and So, the name of the child. When a reasonable period of time passes after marriage, couples who do not have children often take on the names of hoped-for children, *Abu Ahmad* for example if an Ahmad is desired or they may take the name of a relative child for whom they have assumed part- or full-time care. It is not uncommon to find a childless woman referred to as *Um Ghaib* (mother of the missing one). Since women retain their own names upon marriage this assumption of a child's name brings the father and mother together with a common appelation.

A few people go as far as to assert the extreme view that until boys are produced, the essential needs of parenthood are not met and the marriage remains precarious.

A farmer sitting in a group of neighbors and visitors was describing the problems faced by villagers. "My problem," he noted, "is the fact that my wife has only produced four girls. Now she is pregnant for the fifth time and if she doesn't deliver a boy I will have to divorce her and try to have sons with another woman. A man without sons is to be pitied—there will be no one in his old age to support him and no one to take care of the burial arrangements when he dies. I am concerned that this will be my case." Several of his neighbors disagreed with him:

"Your daughters will see that you are properly buried and not leave you in your old age. It would be sinful for you to divorce this woman you have lived with so long."

A common practice in the past to protect boys in the family where there were a number of boys was to give them different names so it appeared that they came from different families. It was thought that a family with so much good fortune might attract the evil eye.

Structural Definitions of Family

Definitions of family that have agreed-upon parameters are structural definitions. They are useful in giving some constancy to people's images of family. The Egyptian image of family noted above, for example, commonly reflects such factors as who resides together, who eats together, or who is related by blood connection. But when a definition of family is reduced to a count of the number and kinds of persons living together it leaves unanswered important questions of why people organize family residential units in a certain way, whom they expect to perform certain tasks, and what kinds of conditions force restructuring of their expectations. A particular composition of household members can be affected by a number of factors: economic imperatives, housing scarcities, the need for females to receive male protection, and the desire of unmarried men to receive the daily care of female relatives.

Since there are limitations on how much can be known about families from structural definitions, it is useful to look also at how people operationalize their family relations. These manipulations are characterized by both an *ad hoc* quality that responds to conditions of the moment and a more stable set of principles and their implications that tends to channel behavior in certain ways. For example, people can talk about the primacy of male relatives while still giving equal time to activities with female relatives. They can talk about blood passing down through the male forbears while still including females within the circles of those whom they consider close kin. Structural definitions establish predispositions to behave in certain ways, but they do not guarantee the final behavioral outcomes. Operational definitions combine the exigencies of the moment with the long-term expectations of people.

Official Pronouncements on Family

Officials recognize the importance of authoritative statements in creating a degree of stability to an institution. The Egyptian Constitution of 1971 states: "The family forms the basis of society. It is built on religion, morality and patriotism. The state is concerned with the preservation of the authentic character of the Egyptian family and the values and traditions it represents, in addition to affirming and developing this kind of relation within Egyptian society." (Article 9)

The statement, like the terms Egyptians use for family, makes no comment about what the family is or how it should be composed. Rather it stresses the qualities families should possess and the importance of extending family-like relationships to society as a whole.

Characteristic of this constitutional statement and others (see Chapter 12 on women's employment) is the emphasis on family as the basic unit of society rather than the individual. When rights are guaranteed by the Constitution, people assigned the rights are normally referred to in terms of their roles as citizens, as workers, as nationals, or as family members. Article 7 of Part II of the 1971 Constitution reiterates this point by stating that social solidarity is the basis of society. In a 1956 version of the constitution, written shortly after the revolution, what appears to be a manifesto of individual rights guaranteeing liberty, security, safety, and equal opportunities, was reduced to guarantees of equal opportunities in the 1971 constitution.

Islamic Models

Implicit in earlier sections is the importance of religion and particularly the sharia legal prescriptions in defining the characteristics of family life in Egypt. A widely disputed article of the constitution is one that in 1956 stated only that "Islam is the religion of the State and Arabic its official language." Purists wanted to give a stronger Islamic character to the legal system of the country. In 1971 legislators added "and the principles of the Islamic sharia are a major source of legislation." In the spring of 1980 the statement was strengthened to say the sharia was *the* main source of legislation. Religious conversatives saw this change as paving the way for broader legal reforms more consistent with the sharia. Because sharia influenced law had been reduced over the years from more comprehensive areas of competence to the specific area of personal-status family law, the changes in the constitution did little more initially than reaffirm and support once again a concept of family based firmly on religious principles.

The significance of the constitutional modifications lay primarily in their potential to change other legal practices. Critics of the new interpretations, fearful of such changes, argue against a return to harsh Islamic penalties for apostasy, criminal acts, and for certain international business practices that have become common in Islamic countries. They rationalize that for the most part modern secular legislation is compatible with a liberal interpretation of sharia and, therefore, there is no need to expand the areas of jurisdiction sharia now covers. Even the most liberal critics do not challenge the importance of maintaining sharia as a basis for family law though some would like to see some reinterpretation of divorce, polygamy, and child custody provisions.

Minority groups are the most uneasy about the prospect of reform: they worry that if sharia becomes universally applied in Egypt they will lose the right to follow the personal status provisions of their own religious communities. Some of their practices, such as limitations in obtaining divorce, directly conflict with Islamic practices. Moderate Muslim supporters of the changes, on their side, see them as a return to a more authentic Islam and try to reassure the critics that Islam has the flexibility not only to solve modern problems but also to show tolerance to other groups' personal status differences. It is only a small number of radical reformers that hope to use the constitutional change to press their view of an Islamic society on the nation as a whole.

What is the Islamic concept of family? One Egyptian sociologist summarizes the key features:

> The family is perceived as being the basic unit of Muslim society. Its soundness derives from strict observance of *shari'a* values and regulation. Authority and production flow from the male head of a household down to females and the young; respect and obedience flow in the opposite direction. In short, the Muslim family is built around obedience, complementarity, protection and respect—not around equality, competition and self-reliance. (S. Ibrahim, MESA conference paper 1980)

Another definition can be derived directly from sharia provisions. Family (*usra*) consists of husband, wife, children, ascendants of a married couple including their collateral relatives (*hawashi*), their brothers and sisters, their paternal uncles and aunts, and their maternal uncles and their children who though related through the female side of the family have moral and material rights in that set of kin. Property relationships make this group a cooperative economic and social unit. Mutual financial assistance includes the following obligations: (1) to pay for the penalties of crime, an obligation that rests on the blood relatives (*aqila*) of the same clan (*asaba*)—that is, relatives related on the male side; the strongest responsibility rests with those closest in the line of inheritance; (2) for the wealthy members of the family to support poor relatives whatever their degree of relationship; (3) for all those mentioned to stand in the line of inheritance, with priority to those closest in degree of relationship (Abu Zahra 1955: 158).

Selected examples of the sharia and explication of their implications illustrate how much the composition and character of family and family relations rest on the tenets of Islam.

Principle: The marriage agreement is a contract and not a sacrament.
Implication: Individuals are joined for the purpose of procreation by mutual agreement and under given conditions. They are not joined indivisibly as in the Christian marriage ceremony.

Principle: There can be no marriage to someone within a prohibited degree of consanguinity, affinity, or milk foster relationship.
Implication: The circle of most intimately interacting family is designated by this prohibition. This principle reduces tensions within this group by suppressing the members' sexual attraction to one another.

Principle: A man is forbidden from marrying two women who would be prohibited from marrying each other if one were male.
Implication: The principle recognizes that two such women may have stronger loyalties to each other than to the man. It reduces the chances for major household divisions to occur, either between the man and his wives or between the sisters themselves who rightfully should continue to maintain their natural loyalties.

Principle: A Muslim woman cannot marry a non-Muslim man, though a Muslim man can marry a non-Muslim wife.
Implication: Paired with the rule that children follow the religion of their father, the principle defends the boundaries of Islamic community by assuring that the households of all followers will practice Islam.

Principle: A marriage is declared invalid if: a woman below the age of competence is given in marriage by other than her father or father's father or person designated in their place; a woman marries someone not her equal; a woman is given with inadequate dower; or a husband is unable to consummate the marriage.
Implication: This principle confirms the responsibility of families to marry their daughters; recognizes the significance of individual marriages to the entire family group; reduces the chances of poorly matched individuals; secures a material base for the woman; and stresses the procreative function of marriage. Over all, the principle provides means of control over the important family event of marriage so that in the heat of decision making certain minimum standards are met.

Principle: A wife must obey her husband in every lawful demand he may make provided he has given her her dower. In return the husband is obligated to provide her with suitable maintenance and support. *Implication*: The complementarity of roles of husband and wife re-inforces cohesiveness and the mutual need of the partners for each other. The principle stresses the material base of contractual relation-ships that break down if the concomitant material goods that are evi-dence of good faith have not been exchanged.

Principle: A man has the right to marry additional wives, to decide where the family home will be, and to control wives' social and pro-fessional activities.
Implication: If carried out, the principle would allow for the protec-tion and marriage of the largest number of women. It establishes clear authority lines in the family unit.

Principle: A husband has a much freer right to divorce his wife than she has to divorce him.
Implication: Other provisions, including those that make it expen-sive, discourage divorce and, therefore, keep the principle from being as devastating to family unity as it might otherwise be. Nevertheless, the possibility of divorce hovers over women, constraining their be-havior toward appeasement of and accommodation to their husbands. Ideally, divorce provisions are meant to provide for dissolving an im-possible marriage and contracting a happier, more stable one. The woman's restricted right of divorce recognizes the large sums a man has paid for dowery and her support. In cases where she seeks a di-vorce she usually needs to provide at least token restitution of these sums if he has otherwise met the requirements as husband.

The *sharia* principles which to a large extent have molded Egyptian Muslim family life have tended also to shape Christian family life (see Chapter 10). This is particularly true in areas of family life where Chris-tians have no authoritative competing theological principles. An area where there is direct coincidence of principle by Egyptian law is that of inheri-tance. If there is a single principle that comes closest to a quantitative evaluation of family obligations it is the Muslim inheritance rules:

Principle: Property is inherited by persons in relationship to the de-ceased according to specified ratios.
Implication: The ratios set up a scale of obligatory relationship be-tween the deceased and his or her relatives.

Principle: A daughter under most circumstances receives half the share of her brother.
Implication: A woman's financial obligations are not as great as those

of a man, and she is entitled to call upon male relatives to support her. Therefore, she does not need as large a share in the group property as a man needs.

Principle: Up to one-third of property can be freely obligated; the rest must go to the designated individuals according to their specified ratios.

Implication: The principle recognizes special circumstances but stresses the general rule that family obligations are foremost and cannot be abrogated.

Sharia provisions include at the same time models for right living and a structure of minimal limits for moral behavior. They contain enough flexibility so that under most circumstances people can find a way to meet their own pressing needs, and they provide a long-term stability so that family retains a recognizable shape.

Operationalizing Definitions of Family

An Egyptian farmer standing in a field overseeing a group of workers harvesting his crops may, with a wave of his hand, say, "These people are my family!" His definition of family in this instance is one based on effective criteria: people who will readily respond to his need because of a sense of kinship obligation. At the moment when he is thinking of family as an economic work group he may exclude a number of other blood relations whose loyalties to other working groups make them unresponsive to his call for laborers. If they are to be defined as family, it must be by other criteria, strictly blood relation, for example, or because they can be mobilized for other purposes, such as to support the general political interests of the group.

A person conceiving family in this way for momentary purposes may define the nuclear family not as a static entity composing husband, wife, and children but as a unit where the complementarity of roles is fulfilled within some kind of legitimizing framework. A widowed woman and her grown employed son living together, for example, might comprise the minimum definition of family under these terms. They cover the two main components of household function: protection (both physical and financial) and household task responsibility. Their relationship as mother and son puts the legitimizing frame around their co-residence. A widow living alone would not define herself as a family. She would usually claim that others residing elsewhere are her minimal family, even when she is assured sufficient support by inheritance or pension. She wants to feel that the protective capacities of a male or the supportive concern of other females are available to her. Two sisters living together are an incomplete family just as are two brothers or any number of other combinations of relatives living together who do not meet the minimal requirements of complementary function and legally legitimizing tie. Operational definitions of family work within the limits of strictly structured definitions but give greater cognizance to the effect circumstances play on who actually takes advantage of their ties. Blood, residence, and other factors play an influencing role but are not the main criteria by which people are included in a particular effective circle of kin.

An extreme case where operationalizing relationships focuses so intensely on effective aspects of relations that it exceeds the boundaries of static criteria is the case where people assign fictive kinship to others who, strictly speaking, have no rightful claim to a kin status. It is probably not much of an exaggeration to say that Egyptians understand best the behavior appropriate to the two categories of kin and stranger, and active relationships in between are either moving toward or away from these polarities. Kin in effect become, by a loose definition, those who have Ego's interests "in their eyes" as the Arabic expression goes, and strangers are people who at their best are neutral and at their worst are hostile.

Um Gamal and Um Fawzi have lived together on the same alley most of their lives. Their homes are not in the same building but rather diagonally across the street from each other. It is almost always possible during the day to find them together in one of their flats. When they were younger their children spilled out of one flat and into another, sleeping where they found themselves at night until it was impossible to tell which children belonged to which house. Um Gamal would run errands for both households and Um Fawzi would watch the children and next day they might reverse these tasks. They would first clean one flat together and then they would clean the other. They baked bread together with Um Gamal mixing the dough, both shaping the bread, and then Um Fawzi poking the bread in the oven in just the right way. At feasts they cooperated in the preparations together. Though they are older women now and most of their children married and gone they like to talk about their relationship as it has been over the years.

"She is my *habiba* [beloved friend]," Um Gamal will say about Um Fawzi. Then she will add, "She is my real sister — closer than anyone in my own family now that my mother and father are gone." The two women take pride in the fact that Um Fawzi's daughter married

Um Gamal's son. They point out the daughter industriously scrubbing the floor of Um Gamal. Um Fawzi comments,

"Look, she cleans the floor for her 'mother'!" to demonstrate how close the ties are of all those concerned. Um Gamal is now a widow and suffers from a weakness in her legs that makes it difficult for her to walk. It is only the help of the daughter-in-law and Um Fawzi that makes it possible for her to continue living alone as she does.

Over the years the relationship between Um Gamal and Um Fawzi has been transformed into a kinship-like relationship. Unless pressed by an outsider for details, they do not stop to draw lines between kinship and friendship. They have in effect become family.

The purpose in showing the variety of ways family is defined in Egypt has been twofold. First, the variety demonstrates that it is not necessary for an Egyptian to have a set definition in order for the institution of family to exert a strong hold on its members and on society as a whole. On the contrary, the combination of flexibility within a strong structure of expectations allows a manipulation of family to meet both old and new needs more effectively.

Second, the discussion has attempted to distinguish between what remains a stable but not immutable basis for Egyptians' perceptions of family — residence, commensality, blood relationship, and a sense of mutual obligation — and what is viewed as the effective relations of family as circles of people who respond to the special needs of one another at given times and under given conditions. The significance of the distinction becomes apparent when we discuss the trend toward the nuclearization of the family. Then it is possible to talk freely about who resides together and who functions together as two separate but related aspects of family.

5

Roles

"Turn the jug on its top; the daughter becomes the mother"
—Arab proverb

IF WE AGREE that husband, wife, and children make up the most enduring image of family for an Egyptian, then it follows that household
organization to a large extent becomes a function of the expectations people hold for these family roles. As was true for the definitions of family,
roles have both a structural and an operational aspect. There is behavior
considered appropriate to a role and behavior a person chooses to use when
he occupies a particular role position. Roles have also an ideal and a general character. In a later chapter, we will discuss how people set priorities
for their roles or even redefine them when two or more family roles conflict. For example, if a woman is at the same time wife, mother, and employee, all roles that consume considerable time and energy and in some
cases require mutually contradictory behaviors, she must somehow resolve
these difficulties in ways that are compatible with her sense of family values or she must learn to live with the contradictions.

In male-female, husband-wife, or any culturally structured set of relations, there are certain possibilities open and certain limits beyond which
an individual cannot effectively operate. It is more efficient for people to
discover the possibilities and limits, whatever they may be, and behave accordingly. By so doing they not only gain their community's approval but
also are able to tap more effectively some of the reciprocal rights that are
implicit in their relationships.

The following illustration gives an idea of how roles are perceived
in their generalized and in their idealized forms in one Egyptian commu-

69

nity. The behavior of the man in the short play represents generalized appropriate role behavior; it is well within the limits of what might be expected of a father-husband but would not be held up as a laudable model worthy of emulation. The woman by contrast represents the idealized expectation of mother and, most of the time, wife roles in their best aspects. This drama was produced spontaneously one day, during their break, by girls of a literacy-handicraft class in a social welfare center of Bulaq. The girls ranged in age from about eight to eighteen.

The play starts with four children asleep around a bench which is intended to act as a wall separating two rooms. Their mother is sitting nearby. Soon the father comes in with a sack of food that he hands to the mother. Kicking one child with his foot, he asks why all the children are sleeping. "Let them sleep; they are tired," answers the mother. Her husband says, "Come then — let's go inside to the other room and 'sleep' together." They go in and lie down with their arms around each other. The husband kisses his wife. [The audience roars with laughter.] One of the sleeping children awakens, gets up, and tiptoes to the "door" separating the room. She peeks at the parents. The father jumps out of bed and shouts at the children to go downstairs and play. After they leave he goes back to his wife. Later when he is asleep, the mother gets up and calls the children back to have tea with her. The children ask their mother for money to buy sweets. She replies that they must have the permission of their father before she can give them any money. They wake him up with their request, and he shouts that he has no money because he has given it all to his wife. That reminds him that he needs 50 p. to go to the coffee shop. She gives the money to him reluctantly but without complaint, and he takes a swat at the children as he goes out. [Some of the audience of little girls cringe and scream out with fear almost as if they were experiencing the blows themselves; they are intensely involved in the drama.] Either there is no money left for the children's sweets or their demands have been forgotten in the interim.

Next we see the husband at one corner of the room in a coffee shop playing a betting game with a friend. They keep telling the waiter to bring some more "water" which they drink down quickly, both becoming drunk in the process. Meanwhile at home there is a peaceful scene of mother and children sitting cross-legged on the floor around the kerosene cooker, drinking their tea. They are speaking quietly and pleasantly to one another.

The father weaves drunkenly home, his money gone, and bursts in upon the peaceful scene. He scatters the children with blows and kicks, directing a few also at his wife. He shoos the children downstairs again and insists that his wife come sleep with him. She complains about the children being sent out in the dark streets and this time refuses his demands. They begin to quarrel. He says he is finished with her, pronounces the three-fold divorce phrase, and walks out. The rest of the story moves along rapidly. The mother buys a knitting machine with the money she has saved and begins to make sweaters and other woolen clothes. Soon she becomes rich while the husband is seen wandering the streets—poor and unhappy.

The roles of husband-father, wife-mother, and, to a lesser extent, the children are neatly described by this play. The husband is breadwinner; he brings home the groceries and the money, but he is aggressive, authoritarian, temperamental, and self-interested, insisting that his desires be constantly gratified by all members of the household as though this were his right in exchange for his breadwinning services. This lack of self-control and need for self-indulgence extends to his habits of gambling and drinking where he squanders what little money the family possesses. Though this is definitely an extreme portrayal of the father-husband role, it is not so far off the mark that the audience does not find something familiar in the portrayal. To portray a woman in this kind of role behavior would so stretch the credibility of the audience that they would either lose interest or roundly criticize the presentation.

The woman in the play is portrayed as self-denying, patient, persevering, constant. She is expected to gratify the desires of others, to make peace, and to mediate the difficulties of family members. She should be resourceful and economical, keeping aside a little extra money for when crises arise. The only point in the play where she does not conform to the ideal pattern is when, the second time, she refuses the sexual advances of her husband. In the overall context of the play she is excused this "lapse" because of her concern, as mother, for the children sent out in the street. This action on her part leads to the rift with her husband and allows for the wish-fulfillment scene in the end. The young feminine directors of the play have obviously created a denouement that appeals to their own sense of the heroic. Indirectly their portrayal of mothers and fathers, though biased, probably reflects quite accurately the stronger bond they, as young girls, feel for their mothers.

The children are not as deeply portrayed as their parents in this play, but it is evident that they look to fathers to provide for their financial needs and to mothers to provide emotional support and affection. Children appear to be the unwitting recipients of their father's unpredictable attentions while the mother's attentions are long term and directed toward their welfare. The attachment between mother and children is recognized by the play as arising out of the mother's ability to accommodate her own needs to those of others, while the father is seen as a rather isolated figure who, by his own temperament, is prevented from having lasting affectionate relationships with others. Again it should be pointed out that this is an overstatement to make the point that men are given much greater latitude than women in gratifying even their most superficial needs.

From the playlet it is apparent that at least three kinds of expectations are in force within the family: those related to sex roles within the context of family, those related to gender in a generalized way, and generational expectations.

SEX ROLES WITHIN THE FAMILY

The rigidity of sex roles within the family has often been underemphasized by writers focusing on the increasing number of Egyptian women receiving extended educations or engaged in full-time employment outside the home. It is true that there is evidence that the segregation of household roles is not as complete in families of the educated, professional classes, but Egyptian men and women as a whole are still a long way from exchanging tasks freely within the household economy. An in-depth study of four upper middle-class families where both husband and wife worked and were highly educated showed that attitudes toward women's work, though clothed in new verbiage, still reflected the value of separate roles for husband and wife. The husbands commented that their wives only worked because they wanted to, that they should not work if it interfered with housework or child care, and that the money they earned should be spent on extras the women wanted rather than on the daily expenses of the household. Most of the men were unwilling to help around the house in any but the most minor ways, and some felt it was the wife's duty to be at home with meals prepared at any time the man wanted them (Stino 1976).

One woman whose personality clearly dominates her household comments:

> As to being equal with men, this is another matter. Men don't like strong women. Any woman who takes on man's work is permeated with a masculinity that repels men. They like women to be weak. What's the point in a masculine woman? It would be as if a man were married to another man. A woman lawyer, for example, assumes masculine qualities, and a man's appetite is closed for this kind of woman. A

woman has to be fine and weak. No man likes a he-she. A man loves a woman's tears. He loves to see her helpless, and he loves her tears. God created men to be lawyers and engineers and doctors, although some women can be doctors. But I feel there is man's work and women's work, and the two should be kept separate, although women should not be entirely dependent on men. (Atiya 1982: 53)

Among the lower classes fairly rigid segregation of roles is still the rule. Consider the following newspaper articles:

A farmer's wife met her death because a cut in the water supply caused her to be delayed in preparing dinner for her husband, a police source said. (*Egyptian Gazette,* December 21, 1979)

A woman in Menufia committed suicide after her husband refused to give her the money to buy a cabbage . . . .The husband told police he did not have enough money for a cabbage. "She began shouting hysterically, accusing me of being unable to face life and its responsibilities," he said. (*Egyptian Gazette,* March 17, 1980)

A wife who dedicated herself to the service of her four children tried to commit suicide, because her husband refused to increase her housekeeping allowance. Her husband used to give her £E 13 a month to feed the entire family. But now it cannot begin to cover all living expenses. . . . One night the children asked her to cook them something to eat. With no money to buy any food, she went into the bathroom and swallowed some insecticide. (*Egyptian Gazette,* May 15, 1980)

In each of these situations, males or females did not fulfill the responsibilities expected of them by a spouse. It was unthinkable for the husband in the first instance to help his wife prepare dinner, or for the two women in the last illustrations to go out to work in order to earn the money necessary for the family. In the three cases, they all took extreme measures to show their displeasure with the spouse (or, of course, they would not have appeared in the newspaper).

This rigidity in the sex roles of husbands and wives has, besides the kinds of negative consequences in the cases above, important implications for family cohesiveness in general. The roles of husband and wife complement each other making it impossible for a man to live alone and difficult for any but a mature woman with assets of her own to do so. People find it almost impossible to live in any but a family unit of some kind. Among the lower classes, as a consequence, one sees amazing evidence of family solidarity even in the face of the potentially diastrous conditions of poverty. The very fact that the rigidity of sex roles is the strongest among the lower classes tends to act beneficially to make their family institutions particularly strong so that one does not find in Bulaq, for example, the kind of family disruption often seen in poor quarters of the United States.

There are similarly distinct sets of ideal personality attributes expected of husband and wife in their relationships with one another that were in evidence in the Bulaq play. Like the segregated task roles of husband and wife they are complementary. Male dominance is matched by female accommodation, male authority by female obedience. An Egyptian journalist in an article in *Al-Ahram* newspaper comments on how women are trained to become good wives:

> We Egyptian women must learn first to control our desires, our anger, and discomfort. We are told to be patient. And when we are married, we tell our daughters the same: "Don't express your feelings. You need a house and a man to spend his money on you even if he is a bad man." And so in this way women must bear the problems and the quarrelling of their husbands without expressing their feelings. (Translated and paraphrased from Gazbiya Sidqi, *Al Ahram,* March 27, 1977)

The journalist, in this case, is suggesting that women may later have problems from playing a role of accommodation so much of the time. One outcome of this suppression, she notes, is seen in the popularity of *zar* (devil placation or exorcism ceremonies), especially among the lower classes but also sometimes among the middle classes.

A social scientist similarly finds evidence of supressed feelings of women emerging through *ozr* (an illness caused by the intrusion of spirits). The researcher finds that a person, usually a woman, becomes possessed when she deviates from expected social roles, as for example, a woman who is barren, a wife who does not respond to her husband's sexual advances, or a woman who does not perform the tasks expected of her by her mother-in-law. The illness becomes a socially accepted excuse for the deviation. The researcher suggests that such illnesses are found more frequently among those who occupy subordinate social roles in society, whether they are men or women. The widespread nature of such illness among women suggests some of the frustration with their roles at certain levels of the society and at certain periods of their lives (El-Bayoumi 1976).

Fortunately the extreme values preached about wifely ideals are not always sustained in real life and women find alternative modes of expression that relieve their tensions. The brash, backtalking, swaggering, aggressive female who stands no nonsense is a valued sub-cultural personality in lower-class Bulaq as is the strong, dominating mother figure. These women are usually clever enough to give men their public due while in private running the household much as they choose. Middle-class women similarly find ways to follow the "letter of the law" while achieving their own purposes. Passing a house one day, my companion commented:

> There is a woman in that house who really knows how to make her husband love her. She listens to every word he says; she brings him good food and wears nice clothes to please him. She married him after his other wife died, but she was careful not to throw out all the other wife's things right away; she slowly replaced all of them with new things of her own. She keeps her house open for his guests at all times of the day or night, so he doesn't have to go to the coffee house like a lot of other men. He loves her very much for all the things she does for him.

Implicit in the word *love* here are a whole host of reciprocal commitments: money for clothes, food, and furnishing, sexual favors, and gifts. Important for the wife in this case are the dependency structures she has erected for her husband which give her the ability to influence where he goes and what he does. Women sacrifice much in building such dependency structures, and they may not seem worth it on another culture's scale of values. In the Egyptian context, however, they put a woman at the heart of where the action lies — in control of family activities and in control, to a much greater extent, of her own future security.

The ideal of an obedient, quiet, subservient, self-denigrating wife, present as an abstract model in the consciousnesses of people, is found in practice most consistently among newly married brides, who in their anxiety to please often become a caricature of the ideal.

> Magda greeted us and ushered us into her new apartment, a much grander place than her family's home in Bulaq. It was not that the family did not have enough assets for a better place but rather that they were attached to the neighborhood and could not find more spacious living quarters. Magda in fact had a better background than her husband, but he and his brothers were known to be industrious and were quickly becoming "rich" by the standards of the quarter. Magda's new apartment was clean and neat. We sat in the "salon" furnished with gold gilt chairs, red satin seat covers, and plastic coverings to keep

them clean. Magda had embroidered a picture of designs with sequins that hung on the wall high up but with a nail pushing in the lower rim to make it easier to see. She was dressed in one of the nightgowns and robes we had seen in her trousseau at her mother's house before the wedding. The custom is for brides to put on make-up and wear a different gown every day for a week after marriage, so that when their friends come they will look as if they just stepped out of the bedroom and are ready to go back in again. Magda was sitting demurely with her hands folded in her lap and her eyes turned modestly toward the floor. She was quite a different Magda from the natural young woman who had enthusiastically dumped trousseau items in our laps several weeks before. The conversation lagged considerably while she was in the room, since she spoke only when spoken to, but it picked up when she went out to bring us sweet drinks (for the happy occasion) and cakes. These were brought in to us suitably arranged on a new shiny tray. After enjoying her hospitality we were shown the immaculate rooms of the rest of the apartment (dining room, bedroom, kitchen, and bathroom), the trousseau again, and the bedding already prepared for the first "nunu" that everyone hoped would appear within the first year.

Magda's self-conscious attempt to fill her new role in as perfect a way as possible was painful in the extreme. No one would expect her to sustain such perfection very long. Furthermore, as she bears children and grows older, her position will permit freer exercise of her own personality within the household and even, to a certain extent, within the community at large.

Despite the difficulty, if not impossibility, of upholding such stringent ideals, people are nevertheless faced with behavioral models of the ideal spouse wherever they turn. Much of it comes in the way people talk about themselves, in the images they try to project:

"I must get home now so dinner will be ready when my husband gets home."

"I will have to ask my husband if it will be all right for me to do that."

"My husband is not very fond of eating that so I never have it around the house."

"No, I'm afraid I can't come at that time since my husband will be at home."

Ideals are also revealed in the way people talk about each other, what they praise, and what they criticize.

Television serials are a constant source of value training. Since much more hangs on the correctness of women's behavior, women in television dramas are clearly defined as good or bad so there will be no mistake made by the viewers. A common theme finds a patient, understanding, sympathetic woman whose life is devoted to husband and children beset by fateful circumstances and a temperamental husband who must be constantly mollified. The plot in such a case may turn on his accusation of her wrongdoing or the wrongdoing of his children, who are, of course, blameless. The wife's constancy eventually restores her innocent reputation, or her perseverance reconciles father and children, and a happy ending results.

In interviews of educated Arab young people conducted almost 30 years ago, in 1955, by a psychologist, the description of the ideal traits of mothers remains much the same as that expressed now. The major difference is that certain traits which were formerly norms of behavior—the woman staying at home, for example—have in some cases become sought-after ideals. The psychologist notes: "The mother is described by both men and women as a patient, affectionate, forgiving, sacrificing creature devoted to her home, children and husband. . . . Her world is almost exclusively the home. 'She has no activity outside the home' is the common statement. . . . The image of the good wife is . . . not strikingly different from that of the mother" (Pergrouhi 1959: 37–38).

GENERALIZED GENDER EXPECTATIONS

There are certain expectations of the sexes that hold true both within and without the household. For example, there is thought to be a stronger bond that can develop between persons of the same sex than between those of opposite sex. In the family the mother is closer to her daughter and the father closer to his son. This carries on to other generations when women are said to prefer the children of their daughters to the children of their sons, since the latters' children are "borne by a stranger." Men are said to prefer the children of the son, "who carry on the name of their grandfather."[1]

It is not difficult to find examples of same-sex closeness. If women are absent from their homes in Bulaq and are not simply off on an errand, it is common for neighbors to explain that they are out for a visit at the homes of mothers or daughters. In a sample of 175 families in Bulaq the number (9) of mothers living with married daughters, once-married daughters, and/or members of the daughters' families was the same as mothers living with their sons (Rugh 1978). Given the norm that daughters or their husbands should not be called upon to support daughters' parents and sons should support theirs, the numbers become significant. Over-all in the cases of family disruption a woman and/or her offspring almost always turn to her own natal family. Since few men of the lower classes outlive their wives,[2] and their longevity rates are significantly lower, in the greater number of cases it means that women are returning to their widowed mothers and children to their maternal grandmothers.[3]

Superficial observation of people involved in normal daily activities reveals the extent to which the lower class, especially, divides itself into separate worlds of men and women. It is not the kind of self-conscious separation that sends women scurrying for cover as in Saudi Arabia when men appear. Rather it is largely a matter of mutual interests and ease that bring the same sex together. There are fewer constraints on the behavior of people when they gather in groups with their own sex. Women touch each other constantly, insult each other, joke, exchange and nurse each others' babies, and continuously do small services for one another. Closeness involves more unrestrained quarrels and disagreements as well as mutually supportive actions. Men enjoy comparable intimacies. In mixed company, the sexes engage in word play of a more restrained nature, less warm and less complementary to avoid the appearance of inappropriate intimacy. Public displays of affection between adult males and females who are married or who could potentially marry are generally taboo. It is only a few "modern" middle-class couples (usually engaged) who stroll hand-in-hand along the banks of the Nile in the evenings.

Part of gender cohesiveness naturally emerges out of similar preoccupations. Food preparation, for example, is an exclusively female occupation that separates the female from the male members of the household. The daily routine of squatting around a kerosene stove or standing before a butagaz one and meticulously cutting the vegetables and preparing the dishes together seems to forge strong bonds between women. In the same way bonds grow between female neighbors as a result of their shared tasks, similar problems, and same-age children. The men of the household find their common interests in offices outside the home, in coffee houses if lower-class and if middle-class, perhaps in politics or business. In many instances their male children accompany them in these pursuits and forge bonds similar to those of mother and daughter.

During the day it is mostly the women who occupy residential areas, relaxing the restraints they feel in the presence of men. The density of popu-

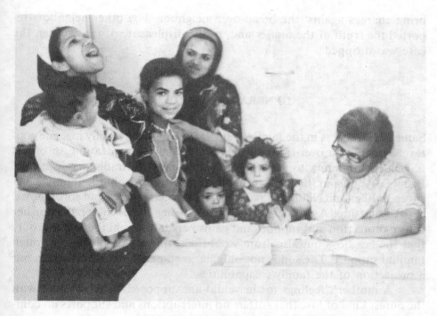

Lower-class women use a clinic serving their health and family-planning needs.

lation in areas like Bulaq means that people cannot avoid seeing each other on a daily basis. Their lives are so public, in fact, that few secrets can be hidden for long. Perhaps because it is useless to hide anything women often share the most intimate details of their lives with other women, sometimes even ones that they do not share with their husbands. Most secrets told to other women will not pass the sex barrier, though they may well find their way through the larger network of female communication.

Women usually trust each other to provide support when it is needed. A woman out on an errand without her husband's permission, for example, can usually count on a neighbor to provide a convenient excuse if it is necessary. Women are aware of the repercussions of unhappy husbands. On the other hand, a quarrel between neighbors of the same sex can sometimes become as violent as one between husband and wife. In one apartment building in Bulaq a quarrel erupted when one woman wanted to place her chicken coop in the hall next to the bread baking oven of her neighbor who objected. After months of sporadic quarrelling the woman with the chicken coop gashed her own head with a rock and ran to the police to bring charges against the bread-oven neighbor. The other neighbors reported the truth of the matter and, to the displeasure of the accuser, the case was dropped.

GENERATIONAL ROLES

Same-sex closeness in the family, though stated unequivocally in some contexts as being an over-riding principle of family organization, in others is seen as secondary to a stronger and partially contradictory principle. People often claim that the strongest relationship within the family is between mother and child, and particularly between mother and son, a cross-sex relationship. A mother invests many of her hopes in her son for her future protection and support and gains her status from the fact not only that she has boys but also from what the son is able to achieve through familial support. The son is not only her own personal ego extension but a projection of the family's capabilities.

A mother's feelings for her child are supposed to be suffused with the purest kind of love that suffers no interruptions and supports no competing interests. Dr. Samira Bahr writing in *Al-Akhbar* newspaper suggests that maternal care "offers the child its first lessons in love, trust and optimism." But she cautions against the kind of excessive tenderness that sometimes characterizes mother love and leads to male inadequacy. She considers "paternal love inferior to the utterly selfless devotion of the mother to the welfare of her offspring, for the reason that the focus is divided between care for the wife and care for the children."[4]

Mother-child relationships are expected to prevail over other relationships even when their survival requires a heavy price, as in a film, *Woman in a Whirlpool*. The plot is as follows:

Nadya finds herself pregnant after her fiancé is killed in a car accident on the way to their wedding. Her widowed mother who is an employee in the hospital where Nadya is delivered of a daughter switches the baby with the dead child of a rich couple eagerly looking forward to parenthood after ten years of a childless marriage. Nadya is grieved by what she believes is the death of her child, but her mother Amina sees it as the best solution to a difficult situation. The two women move to a new area where Amina's sister's daughter lives, and Nadya finds work. Everyone is told only that Nadya's fiancé was killed. The two cousins become friends with two young men neighbors. Meanwhile Amina keeps in touch with her grandchild, always visiting her on birthdays. The young child, Tuha, loses her "mother" and the father marries another woman who proves to be very cruel to Tuha. Concerned for the child, the father divorces the new wife. Nadya in the meantime accidentally meets Tuha, and through her work in a toy store has the excuse to visit the child. There is instant rapport between Nadya and the child though neither know their true relationship. The neighbor friend upstairs asks Nadya to marry him, and she tells him the whole story of her pregnancy, but this does not alter his feeling for her; they become engaged. Soon after, at Tuha's birthday party which this time Nadya attends, Tuha's father, seeing Nadya's concern for the child, also proposes, declaring that he wants "to find a good mother for Tuha." In the final scene, Nadya, the father and Tuha are saying goodbye to Amina from a train window while at a distance, the real love, the forsaken neighbor, catches Nadya's eye and brings tears.

A close cross-sex relationship is sometimes said to exist between father and daughter but is thought not comparable to the strength of the mother-child relationship. A father is supposed to keep tight controls over a daughter particularly after she reaches puberty, but often he cannot resist indulging his emotional feeling toward her. After all, as people say, "Who serves her father willingly and will always be the one that loves her father no matter what?" Mai Shahin writing in *Al-Akhbar* urges fathers to develop a more lenient and merciful approach of this kind toward their daughters. She says, "Many Egyptian fathers treat their daughters cruelly because they are afraid for them and anxious to see them protected from the evils of society. Accordingly, they either lock them up or seek various ways of secluding them from male companions. Such harshness and cruelty in the treatment of girls usually has adverse effects and can lead to neurosis or delinquency,"[5] she concludes. The father who has an overt, loving, indulgent relationship with his daughter is seen, therefore, as more of an anomaly than normal in the structural sense, while the mother's loving relationship with her children is seen as natural and expected.

If the two principles of same-sex closeness and greater closeness with mother are carried to their logical conclusion, one might then postulate that the inherent conflict in family life involves the father-son relationship, which though strengthened on the one side by same-sex closeness runs into difficulties with not only the son's greater attachment to the mother but also the greater demands placed on him by the father to maintain certain ideals of the filial position (proper respect, promoting the good name of the family, etc.). A contributory factor is the competitiveness that fathers and sons feel toward each other — competitiveness over the affections of the mother, over their personal achievements, and over the need

to assert hierarchical positions within their own and extended kin households. Eventually, the son knows he will take over the position of dominance within the household, but he is expected to suppress his desire to
control until the appropriate moment comes. This process of role substitution is illustrated in a television serial called "The Straight Family" where
the eldest son is portrayed first as a young man who, with his brothers
and sisters, make impossible demands on their father's affections and finances. In trying to meet their demands, and incidentally his own sense
of masculine pride, the father becomes exhausted and dies. The elder son
takes over the responsibilities of the family, and as he molds himself to
this new position of authority he recognizes the miserable situation his
father had to contend with. In his relationships with the younger children
he assumes the father role and along with it the ambivalence of sustaining
at the same time a sense of love for his siblings and a need to discipline
them.

Within the family, therefore, the son becomes the object of the competing loves of the father and of the mother—the father feeling restraint
on his indulgence by the need to raise his son to reflect credit on the household, the mother feeling unrestrained love and affection for the son. If
the son turns out poorly the mother may be blamed for her over-indulgence
of the boy, or she in turn may blame the father for being overly strict with
him. There is an underlying urgency to the mother's need to co-opt her
son's affections. If something should happen to her marriage and she
should be divorced, her security rests with her son's desire to stay with
her and support her.

The mother-daughter relationship in the household is one of extreme
closeness. Women in general usually minimize hierarchical distances between each other, even when there are significant differences in socioeconomic status or age. Mothers also commonly require less respectful
behavior of children in the household than fathers do, treating children
generally in a fairly egalitarian manner. In lower-class households mothers are even sometimes insulted or treated like contemporaries by their children, though this is not considered ideal behavior. Middle-and upper-class
families usually require greater respect from children toward their mothers, but mothers in these classes still have much more egalitarian relations
with their children than fathers normally do, and children are able to con-
fide in their mothers almost as if they were equals.

The relationship of mother and daughter in an Egyptian household
is quite different from that existing in the American household. In the latter a tension is created by the daughter's need to break away from her
mother in order to become a mature adult, while at the same time the

A middle-class mother enjoys a close and affectionate moment with her young son.

mother may be trying to compensate for her own frustrations and disappointments through the achievements of the daughter. The American
daughter often sees in her own mother the dependent, restricted figure she
does not want to become. In Egypt the closeness between mother and
daughter occurs "as a sympathy in the face of mutual misery and the inevi-
tability of their separation," as one Egyptian social scientist put it.[6] Daughters are expected to leave home and go to their husbands' homes. They
depend on their mothers, and do not want to be parted from them. They
hope the physical distance between their parents' homes and husbands'
homes is not great because they still expect the help and support of their
mothers after marriage. In one family, as illustration, a young woman broke
her engagement three times because, as she said, "I can't bear the idea of
leaving my mother. Even when I visit relatives for a few days I become
so homesick for my mother that I sometimes cut my visit short to return
home." When we discussed a current American book on the need for daughters to separate from their mothers to become independent adults, she replied, "It would never work here! I am my mother and she is me. Why
should we want to break what is such a warm and loving relationship?"

Observation of daily life in Bulaq and Shubra tends to confirm that
real relationships follow to a considerable extent the expectations people
articulate. Mothers and daughters appear to have close and enduring relations while sons' positions in the household appear to become much more
strained as they grow older. Sons experience the entire spectrum of complete indulgence by parents as young children to ever-increasing restrictions and demands made on them as they grow older. With their salaries
lower-class men are usually expected to help maintain parental households
with little thought to their own hopes for early marriage. They may be
required to support siblings through schooling and help marry off their
sisters before they themselves marry. When their own families require all
the money they can earn, they still must help support their parents. At
the same time they resent any withholding of family money that prevents
their own aspirations from being realized.

If crimes can be considered a marker of where some of the tensions
in the family lie,[7] then one finds that between sons and their parents, the
violent crimes almost always involve crimes between fathers (or father sur-
rogates) and sons and usually are perpetrated by the sons on the fathers.
The main cause of the initial dispute is money or property. The following
newspaper excerpts indicate the kinds of problems that arise:

> Two brothers were arrested by the Giza police earlier this week on a
> charge of stabbing their father to death because he had refused to give

them money to help cover the expenses of getting married. (*Egyptian Gazette,* September 1, 1981)

Overcome by despair he took his gun and shot his brother to death. So that was the end of the long wait. . . . Mr. Khalid had been trying for the past five years to make his older brother, who ran the family's properties, pay the necessary costs for his marriage before his sweetheart was pressed by her conservative father to marry another. (*Egyptian Gazette,* December 18, 1980)

A Cairo engineer killed his farmer brother over an inheritance dispute. The murder was committed when the daughter of the farmer invited her father and uncle to a banquet to reconcile them. (*Egyptian Gazette,* May 3, 1981)

The primary causes for crimes that involve parent and daughter are of a wholly different nature than those involving parent and son. They normally concern controls over the girl's morality and are almost always crimes committed by parents (usually the father) or parent surrogate (usually a brother) against the young woman. The first example entitled "Willful daughter stabbed" is an exception to the usual examples of morality cases:

Cairo Criminal Court yesterday sentenced a man to 5 years hard labor for killing his daughter who had refused to live with him since he divorced her mother. The girl went to live with her grandmother and when she refused to return to her father's flat he stabbed her. (*Egyptian Gazette,* March 16, 1980)

A Bedouin strangled and then electrocuted his 16-year-old daughter because she had been raped and brought him disgrace, police said. (*Egyptian Gazette,* May 9, 1981)

Police investigating the death of (a girl) . . . found slain in (a) cemetery . . . arrested the girl's brother . . . According to the police he claimed that he had killed his sister because she had sinful relations with one of the young men of the village, and had become pregnant. (*Egyptian Gazette,* April 11, 1980)

Police investigations have proved that the suicide of a young girl . . . was but a predetermined murder because the girl got pregnant after being raped by a neighbor. . . . Thinking of a way out the brother got a chance when the poor sister complained of a colic. He put an insecticide in a cup and gave it to her for a medicine. (*Egyptian Gazette,* September 19, 1980)

A brother's or father's obligation for preserving a young woman's moral character continues even after her marriage:

> A young wife . . . left her husband's house . . . because of their continual quarrelling. Her family searched for her but with no success till two of her brother's friends chanced to see her in Saida Zeinab. The brother hurried to the place where he found his sister in the company of two young men . . . the brother planned his revenge and after a while he phoned his sister and told her that he had forgiven her and she could return to her father's house. In his father's house the brother killed his sister. . . . [He] gave himself up to the police and told the investigator that the killing wiped out the shame which his sister brought on him and his family. (*Egyptian Gazette,* October 26, 1980)

There is no doubt that the majority of instances involving parents and children with similar provocation are solved in less drastic ways. The main point of the illustrations above is to give a sense of what people see as the obligations and responsibilities of people in particular role positions. Without doubt each aggressor felt that his right or a principle he valued had been willfully violated to the extent that he was morally obliged to take the action he did.

From details of the cases not reproduced here it is evident that most involve people from the lower social classes. The middle classes may have more subtle ways of committing crimes of this type, they may be more successful at keeping them out of newspapers, or they may simply restrain themselves to a greater extent in an attempt to avoid inevitable punishments. Their moral objections to the provocative behavior of the victims are the same, however.

The conditions of middle-class life to a large extent have softened the extremes of authoritarianism and indulgence that formerly characterized male and female roles for these families. If men are away working at two jobs a day, women must take over some of their supervisory and disciplinarian tasks. If women are at work, men must assume some of the child-care responsibilities. Writers tend to associate the increasing numbers of women working with a reduction of male authority and dominance in the household.[8] A recent study (1981) by the Higher Institute of Social Work in Cairo concluded that mothers were disciplining their children now more than fathers in reverse of the traditional expectations. Beating was a common punishment where children told lies, stole something, or uttered insults, but was not normally used when "children were unwilling to eat or [for] those who usually scream or cry. . . . " The study notes that the mother's position in the family is usually more effective and impressive to the child than that of the father, and that most children prefer to handle private business with their mothers. Of the fathers questioned 75 percent said that the mother is the one responsible for bringing up children. A review of the study ends by commenting that when a mother adopts a tough stance in treating her children, "it has obviously affected the child's attitudes, resulting in children giving more obedience to their father" (*Egyptian Gazette,* October 23, 1980). The commentator and/or the researcher sees the new trend as bolstering the old value of obedience to the father.[9]

Middle-class goals of respectability, including extended education and white-collar employment, similarly affect the way parents deal with their children in these classes. Parents tend to require fewer household responsibilities of children so the children can concentrate more fully on their studies. An adult almost always spends several hours a day "studying with the child," an activity that brings child and parent into close contact over something that is the province of the child.

In order to keep up a middle-class image of a well-dressed, well-behaved, morally upright family, middle-class parents control the public behavior of their children fairly strictly. This requires a great deal of the parents' time taking them on visits to appropriate places and people or seeing that they have some kind of entertainment at home. Middle-class parents work much harder controlling their children in the interests of the children's futures than do most lower-class parents who despite their greater authoritarianism often work more as a team with their children to satisfy the present needs of the whole family. A middle-class father who expressed extreme dissatisfaction with his job, noted, "It really doesn't matter how I feel about the job; I get paid well for it and that's what counts as far as what I can provide for my children is concerned. After I have given them all the opportunities I can, then I can think about taking another job that suits me better." The child's future commonly becomes the family goal in the middle classes while the family welfare as a whole remains the concern of the lower classes. The lower-class parent normally does not feel the same compulsion to define his child's future as bound up in long-term education and, in any case, that parent expects a good part of the effort toward his future to come from the child himself. When the lower-class parent develops middle-class aspirations for his child, then his own behavior changes markedly, shifting to a much greater sense of his own need to sacrifice in order to provide what the child must have. Long-term education requires supreme efforts on the part of almost any Egyptian family that wishes to obtain its benefits. In a later chapter we will look more closely at the effects extended education has produced on the organization of family life in general. Here, it has only been mentioned briefly to show how markedly it can affect the relations of parent and child.

A final fact of middle-class life affecting the relations of parent and child is the impact of individualized salary and eventually individualized pension that the large number of government workers in this class receive. Salaries are so small as to make it difficult for grown children to support themselves, let alone their parents or other relatives. Individualized wage or salaried labor encourages the nuclearization of families and discourages the concept of family in its long-term aspects as a substitution process of children taking over the support functions of extended households as parents become older and incapacitated. Fortunately pensions, small as they are, give many old people an opportunity to support themselves. Thus some of the tensions between parents and children are reduced by this condition.

In general middle-class parents do not require such heavy household responsibilities of their children as lower-class parents do, and they are more indulgent toward their needs. In this way they avoid some of the conflicts that arise out of children's frustrated needs or their inability to meet the heavy demands placed upon them. This is not to say that the demands made upon middle-class children are not great — every child who does not become a doctor or engineer in effect disappoints his parents; it is rather to say that the demands are of a different kind and can be construed to be in the interests of the children themselves.

The expectations of Egyptians about family roles in large measure influence the organization of family life. No matter what aspect of roles one considers, features appear that lead to or protect family cohesiveness and solidarity: the complementarity of husband-wife roles, the focus of middle-class families on providing opportunities for their children, of lower-class families on meeting the needs of the household group as a whole, of same-sex closeness, of mother and child attachment. Even when contradictions arise in stable values or expected role-behaviors, people insist that both contradictory factors enhance the ideal goal. Paternal discipline or indulgence toward daughters, for example, are both said to enhance close family ties. The test comes in the results. If the results support the goals of family cohesion, the behavior is applauded; if it ruptures family ties then it was extreme and not appropriate. Expectations have this sensitive character: they are part of a belief system that for the most part produces self-fulfilling outcomes, but if not, there are also provisions to explain the negative consequences.

6

Ties

"There is neither sister nor mother to share my misery"—Arab proverb

WHAT ARE the mechanisms that draw the members of the Egyptian family together in the strikingly cohesive way discussed in the previous chapter? Part of the answer most certainly lies in the complicated pattern for familial and other personal relations that is part of every Egyptian's conscious knowledge. At the heart of this conceptual framework — or cultural grammar — is a system of rights, duties, and favors that, seen as a whole, provide the overarching principles for human interaction. People come to think of them as naturally correct and necessary in order to achieve such "strong" values of the society as family solidarity and harmony.

JURAL AND AFFECTIVE RELATIONS

People tend to characterize their enduring relationships in two qualitatively different ways — as possessing jural elements and affective elements. Jural aspects of relationships include the specific rights and obligations people of the society attach to particular, structurally defined relationships like those of father-son, husband-wife, or simply of friend to friend. The jural relationships normally include rights to property and services expected and definitions of who has the right to exercise authority over another. Usually jural expectations are accompanied by sanctions that reinforce the commonly held views defining the relationship.

Sanctions against breach of the rules are normally of at least two

89

degrees in a society as socially complex as Egypt. There are those that are legally codified and reserved for the breaches the society takes most seriously, and there are those that are evoked informally and applied with more variability through a range of social pressures.

In Egypt an example of the first kind of jural-legal relationship is found when the husband-wife relationship is defined in its most minimal terms. By law the husband is required to support his wife; she in turn is required to obey him. Similarly, a father has a jural-legal duty to support a child. The male child is a jural asset to the father, carrying on the family name and property and helping in the support of family members as he grows older. In Egypt many jural-legal aspects of family relations are defined by Islamic law while other jural-legal relations are governed by civil and other codes of law.

The jural aspects of personal relations that, rather than being codified, depend for their existence on social understandings can best be observed in the exercise of everyday obligations people feel for each other. These jural-social relations differ from jural-legal relations in that their breach evokes social rather than legal sanctions. Jural-social relations may bear much the same force for compliance as if they were accompanied by jural-legal sanctions. Not carrying the legal sanctions, however, means that they depend for their strength or weakness on the social understandings of the moment.

Loosely defined, a jural-social obligation, *wagib* in Arabic, is that service, gift, money, or action initiated between two persons because it is believed to be owed by one to the other. In certain roles specific rights and duties are implied. A son owes certain *wagibs* to his parents (support, visits, gifts on special occasions, etc.). A friend is expected to pay condolences to a friend who has a death in the family. A stronger person is supposed to come to the aid of a weaker person. Sharkawi's character in the classic novel *The Egyptian Earth* expresses *wagib* relationships when he retorts to the grocer who is questioning where he got some stolen corn he wants to sell: "'I'm brave! Yes, indeed. But I swear by the Prophet that not one of these comes from a friend or from someone whose salt I have eaten, or from anyone who's hard up'" (Sharkawi 1962: 156).

It is in the nature of *wagibs* that they are fairly specific, not as much in terms of the content of the behavior itself as in the personnel involved and the direction in which goods or actions flow. The duties of relatives are particularly clearly spelled out. It is an idealized system that is honored perhaps as much in the breach as in the practice. The fact remains that people who are entitled to certain *wagibs* from others and do not receive them feel offended or hurt and may feel it desirable in some way to reduce their attachments or punish those who have neglected them. In the words of one woman, the bitterness is evident:

> If a woman is totally dependent on her husband as I was in the early years of marriage, then she longs for sons. She prefers them to daughters because she feels they'll stand by her in time of need — they have the means to stand by her. My hopes were disappointed in the case of my eldest son and it is my youngest daughter who asks after me and insists on sending me £E 5 from her paycheck. This is unusual because custom dictates that a daughter's allegiance will be to her husband's family when she marries. Boys are expected to give money to their parents once they're employed. They support their parents in their old age and look after the well-being of their married sisters. This is important because a girl who has men folk behind her is better cared for and respected by her husband than one without men at her back. (Atiya 1982: 48, 49)

The extent to which relationships remain strictly jural and expressed primarily in *wagib* terms is the extent to which they remain formal, impersonal, and highly structured. What adds depth to personal relationships are the affective aspects.

In affective relationships people evaluate their emotional involvement with one another over the long term to determine the extent to which their relationships require unique demonstrations of good will that are different from those their structural relationships strictly require. In such cases the jural-legal or jural-social expectations are either put aside or modified in favor of a more flexible interpretation of the relationship and the exchanges required.

In Egypt affective relations find one form of behavioral expression in the offering of a favor (*maruf*). Like a *wagib,* a *maruf* may be a kind of service, gift, money, or action initiated between persons, but instead of being formally required, a *maruf* is given "from the heart." A neighbor who sends over unsolicited sweets on a feast day, for example, is doing a favor. But her *maruf* in this example normally then sets up a *wagib*: the favored person has the duty to return the favor with something of equal value or preferably of a little greater value. A *maruf* does not always require a return, especially in cases where there are status differences between the two involved in the exchange or where genuine deep feeling precludes keeping account of every transaction.

An Egyptian journalist in attempting to explain what friendship meant to him was in part describing a relationship where affection made the return of *maruf* unnecessary:

> A friend to me is someone I can just reach over and take a cigarette from without asking. He is someone I can take home for dinner without letting my wife know beforehand and he will accept whatever we have available. He is someone I can ask to write an article for me when I have something more pressing to do elsewhere. He can also ask any of these things of me and I will gladly oblige him without thinking that he should return some equal favor to me.

The illustration points out that *marufs* can also be demanded of those with affective ties to oneself, and by doing so one underlines the quality of the relationship. If *marufs* are demanded of strangers or casual acquaintances, however, then the tone of voice must be conciliatory, the person must possess a rank that entitles him to such services, or by contrast one must be "helpless" (a foreigner or a beggar, for example) and, therefore, owed help as an act of hospitality or charity; or the person must be in a position to return an equal or greater favor at some other time. There is nothing in the relationship between strangers that automatically requires a service though people are usually willing to extend such help in any case.

The systems of *wagib* and *maruf* are connected when, as sometimes happens, a *maruf* elicits a *wagib*. They are also connected in the sense that *maruf* in one form is the reverse of *wagib*. This can be best illustrated by an imaginary example:

> *Wagib:* As a young bride, Muna's *wagib* is to help her mother-in-law, serving in every way possible to relieve her of the more arduous tasks of housework. Muna's husband also is expected to give gifts to his parents, visit them frequently, and support them financially if that is necessary. Now that the young man is grown, the parents have no major *wagibs* they owe him nor are they expected to return the services or the money he gives them during their lifetime. (The son will, of course, share in inheriting any property that exists after their death.) Muna's own parents, on the other hand, have a *wagib* to help their daughter in every way they can to provide a good image of their family in her new home: they bake cakes on feast days, give gifts to her children, take her place in housekeeping chores if she is incapacitated by childbirth or illness. Any *wagibs* Muna owes to her parents are largely superceded by her obligations to her husband and in-laws.

A young woman of the lower classes returns home after delivering sweets to her neighbors.

When Muna performs her *wagib* to her mother-in-law she only does
what is expected of her and no thanks or special acclaim are due her,
though she may be spoken of with admiration as "one who does her
duty."

Maruf: Perhaps on a feast day Muna takes the extra time to make
her own mother some cakes or another time Muna's mother is sick
when Muna has a baby and her mother-in-law comes instead to take
care of the house for her. Both of these examples reverse the natural
flow of expected *wagib* and, therefore, can be technically known as
maruf.[2] They are *marufs* because they are performed out of generosity and are not required. They are seen as conferring special credit
on the doer.

Balance is achieved when *wagib* and rights (which are the reciprocal of
wagibs) are looked at in their totality. Balance means that the arduous-
ness of duties required of an individual is fairly equally offset by the advantages of rights received.

From Muna's required *wagibs* it is obvious that she is not expected
to get as much in return for what she does for her mother-in-law as
she gives. The relationship is unbalanced in favor of the mother-in-
law. For Muna herself the balance is ideally restored by the services
she receives from her own mother.

Because of their greater specificity and unbalanced reciprocity, familial relations are particularly prone to imbalances. The following is an
illustration of a young woman not only burdened by her own obligations
to a mother-in-law but also that mother-in-law's obligation to her own
daughter, without the compensating support of a mother's services.

Gamallaat was tired, a haggard version of the vivacious, enthusiastic
young woman she had been only a few months earlier. Then, planning every detail of her trousseau and wedding, her disappointments
came in the way she had to cut corners wherever she could — wearing
second-hand shoes at the wedding, making her sweets at home rather
than buying them from a store, and accepting the fact that her furnishings would consist of no more than the pieces her mother had
stripped from her own simple room. These disappointments were nothing when compared with the hopes Gamallaat had for her own future. True, she and her bridegroom were unable to afford their own
apartment and would have to live in one of the rooms of her mother-

in-law. Like her own father, Gamallaat's husband was a fruit and vegetable peddler, but he was young and more aggressive as a salesman.
With her help she was certain that he could do well.

Now a few months after the wedding she was finding life unex-
pectedly difficult. She accompanied her husband to the wholesale
market every morning to help him bring home the boxes of fruits and
vegetables for his cart. Before he set out she washed and scrubbed
everything to give it more eye-appeal for the customers. When he was
gone she spent the morning cleaning both her own and her mother-
in-law's rooms, washing their clothes, and bringing water from the
pump for both households from some distance away. By the time her
husband returned he expected a tasty dish on the table. Gamallaat did
these chores cheerfully on the surface because she knew her responsibilities to her mother-in-law, and as a young bride she wanted to
please, but as time wore on, the hard work began to tell on her spirits.
People were beginning to ask also why there were no signs yet that
she had become pregnant. The pressures mounted on all sides, and
what was hardest was that her mother lived in a district so far away
in Cairo that it was impossible for her to give encouragement or offer
her help. Very soon in fact after the marriage of Gamallaat, her mother,
relieved of her most important obligation — to marry her daughter —
announced that she was off to Upper Egypt where she could now die
in peace (conveniently at little expense in the village). She did just that,
leaving her grieving daughter alone and feeling more abandoned.

It was at this point that we visited Gamallaat one day, just before the feast of *Bairam*. We talked first with her and then went to
visit her mother-in-law in the next room. Visiting also at that time
was the old woman's daughter bringing flour and other ingredients
so that the feast cakes could be made in the old woman's house for
the daughter's household. The daughter explained that she had saved
the money for the ingredients without her husband finding out, so
that when the old woman presented the cakes he would think them
an outright gift from her. The daughter eventually left and in our
presence the old woman turned the flour over to Gamallaat so she
could bake an extra portion in addition to the cakes she would already prepare for the family.

This case illustrates the key point that when a close relative is missing for
whatever reason, a gap is left in the balanced whole of the personal networks affected. Individuals feel the loss keenly, particularly in a society
that is set up to operate with a continuous round of publicly exchanged
evidences of relationships. The individual is not forgiven his or her obligation simply because the credit he or she draws from others is diminished.

People have different generalized expectations for how *wagibs* and *marufs* should appropriately be carried out by men and women. The expectations correspond to male and female roles in society. Since the man brings home income, a man's expected *wagib* tends toward cash gifts or material goods. The woman, whose role it normally is to convert income or raw food products into edibles and to serve the daily nurturing and household needs of a family, is expected to fulfill her *wagibs* by time given to help in work, such as in baking sweets or in some kind of nurturing task such as care for the elderly or the indisposed. These different expectations are not inviolable. For example, women give each other gifts of material goods when they return from travel. As incomes increase, time becomes a more precious commodity that the obligated person buys by substituting store-bought goods for home-produced items. With the new admiration of ready-bought products, these kinds of gifts tend to be more appreciated.

In generalized relationships there are also different expectations for men and women. A husband, for example, is permitted greater recourse to strictly jural aspects of the marriage relation. If he follows the letter of the law and supports his wife, public opinion does not find him negligent even if he invests very little emotion in the relationship. Public opinion, on the other hand, judges the wife by the quality of the emotional content she brings to the relationship. She is faulted if she neglects the loving, affectionate qualities of service — as she brings the tea and is attentive to the needs of her family. Women are generally held responsible for the atmosphere of affection in a household. If there is a warm, closely knit family she is expected and usually is found to be at the emotional core, orchestrating the concern and quality of relationships. Carrying these expectations one step further, one finds in this idealized scheme that the relations of children with their fathers are thought to be characterized more by jural aspects while affective aspects are considered to dominate the relations with mothers. In this way, children go to mothers for requests they fear their fathers will turn down. Young women tell mothers about boys they meet in the club or elsewhere when they suspect the fathers would object. Mothers in many cases become the affectionate mediators who can be counted on to plead the child's case with a father.

The father may not be temperamentally disposed to take the stern, authoritarian role that is offered him; mothers from their side often do much to heighten the image, at least partly from the good faith view that the family runs better that way and that the public reputation and honor of the family is better maintained with an *éminence gris* in the background. Middle-class fathers tend to have more latitude in whether or not they conform to this role than lower-class fathers who feel more keenly the need to demonstrate their masculinity with a show of authority. Exceptions, however, are not uncommon even in these classes. This expectation does not prevent fathers from taking a sympathetic and affectionate stance toward their children, but it does define where fathers are expected to draw the line and do "what's best" for them. The father in theory lays down the law and the mother soothes the disappointments of the children.

When a family is missing a father, women in television dramas and in real life often become less indulgent and more strict in disciplining children in an attempt to compensate for the missing authoritarian element. One television drama builds its theme around this issue. A widow left with four daughters takes her responsibilities so seriously that she denies herself the chance to fall in love and marry. With each of her children she exerts such strict controls on where they go and whom they see that they have difficulty in carrying on normal relations with their friends. The girls are confused by their mother's transformation from a sympathetic friend to a harsh disciplinarian.

The Higher Institute of Social Work in Cairo conducted a survey of lower-class families and discovered that mothers are taking an ever-increasing role in the discipline of children, a task generally considered the province of men. It is possible that this might be related to the increasing role women are taking in supervising children with their homework — "studying with them." Women now tend to be blamed if children do not do well in school; and a new rationale for extended education of women is that they can aid children in homework. (See Chapter 5 for details of the study.)

In the relationships of siblings, the sex differences continue to hold sway. The jural duties of brothers to sisters are emphasized while on the sister's side the affective nature of her feeling for her brother is stressed instead. Brothers are expected to have strong feelings for each other, simply as family members, but their jural rights and obligations within the family are recognized as giving cause for contention. Sisters' bonds are considered stronger because of their unhindered affective relationship. The unfettered love of sisters demonstrates how in any cultural setting one finds the ideal ignoring some aspects of relationships while stressing others. In another context, sisters might be seen as competing with each other for a mother's attentions or for family resources to take into marriage. Here, however, the ideal invests females with a sympathetic outlook and prefers not to reveal the other side.

In the circle of wider kinship, some of the sex differentials are carried a step further. Relatives of the mother assume the affective nature of her relations with the child. Paternal relatives assume a more jural rela-

During the day lower-class residential areas, empty of men, becoming the domain of women and children. Women's common activities foster strong bonds of cooperation and dependence across generations.

tionship with the child. In both cases, the generalization holds true whether the relative is male or female with the only qualification being the extent to which men and women are able to demonstrate these two tendencies. One person in commenting upon the difference in paternal and maternal relatives said, "In the home of my mother's relatives we can go right to the kitchen and carry on a conversation there. In the home of my father's relatives we usually stay in the sitting room."

It is common for people, especially those in the lower classes, to extend these distinctions to non-relatives. A younger woman passing an older man might respectfully greet him with "Good morning, Amm [father's brother] Bakheet." If the person is an older woman she would greet her as "Khallt [mother's sister] Zahiyya." In both cases by making the reference specifically to a maternal or paternal relative she preserves the appropriate distance required by her sex, while claiming a reciprocal relation that is respectful and protective from the man and affectionate from the woman. Under the same circumstances, young women in Saudi Arabia address older people as father's brother or father's sister, emphasizing instead their respectful and deferential posture toward these individuals. Such differences in the customs of the two countries underline basic differences in their conceptual frames: Saudi Arabian familial structures are much more subject to patrilineal and Egyptian to bilateral organization.

Wagib and *maruf* play an important role in interfamilial and community relations as well as private family relations. Within the family, few *wagibs* are formally defined as equal. Even between sisters, which is the closest to being the exception, age differentials technically require different behaviors from each. It is only in relations between families as groups or in relations with those wholly outside one's own family that equivalency in *wagib* is found. Where it is found one finds also a relationship that is defined as equal. For example, friends, neighbors, professional colleagues, and others in relationships not complicated by status disparities of sex, age, educational, economic, or other factors normally sustain fairly balanced *wagibs* toward one another. If equal statuses do not exist, then a patron-client relationship may ensue with the better-endowed giving *wagibs* or *marufs* of more value, and the less-endowed either giving nothing or something of lesser value. In this way, the ability to perform *wagibs* properly (the rich giving alms to the poor, for example) is minimal to fulfilling a particular position in the social order. On top of that, to be generous with one's optional *marufs* allows one to raise that position. To cut back on *marufs* at a later stage is to redefine a position or reassess a relationship.

It is difficult to define precisely the categories and values of status characteristics. Every situation involves numerous impinging values that need to be evaluated according to appropriate criteria of the moment. For example, in one situation it might be expected that a woman defer to a man's opinion because all other factors being equal a particular public context prefers a male voice. In another public context a woman of higher socioeconomic or political status is given deference by the males of the audience. Add to the equation other factors and the expected outcomes become ever more complicated. The member of the culture sifts the factors with computer-like ease and speed and responds immediately, but he or she has learned the social meanings much as one learns a complicated word, by experiencing them in a vast array of contexts where the subtlety of meaning comes more clearly. The American can fall back on the informal, "we're all equal" stance when engaging a stranger, but for an Egyptian this never works. He or she must evaluate the signs thoroughly and respond correctly to status level in order to avoid unnecessary trouble. On the other side, the stranger wears his status "on his sleeve," to avoid just such mistakes. The markers are his dress, their style and cut, language, mannerisms and manners, mode of transportation, and endless clues. The delivery boy careening through the streets on his bicycle with a stack of hot breads, shouts: "Watch out, *Haga*" (title for a female who has been on pilgrimage — usually used with the lower classes). "Watch out, *Sitti*" (the equivalent of Madam for the lower classes). "Look out, Madam." "Look out, *Maallam*" (master craftsman). "Watch out, *ya Bey*" (Turkish title of the influential). Each term of address is carefully graded to its recipient's position.

Exaggerating the person's prominence is one way of assuring that error does not occur on the side of underrating a position. Intentional exaggeration, as in calling a person a "skilled master" when he is a street cleaner with no particular skills, is a common form of politeness. It still implies knowledge of the correct status.

In more intense relationships than those of the boy on the bicycle, people first evaluate their relative statuses and then apply the schedule of *wagibs* they feel are appropriate, leaving to the system of *marufs* the flexibility to deepen the commitment.

A *wagib* often needs to be publicly exposed in order for others to realize that an obligation has been fulfilled. This may occur even when the underlying reality is different from the public event. A married daughter who is more affluent than her mother may give her mother money from the household account so the mother is able to buy gifts for the daughter's family. This allows the mother to publicly save face by fulfilling her *wagib* without the daughter's husband knowing what has happened.

At marriages and funerals where gifts of food and money are generally required, the opportunity for public accounting of *wagib* is provided. If one family gives 2 £E and a specific list of food stuffs, that amount or possibly more is carefully returned to the donating individual's family when the first opportunity of the same kind occurs. Friends of a bride may even go and claim the amount if it is not presented.

The whole system of jural and affective ties, of *wagib* and *maruf*, is not a fixed, immutable structure. In some cases *wagib* is suspended because other duties conflict. For example, mothers never expect *wagibs* of their daughters to be fulfilled with the same intensity when the daughters marry and are trying to please their husbands. Similarly, affective ties and the system of *marufs* are variable, unpredictable, and unquantifiable. Their character determines much about the outcomes of relationships. Affective ties overlay jural ties to strengthen and reinforce them. Particularly within the intimacy of family living, relationships assume a many-layered character, reinforced even further by the multiplex connections of common interests, common economic endeavors, similar circles of friends, and a number of other factors. Every relationship is in a state of constant flux. Layers of affective content tend to be added over time and with mutual experiencing of common events. Other relationships, bankrupt for whatever reasons, roll back the affective layers and either remain stripped to their jural essentials or dissolve themselves for all practical purposes. Friendships having no jural-legal essence are more vulnerable to this final kind of dissolution than family ties which can be dormant for a period and be rekindled when it becomes important.

Family ties, to sum up, are reinforced on one level by legal definitions with legal sanctions to back them up and on another level by social obligations producing a cluster of asymmetrical expectations around any pair of kin. The asymmetry builds a tension for a wider set of kin relations to offset the imbalances of single relationships. This can best be achieved with an extensive kinship circle physically present and complying willingly with obligations expected of them. (The implications of a complete circle of kin will be discussed later, in considering the effects on the family of urbanization and migration.) In this way duties are balanced with rights, and restrained behavior is balanced with acts of love and indulgence. Social expectations invest women with a stronger, but of course not exclusive, role in bringing emotional content to the bare bones of jural relationships. They supply the loving nurturing aspects that give quality to everyday life. The Arab proverb at the beginning of this chapter describes the ultimate in despair: "There is neither sister nor mother to share my misery."

Together, these unequal expectations of several orders create a bonding in familial networks, more intense in the core of the nuclear family and decreasing in intensity as the levels of relationship recede. Every individual sits at the center of a complex web of relations pregnant with inherent possibilities. People are not equally defined within families or within the society as a whole. The Western attempt in theory to reduce everyone to the same common denominator regardless of income level, educational attainment, race, creed, sex, or any other factor is not seen as valid in the Egyptian context. People play complementary roles toward one another, each important in his own way but of necessity impossible to reduce to a single denominator. The fact that personal exchanges are unequal, that they are open to manipulation, that relationships are subject to redefinition, and that obligations to a person on one side or rights received on the other may not be honored keeps the system from being overly rigid. It also makes it unlikely that there will be rigorous conformity in the real world to the idealized pattern.

MOBILIZING THE NETWORK

In Egypt vitality in social relationships is tested with constant visible reminders that the relationships exist. *Wagib* and *maruf* systems provide Egyptians with the opportunities for the continuous rounds of exchanges and aid that make up daily life. They provide the means by which to convince others that not only is the individual honoring commitments in the system but is doing so with the expectation that the commitments owed to him or her will be similarly honored. The impressive willingness to spend considerable time and effort running "other people's errands" attests to the important nature of the obligation. Ceremonies, special events (births, deaths, marriages, seven-day-after-birth parties for babies), and holidays are also recurring opportunities to confirm allegiances and show priorities with *de rigueur* visits and gifts.

Under certain special conditions, people may feel the need to affirm the instrumentality of their relationships in less formal ways. They may doubt the strength of their bonds with others, or in some other way feel insecure about them. There are several ways to test whether people will honor their commitments. The individual can: (1) demand his or her right by asking a favor and assessing whether the response meets the degree of expectation; (2) threaten sanctions if normal obligations are not met and wait to see if the person responds (as, for example, when a mother withdraws her love from a grown son who does not make frequent enough visits) and; (3) initiate a *maruf* and see if a *wagib* is returned.

The following example illustrates how a whole network of relationships can be mobilized by provoking a crisis that elicits *wagib* visits of consolation:

Ibrahim was a worker who at the time of this event was working in Libya. His wife Muna and their two small children remained at home in Egypt with his mother, Um Ibrahim. Over a weekend in the summer Muna and the children spent a holiday with Muna's sister, Nadya, and her family. During a picnic by the sea, pictures were taken of both the families gathered together enjoying themselves. Among the pictures was one of Muna and her children sitting together with Nadya's husband while Nadya snapped the picture. Muna sent the set of pictures to Ibrahim in Libya. For a long time there was no letter from Ibrahim, and both Muna and Um Ibrahim became worried. Eventually a dramatic letter came, telling of Ibrahim's constant faithfulness to Muna, reporting that he was seriously ill, requesting that Muna take care of his children should he die, and enclosing the number of the bank account where their money was kept. Both women were extremely concerned, but Muna, after some thought, realized from the tone of the letter and the fact that the news had been dispatched by letter rather than telegram, that perhaps Ibrahim was not so ill as he reported. She saw in the letter a resurgence of the jealousy he had felt for some time about the possibility of a romantic interest between Muna and Nadya's husband. The pictures had fueled these concerns. Muna was reluctant to tell her mother-in-law the whole story fearing she would give credence to the possibility of a romance and said instead that Ibrahim was only angry with her for not having written frequently enough. Um Ibrahim, however, seized on the uncertainty of the situation to satisfy some of her own feelings of neglect.

In the previous year her husband Abu Ibrahim had died; Ibrahim, who was her eldest son, instead of remaining home with her after his father's death, sent Muna and the children back from Libya to stay with her. Um Ibrahim's other children living far away in various cities of Egypt, came to visit only infrequently. What was more, Muna, after arriving to keep Um Ibrahim company, had proceeded to go out to work immediately, leaving her two children every day from nine to two with the old woman. Though Um Ibrahim accepted this task, nevertheless she felt discontented that her daughter-in-law was not continually present to keep her company and serve her at home. She often expressed her displeasure with her own children and Muna to friends and relatives. In short, she felt abandoned by all those she considered her close connections.

Seizing on the excuse of a possible catastrophe to her son Ibrahim in Libya, she sent back a telegram to him saying the news of his illness had made her seriously ill, and begging him to return home immediately if he wanted to see her alive again. Meanwhile, she sent out word through friends to the local grocery store owner and to those in a neighborhood prayer society she often attended that everyone should pray for her son who was dying in Libya. Muna on her side was trying to assess the seriousness of Ibrahim's condition. She sent word to her brother who was also working in Libya, asking him to check on her husband's health. People began to stream to the house, keeping up a continuous flow of emotional comings and goings as they attempted to console Um Ibrahim. In the midst of these activities a letter came from Muna's brother, brought by a mutual friend. He confirmed that indeed there was nothing wrong with Ibrahim, and shortly thereafter a worried telegram came from Ibrahim himself to say he was fine but concerned about his mother. For several days the consolation callers continued to come, unaware that the news was now good. In all they included Um Ibrahim's sister and husband, her brother, the religious leaders of their community, friends of Muna from her work, Muna's mother from another city, the neighbors from the building, the neighbors of Um Ibrahim's sister who lived a block away, her prospective daughter-in-law and the daughter-in-law's mother, and finally on the week-end, after marathon travelling, her distant children and grandchildren. Each spent a minimum of an hour or more, the women in a particularly dramatic way entering the house weeping and clasping the also weeping Um Ibrahim to their bosoms. Each in turn heard the entire story, embellished by speculation, of Ibrahim's illness as well as the numerous general problems of the abandoned and miserable Um Ibrahim. Um Ibrahim, rather uncharitably, blamed the problem on Muna who, she said, had not been conscientious enough in her duties as a wife and consequently had worn Ibrahim out with his worry about her.

When the good news came from Libya about half-way through the round of visits, Um Ibrahim eked out as much sympathy as possible before revealing that the danger to Ibrahim was over — that "thanks be to God," the news was good. Um Ibrahim's spirits rose visibly over the next few days. After a heated controversy over whether to send any answer to Ibrahim at all, she finally decided to send a letter by slow post rather than a telegram.

This event gave the mother-in-law the opportunity to strengthen what she felt was her sagging position in the wider circle of relations, but the result was achieved only by unsettling a number of her own important close relationships. In the aftermath of the affair a number of relationships had to be put right again by special effort on her part and that of others. Each restored relation among these close family members was then sealed with some visible token. By accepting the token the person acknowledged the reestablished relation.

Muna's mother sat through the consolation sessions of Um Ibrahim, and at one point while helping Muna prepare refreshments in the kitchen she heard the negative remarks about her daughter. She was visibly agitated, feeling keenly her daughter's vulnerable position in the household. Muna, who is an unusually sensible and mature person, preferred to let the matter drop, but her mother, Samia, felt it her duty to give Muna support. Not knowing exactly how to proceed, she tried several possibilities. First, she gave a small sum of money to an old woman who, in return for food and a place to sleep, helped Um Ibrahim with the household chores. Samia asked her to keep an eye on Muna and help her. Then she visited Um Ibrahim's sister and commented on how fond Muna was of her and how "she only has good things to say about you." She hoped the sister would then take the side of Muna in discussions with Um Ibrahim. On the return bus ride to her own home, Samia debated how to help her daughter. First she thought she would write a strong letter to Um Ibrahim defending her daughter. Then she decided to tell Um Ibrahim that she and her husband planned to move to her area in order to be closer to their daughter (an unlikely possibility). In the meantime, she decided that in turn, she, her husband, and Muna's brothers and sisters must visit Muna every month because "when they see we are watching they will be good to her."

Meanwhile Ibrahim wrote to Muna and his mother, sending Muna some money and promising his mother a visit after a month. Ibrahim also sent a very warm, polite letter to Muna's mother. Um Ibrahim bought a special expensive dress for Muna's daughter, and Muna gave Um Ibrahim a gift that had been given to her but which Um Ibrahim had coveted. When Ibrahim's brother married the girl who had consoled with Um Ibrahim, they both were urged by Um Ibrahim to pay a special call on Muna's mother. Muna's mother still agonizes over whether it would not have been better to confront Um Ibrahim over the issue of Muna. She argues that it is better to operate from a position of strength rather than weakness, but in deference to her daughter's wishes she has remained silent.

People avoid leaving unresolved tensions within their circle of intimate connections. One reason is that when tensions exist the person loses the full potential support relationships provide; the person is unable to face the world with a cohesive group at his or her back. A proverb expresses this feeling: "Be on your guard against your enemy once, but beware of your friend a thousand times, for the friend may become an enemy, and he will be best acquainted with where the shoe pinches most severely." The beliefs that the evil eye, curses, spells, and other black magic are most often generated by people close to one another, friends or relatives, reinforces the sense of wanting to remain clear with the immediate circle of contacts.

For Muna's mother the alternatives in healing the breach between Muna and Um Ibrahim were whether to use diplomacy or to create another crisis that would show the strength of Muna's family backing. Muna herself was in the difficult position of wanting to remain on good terms with the two families. She was forced to remain in the home of Um Ibrahim until her husband returned and, therefore, did not want to upset their relationship. At the same time she understood her mother's concern that her own parental family's image would suffer if members allowed themselves to be treated badly without putting up some kind of resistance. The ensuing set of *marufs* (not requiring returns in this case) that were offered allowed everyone to restore relations to the pre-crisis stage.

It is difficult to convey to the non-Eastern audience why a crisis of this kind is not simply a waste of a good deal of time, effort, and emotion. In fact it is the culmination of personal attachments that have been cultivated and developed over a long period of time, prepared for an occasion like this or one that has more serious repercussions. Personal transactions serve to store up or reduce credit, credit being one person's right to call on the support of another for either small or large services. When something serious occurs it is advantageous to have substantial credit available. In a country like Egypt, where a large part of social, economic, and political life is carried on through personal contact, personal credit is often far more significant than material credit. For this reason people prefer to deal through these modalities rather than the impersonal ones that exist in other Western societies.

For Um Ibrahim, this particular crisis may have been used to test out the strength of her connections in preparation for some more serious occasion, or it may have been a genuine emotional crisis where she needed to use part of the credit she had stored away to solve her problems. Being an old woman, her services to people when she was younger serve to exempt her from significant return services now. The crisis made it possible for all the family to vent their long-standing grievances, if not always overtly at least covertly, and receive some kind of reassurance that they were still valued by others of their circle.

7

Marriage: Theory

"The hell of a husband is better than the heaven of a father"
—Arab proverb

MARRIAGES offer an opportunity to develop more permanent ties with other persons and by extension with their kin groups and networks of personal acquaintances. The marriage bond, however, is not like the bond of blood relationships that endures forever. The ties of marriage remain in force only as long as the marriage contract itself is honored. What the contractual agreement provides is the potential for other reinforcing jural and affective ties to develop: a vested interest in children, overlays of emotional attachment, a fund of common experiences, and a common sharing in material properties, not to mention the development of ties with persons in the other spouse's circle of kin and friends.

In real life, choice of a spouse tends to be a pragmatic compromise between actualizing a person's or a group's idealized expectations for a marriage partner and responding to the compelling conditions of the moment. This chapter is concerned with the theory behind marriage choices; the next will take up the practice of spouse selection. Whatever the final choice of spouse, people know the implications of certain kinds of marriage and color their decisions either directly or indirectly by this knowledge.

Individuals do not stand alone in making decisions about their future mates in Egypt. Their family groups are usually actively involved, if not in the selection itself, at least in the negotiations for both sides' approval. At the same time individuals do not escape an appraisal of their qualifications as reflected in the publicly known traits it is assumed they share with their families. It is often more important that a person with

107

the right set of qualifications marries another with equally acceptable qualifications than it is that their own personal traits are compatible. These are sensitive issues to determine during mate selection because they reflect so conspicuously the public reputation of the family groups concerned. In certain respects, marriage choices are the ultimate "score" by which a family is judged successful in creating a respected public image.

Marriages are expected to strengthen families as corporate units (1) by expanding their effective modes of operation through the recruitment of non-kin to positions within the system of obligatory relations, as happens when "strangers" marry; (2) by reinforcing already existing ties through adding new layers of affective and obligatory expectation, as happens when relatives marry; and (3) by satisfying certain felt needs by selection of marriage partners who are thought capable of alleviating those needs. This last is a "vested interest" marriage. Needless to say, all families do not consciously seek corporate strengthening in this way, but all do recognize the implications of these various kinds of marriages.

When people talk about preferred marriages in general or in specific for their own children they refer to various combinations of jural and affective relations that they consider in particular circumstances to be optimal. They generally want a potential spouse about equal to but not much higher in socioeconomic level and other similar criteria by which an eligible member is judged. A woman may marry up the social scale a little, but a family has little advantage, except perhaps economically, if a man does so since children's name and status come largely from the father. A woman richer than her husband is thought to have the upper hand in the relationship. People also want a match that preserves larger family harmony and stability. In real life, some criteria loom larger than others while contemporary tendencies to look with greater sympathy on "irrational" love marriages may render many considerations moot. Nevertheless the criteria above are said to motivate choices in marriage whether they are arranged by parents or initiated primarily by the individuals concerned. Real life behavior bears out the fact that where appropriate opportunities exist, choices reflect the ideals people articulate — or at least they rationalize their choices in terms of those ideals. One way to understand the choices people make is to look at the outcomes people expect from different kinds of marriage commonly contracted in Egypt.

RELATIVE MARRIAGE

The kinds of marriages most frequently mentioned by members of the urban lower classes, rural peasants, and even considerable numbers of the

educated middle classes, as ideal—as providing the potentially best outcomes—are various types of relative marriage. The two following illustrations demonstrate the importance of finding the appropriate relative to
fit the family circumstance.

Um Ali is still relatively young though already she has lost her husband and now must face a future bringing up two young boys alone
in the city. Her daughter Aziza, seventeen, has been a help to her but
she is one more mouth in the household, and the prospects of marrying her without the customary furniture and kitchen utensils are bleak.
Um Ali sells a macaroni dish and little newspaper cones of nuts to
neighborhood children and makes about 30 to 50 p. in profits a day.
This, along with a small welfare payment from the Ministry of Social
Affairs, is all she receives. One day a beaming Um Ali greeted her visitors with the happy news that not only was Aziza about to marry but
she, Um Ali, had arranged the most ideal marriage of all despite their
circumstances, marriage of her daughter to the son of Um Ali's sister.
The bridegroom would generously pay most of the expenses for the
marriage and furnishings, and Um Ali knew she could rely on him
to treat Aziza well.

"What is your news, Um Samir?" "Everything is fine, thank
God. The children and Saad are well and we married our eldest
daughter to a colleague at her work. We also bought the fridge and
the washing machine. And our son Samir will marry his *bint am*
[father's brother's daughter] soon. Come sit with us inside and see the
fridge."

Abu Samir: "This woman! She has accomplished everything we
have by herself. I only sit and drink tea and smoke my cigarettes. She
is so clever at piling together the money that anyone would want to
marry her. But she would never take another man. How could she?
If she got in trouble with him she would have to come to me, her cousin
(*ibn amm*—father's brother's son). She has no family but me. Because
we are at the same time both cousins and man and wife our concern
for each other is strengthened. We could never do anything to harm
each other. Look at what she does; for example, you know that when
a woman of the family marries it is always good for a man of the family to visit her to show she has males standing behind her. Um Samir
always pushes 10 £E in my hand at the feast time and tells me to go
give it to my married sister. Another woman might feel angry that
money of the house was being spent on someone else. But because
we are cousins our concerns are the same. She is a good woman, Um
Samir is, a woman who is known for fulfilling her *wagibs* as well as
providing well for her own house."

Neither of the examples is clear without some general knowledge of how Egyptians conceive of various kin relationships and, in particular, what expectations they hold for various forms of relative marriage.

As noted in a previous chapter, both men and women in Egyptian society feel commitment to fulfilling their formal jural *wagib* obligations to each other. *Maruf* relations built on affective ties are more flexible and voluntary. When many Egyptians speak of ideal marriage, there are two major assumptions underlying the scale of what is most desirable. The first is that males are preoccupied more with strengthening and promoting their jural relationships. This is logical considering that jural relations are intimately tied up with family name, reputation, inheritance, legal responsibilities, and economic working group alliances. The second assumption is that in the case where their economic needs are secured women are more interested in developing their affective ties and to that end elaborate those ties to a much greater extent than they do their jural *wagib* duties. In the second example Um Samir's affective ties with her immediate family might have been expected to overcome her sense of duty to more remote relatives, but she is praised for resisting this temptation to avoid her duties. Her case, by being cited as exceptional, provides evidence of the general expectation. Basically, men and women are expected to and usually meet the separate demands of their sex roles as supporters or nurturers by emphasizing the two different aspects of relationships: jural and affective.

This general consideration applies also to choices in relative marriage. When deciding whether and with which relatives to contract a marriage agreement, families consider some of the following points: First, whether the individuals being scrutinized bear a relationship to their child which is considered primarily affective or jural. Second, they consider the net losses and gains that occur from a particular kind of relative marriage. For example, does a woman enter an indulgent or a severe household when she goes to her mother-in-law? Does a man gain the optimal jural assets he can out of a marriage or does he sacrifice these for other qualities in the bride? Third, what fields of activity will be diminished or enhanced by the new relationship? What activities, for example, will be centered in the husband's or the wife's homes of origin, and will these activities be enhanced by a particular marriage? These are some of the concerns families face when trying to contract marriages most satisfactory for the partners themselves. These concerns are of less importance when a vested interest of the family groups involved obliterates the significance of individual needs.

Given the different social roles and interests of men and women, it is logical to expect that marriages ideal for men are different from those that are ideal for women. Respondents from the lower classes were fairly consistent in listing an order of preferential priority. Choices two and three for the women were often interchanged as being equal in preference:

Preferred Relative Marriage in Order of Priority

For the Man	For the Woman
1. Father's brother's daughter	1. Mother's sister's son
2. Father's sister's daughter	2. Mother's brother's son
3. Mother's brother's daughter	3. Father's brother's son
4. Mother's sister's daughter	4. Father's sister's son

The priority listings are not congruent for men and women nor are they even the reverse of one another. This fact confirms the existence of different guiding principles that determine their order. Additional evidence emerged in a lower-class sample I took of 250 Muslim and Christian women frequenting a social center in Bulaq who were asked if and how they were related to their spouses. Those who were related in more than one way invariably chose to identify their relationship in ways that reflected different preferred marriages for males and females. They would say for example: "I am his father's brother's daughter and he is my mother's sister's son," ignoring the fact that the respondent was also his mother's sister's daughter, and he her father's brother's son. There is pride in the way the women state their dual relationship that does not appear in the cold reality of print. They are boasting about what they consider an ideal condition where not only are both the idealized preferences of the partners realized but also evidence is provided that intermarriage has gone on before in that kin group, suggesting a close and well-integrated family unit.

If the preferences of males and females are compared to the concerns of parents with regard to relative marriages listed above, the parallels are clear. Men are emphasizing their jural ties to male kin for a number of reasons. They derive more jural assets from these associations, they strengthen the patrikin, and they concentrate their primary interests and activities (and those of their wives) in the homes of their paternal relatives. Women's marriage priorities, on the other hand, show a preference for reinforcing affective, indulgent ties with maternal relatives and for increasing the amount of time activities are centered within maternally related households. Marriage for women normally implies separation from kin; at the very least, it means obtaining permission to visit. Any marriage arrangement that makes for greater ease of contact is preferred by her.

The assumption behind these priority listings goes back to the theoretical underpinnings of kin relationships in general: that the character and tone of the relationship with kin outside the immediate family—aunts, uncles, cousins, grandparents—is of the same quality that exists with the father and mother, jural-legal with paternal relatives and affective-indulgent with maternal relatives. Ideally, as was noted, this conceptualization of the world of kin permits each individual, male or female, to carry out both jural and affective roles depending on the relationship with the people concerned. That men and women choose to emphasize different poles of the spectrum is simply viewed as inherent in the separate nature of the two sexes.

Below, each form of relative marriage is taken in turn and its major implications reviewed as they might be found in a classical case where the bride moves into or near the home of her husband's family. In reality this eventuality is much more likely to occur in rural or lower-class urban environments, though even there the trend nowadays is definitely toward nuclear living arrangements.

Mother's Sister's Son—Mother's Sister's Daughter Marriage

Women prefer to enhance their affective, matrilateral ties. This is logical when one considers what these ties mean to women in their daily lives. In the form of marriage where a woman marries her mother's sister's son, the highest preference for a woman, the bride moves into closer relationship with, if not into, the household of a "loving" aunt. The aunt is loving because she is the closest of all kin to being the structural equivalent of the bride's mother. She is, in effect, a mother substitute. The bride's new husband has, until the time of their new relationship, played the role of warm affectionate cousin, a role that conflicts with his new role toward her of economic and jural protector. Calling on their past relationship, she may be able to undermine his attempts to assert an authoritarian presence.

After marriage the normal exchanges of services that occur between sisters continue between the bride's mother and mother's sister and if anything are intensified by the daughter-niece-daughter-in-law relationship of the bride to both women. The bride's mother-in-law, as her mother's sister, encourages the relationship between the bride and her mother and does not attempt to compete with it. The strong relationship between the triumvirate of women at the same time weakens the position of the men in the households since the two men who are related as father and son have permitted their "stranger" (blood passes through the father) mother-wife to strengthen her own ties in opposition to theirs. The bride's close relationship to her mother-in-law makes the hierarchical discipline expected of a mother-in-law difficult. For a husband this kind of marriage does little to further his jural interests. His main consolation is the thought that the women of the family will get along harmoniously. His problems are most likely to be in maintaining his own independence against the pressure of the females in the household. This kind of marriage encourages and justifies a great deal of activity back and forth between the homes of the female members and reduces the conflict caused by *wagib* chores owed outside the household that are found in many other forms of marriage. The work load of the bride is, therefore, considerably lighter and more consistently shared by the women of the household. For all these reasons, young women are thought to prefer these marriages, and men are said to consider them a weakening of their own position.

Father's Brother's Son — Father's Brother's Daughter Marriage

The marriage that is structurally the reverse of sister's children marriage is brother's children marriage. In the rural areas of Egypt where this marriage is most common (see Chapter 8) males often bring their wives home to live in or near the paternal household. If the fathers of the couple, as brothers, followed the same principle, then the couple grew up in close proximity to one another, even perhaps in the same household. As a result, this kind of marriage is the least likely to disrupt the family unit as it has been constituted up to the time of the marriage; marriage may only entail the rearrangement of sleeping quarters. The new mother-in-law of the bride as the wife of her paternal uncle is already in a position where she exerts discipline over the bride. There is, therefore, a congruence in the two roles she plays in relation to the bride. For the new husband this ensures a well-disciplined household with his bride trained by his mother to serve his needs as he likes to have them served. All the women of the household, bride, bride's mother and bride's mother-in-law by nature of their positions either as outsiders or, in the case of the bride, as a blood descendent, have no joint interest beyond that of serving the causes of the men and their households. For the men this situation enhances their authority and the jural interests they invest in family.

For the wife, this kind of marriage is a mixed blessing. On the one hand she is more intimately tied to those whose obligation even before marriage it was to support her, whatever her difficulty. She also does not need to make the psychological break with the household she knows well. On the other hand, she may have assimilated some of her mother's sensitivity as an outsider to her father's family and may resist the discipline

they exert on her to maintain a high standard of conduct for the sake of
the family name. Her real affections may lie with her mother's family (especially her maternal aunt and grandmother) who indulge her without requiring services of her. Any services she provides for their households are
marufs given with love and not required. In this form of marriage to a
paternal cousin, her opportunities for mixing with her maternal kin (except for her mother) are diminished. For her the marriage offers economic
and protective security (the men of the family stand behind her), at the
expense of some of the maternal kin's emotional warmth and support. If
she were choosing a marriage partner herself, she might be more likely
to align with her maternal kin; if others, especially male kin, chose for
her they may be more concerned with the protective capacities of paternal
kin and perpetuation of her line under the same family name. There are
trade-offs required for a woman in this kind of marriage, though not so
for a man who is thought to consolidate his main interests at one and the
same time.

Mother's Brother's Son — Father's Sister's Daughter Marriage

The major problem in this kind of marriage is that the bride and
bridegroom hold contradictory jural and affective ties without greatly enhancing either of their primary interests. In the household of the husband's
parents where he has jural-legal interests, his wife has affective ties. His
remaining affective ties and her jural ties are divergent, invested in people
who are only related tenuously to the other by marriage. For the man, he
is pleased to bring in a wife from his paternal relatives who also has affective and, therefore, harmonious ties with his father. The difficulty is that
his father in his old role towards her was not accustomed to exerting authority over the bride; thus his new role as her stern father-in-law is in
contradiction with the old role as loving uncle. If the old patterns continue to assert themselves, she may continue to honor her jural commitments to father over father-in-law. This may cause problems for the young
husband. Yet on the other hand, for both husband and wife the arrangement means that the young wife, because of her relation to the husband's
father, will be assured a strong if not indulged place in the family. The
severity of in-law roles should be tempered by this fact. The marriage is
not the best for either spouse, but it comes in second best for both. It still
has some of the advantages that people expect relative marriage to hold
over stranger marriages: a reinforcement of jural ties for the groom and
affective ties for the bride.

Father's Sister's Son — Mother's Brother's Daughter Marriage

The same contradictory jural and affective ties for husband and wife exist in this marriage as in the previous one, only in reverse. The man's affective ties are invested in her father, while she has jural ties with his mother. This makes the roles of "stern" aunt and mother-in-law congruent in relation to the new daughter-in-law. It eases for the man his relation with his new father-in-law who is "loving" uncle. This fact should lessen the potential for conflicts between the husband and his wife's father. For the wife, it means that she is surrounded by nothing but authority figures, mother-in-law (also stern aunt), father-in-law, father, and husband (who is aligned with her father). Any conflicts between these authority figures will most certainly cause conflicting interests for her. Hers is a weak position under such circumstances and this is, therefore, for her the least favored relative marriage.

One would expect a husband on his side to feel well pleased with this kind of marriage that strengthens his authority, but there is one major disadvantage for him. Instead of strengthening his paternal relations he has taken from one of his weaker choices and strengthened the maternal, interloper side of his family connections, causing a weakening of the jural concerns that are his main interest. For him it is a third preference.

STRANGER MARRIAGE

There are, of course, no overlapping kin-reinforced affective or jural ties for couples in stranger marriage. There is, therefore, little to recommend these kinds of marriages from the structural side in terms of reinforcing family solidarity. Conditions may be such, however, that the advantages of stranger marriage outweigh those of relative marriage: friends, for example, may want to reinforce their relationship through the marriage of children; property holdings can be profitably consolidated; a family labor unit can be enhanced by bringing in additional members; or a political position can be strengthened by aligning two families. These kinds of vested-interest marriages will be discussed in the next chapter.

Stranger marriage also may be adopted in a case where the young couple for some reason prefers a more autonomous situation without the complicating factor of maintaining close kin relations. This is more likely to happen in urban areas where some of the advantages of close kin ties are reduced and where in any case it is difficult to maintain continuous relations if family members are dispersed and husbands and wives both occupied for long hours by their employment.

The main disadvantage of stranger marriage is that there is no formal mechanism by which difficulties in the marriage can be resolved. To begin with, the marriage partners have no over-arching jural or affective commitments to one another beyond those of the marriage relationship; nor as strangers do they have a larger group interested in their continuing harmony. Their in-laws are also strangers and are therefore expected to cast a suspicious eye on their child's spouse, fulfilling the general expectation that there will be difficulty between married couples and their in-laws. Children are expected to maintain strong ties with their parents, regardless of their maturity. If disagreements erupt in marriages, these ties reassert themselves leaving, in the worst cases, two hostile groups facing each other (see the case of Suna in Chapter 11) with no recourse left to heal the wounds other than yet another "stranger," mutually satisfactory to both parties but tied to neither by kinship, to mediate the dispute.

SIBLING MARRIAGE

One way of creating some of the advantages of relative marriage, when appropriate cousins of the right age and inclination are not available, is by contracting sibling marriages between two unrelated families. In these cases, of course, the advantages of greater solidarity in the larger family group is lost by the "outside" marriage of two family members. Emphasis instead is placed on producing more stable and happy marriages and closer family ties between the couples concerned. This is achieved, according to prevailing belief, by developing a mutuality of interest between the couples so that together they can exert pressure on any erring partner to behave appropriately.

In the following example the two forms of sibling marriage, marriage of a brother and a sister of one family to a brother and sister of another and marriage of two brothers to two sisters, occur in the same family.

Two sisters married two brothers from an unrelated family.
The third brother and a sister of the two men above married a sister and brother of a third family.
When the wife of the third brother died, friends and relatives counselled him to take the sister of his wife "for the sake of the children, since only a mother's sister can love children like a mother." He

resisted at first because he was attracted to another woman but finally succumbed to family pressure. Members of the family explained that the advantage of these marriages were several: first, that children felt closer because they were cousins two times over, and second because the adults were bound more closely together. During feasts and holidays there were fewer other competing relatives so they could arrange to spend more time with each other. In cases when they needed to help each other there were also fewer claims on their time from other sources. [It should be noted that the most frequent visits and contacts were kept up between the families of the two sisters who married the two brothers. One of those sisters was also much more active in keeping up the contacts with her sister-in-law's family than was her husband, though he was active in sending his sister gifts from time to time.] In commenting on whether sibling marriage in fact made families closer, one woman said: "It doesn't always work out. For example, my husband and I loved each other, and so we urged his brother to marry my sister. But she never really loved her husband even up until now, though he seems to love her. And in the case of the other brother, he really felt that he got the worst deal. He said his wife was neither beautiful nor clever, so he sent her back home for several years. Eventually he took her back again but only after her brother threatened to leave his wife, who was, of course, the sister of the rejected woman's husband."

From the example it is obvious that the more interconnected the marriage partners the more opportunity there is to exert the full force of family pressures and sanctions. This can be good or bad depending upon the personal experience of those concerned. In sibling marriage there is no primary group to turn to outside of the marriage; parental home, as represented by siblings, has expanded to encompass conjugal household and provide a social control similar to relative marriage.

In another example the results were even more unsatisfactory than the first. A sister from family A and a brother from family B fell in love and became engaged. Hoping to share their happiness, they involved a brother from family A and a sister from family B, who also soon became engaged. Soon thereafter the brother (A) began to have second thoughts about his bride and broke off the engagement. Though brother B still loved sister A he was forced to break his engagement in retaliation for the affront to his family caused by the rejection of his sister. The sister (A) confined herself to her room for several months and refused to be consoled. This case suggests that involving four people in such sensitive relationships sometimes in the end produces more conflict than one might find in normally stable marriages of unrelated couples. This fact in no way diminishes the high hopes people have for sibling marriages. Their convictions emerge out of the firm belief in the strength of kinship ties. Introducing this element into what is otherwise a "stranger" marriage creates multiplex bonds of relationship that overlap on different levels. The nature of the jural obligations is fairly clear, but the nature of the affective relations is less so. It is determined much more by the idiosyncracies of the people involved and the kind of sibling marriage contracted.

Sisters Marry Brothers

Structurally, the two kinds of sibling marriages have different kinds of advantages. When two sisters marry two brothers, the emotional ties created are expected to be stronger. Siblings of the same sex are thought to be closer emotionally. This means that both in daily life and during special visiting occasions at holidays the same-sex siblings will be happy to get together and share their tasks and their pleasures; the loneliness of out-marriage will be mitigated for the sisters by the opportunity to see each other on a regular basis. Both families will have the same kinds of obligations to the husband's family and will draw on the wives' family for voluntary services. One woman who experienced this kind of marriage commented: "Every time my sister had a baby she came to my house for several weeks, and I took care of her until she was strong again. If my husband had been a "stranger" to her and her husband it would not have been possible, but he was the brother of the baby's father so he had to accept the idea. Our two houses have always been like one." Children will be all related in the same way with "stern" uncles and "loving" aunts, a combination that gives them the best of both worlds.

The disadvantages of this marriage are twofold. First, the bonds between the siblings are strengthened, and as a result their own primary families are reinforced while the bonds of marriage are only indirectly affected. In other words, as couples, husbands and wives do not have mutually overlapping affective and jural ties except in the case of the father–father-in-law where both husband and wife have jural ties to the same man. The second disadvantage is that rather than making *mahr* (bridal payments) easier, the men need to amass a double amount for their brides, and the bride's family needs to amass a double amount of capital to buy furnishings. Thus the bargaining may be equally as intense as for stranger marriages with the added problem that the families may need to accumulate the amounts at once rather than spread over a period of time.

Brother and Sister Marry Brother and Sister

The other kind of sibling marriage, brother and sister of one family to brother and sister of another family, is structurally different. It gives the children of the marriages a "stern" aunt and a "loving" uncle, a weaker combination than the other variety of sibling marriage and one that goes against the "natural tendency of males and females." What is more, visiting and *wagib* obligations of the two households are vested in the different paternal households of the husbands, thus theoretically separating the couples on important holiday occasions. Even when the couples do get together their main link is the weaker one between brothers and sisters. Two stranger women and two stranger men interact. In the two examples cited above, it can be noted that it was marriages of this kind that ran into trouble and not the other kind of sibling marriage.

Given these weaknesses in this marriage pattern, it is necessary to look for some advantages. Basically these are two: First, the jural role of brother as protector of sister's interests is strengthened. He is thus better able to exert his influence in favor of her rights, with his own wife held as hostage against her brother's compliance (see again the two previous examples). Second, at the time of the marriage negotiations, the fact that both families must produce the same amount of *mahr* and capital for furnishings means that bargaining is less intense, and the amounts arrived at the optimum for all those concerned. This brings a more cooperative atmosphere to the transactions before the marriage.

In short, sibling marriage is a way of personalizing stranger marriage when conditions may not be appropriate to marry a relative. The practice demonstrates the importance people place on strengthening ties of marriage beyond their purely contractual jural-legal aspects. In doing so they place a great deal of faith in the hope that people will perform their expected roles as they are characterized in the cultural models for ideal marriage.

8

Marriage: Practice

"If you do not have a good family, marry into one" — Arab proverb

HOW ARE the ideal representations of marriage translated into practice, and what are the constraints that encourage use of one marriage form over another? People recognize that different patterns achieve different ends and consequently that each tends to work better in a context with an appropriate set of conditions. The ideals are built also on certain assumptions about what concerns men and women and their families.

Under certain circumstances these assumptions may be dwarfed by considerations of a more pressing nature. For example, modern élites, though consciously aware of the general public's conceptions of marriage ideals, often reject them in favor of patterns more compatible with the value they place on international norms.

In others, the very real problem may exist that the appropriate people, a father's brother's daughter of the right age or an eligible mother's sister's son, may not be available. Even though human behavior is substantially a product of rational choice, it is never completely so. Variation in response to the same set of circumstances is, therefore, an expected outcome of the human condition.

MATE SELECTION

Matching Critical Characteristics

Most parents are genuinely interested in providing the best matches for their children. Good matches reflect well on the whole family, increasing

121

the possibility that later matches for younger children will also be good ones. A good match is financially and emotionally stable and happy. In general, parents and children believe this state of marital bliss comes about more as a result of carefully matching the characteristics of the couple than it does in finding out whether the couple are temperamentally suited to each other or even currently in love. Some of the relevant characteristics are income, beauty and other physical characteristics, social status, moral factors, educational level, employment potential, and temperament.

In Upper Egypt, according to women in Bulaq, a potential mother-in-law used to come to the house of her son's intended bride to perform a test of her attributes. She is said to have demanded that the girl cook and peel a hard-boiled egg so that no nicks appeared in the white of the egg. When kissing the girl on her departure, the mother-in-law would tug at her hair to insure that it was real and pinch her buttocks to insure that she was pleasingly plump.

The more positive the attributes of the candidate the better, though it is generally recognized that to marry someone much above or below one's own level in such characteristics as wealth is to court trouble. Certain characteristics also have much greater value attached to them than others. Moral behavior is one that is ranked high. Others may vary in their degree of regard depending on the sex of the individual. A woman of great beauty may be excused a number of other faults. A man who earns a good income not only can ask for more in a wife but is excused less agreeable physical or personality traits. Among the middle classes, a strong value placed on women now is the ability to earn an income at a job that has a prestige compatible with her husband's position — that is, not higher than his job but not significantly lower either.

In the following illustration we find Um Fuad engaged at various times in assessing the relevant factors and trying to make the best choices possible for her sons.

As Um Fuad becomes older she feels keenly the responsibility of marrying all her children before her death. Already her two daughters and an eldest son are married. Her two remaining sons are not as easy to find appropriate brides for as her earlier children were. The elder of the two has a good job as a clerk in a store in the central shopping district of Cairo earning 30 £E a month, but he is known for his short temper and drug-taking habits. Um Fuad, who has high aspirations for her son,[1] encouraged his interest in a lower-middle-class teacher in a local school and the two "fell in love" as they met in the street after her work. Um Fuad's eldest son negotiated arrangements with the school teacher's family. After a stormy engagement period, the two finally married and moved to a room on the edge of the city. Um Fuad was pleased with the way this marriage worked out; she ignored their strong personality clashes; and she felt, as did everyone else, that the bride was a step up the social ladder for her son.

Um Fuad then turned her attentions to securing a good bride for the remaining son. There was little to recommend this man as a husband. He was an assistant to a man who sells vegetables, an uncertain occupation at best and one with very low income. He was unattractive physically and had a disagreeable personality. Like his brother much of his money went to maintaining his drug habit. Um Fuad scouted the neighborhood community for some time looking for likely candidates. The first was a girl whose younger sister had married first, a sure sign that something was probably wrong with her. Um Fuad recognized that her son was not a particularly attractive candidate and knew she must be prepared to accept a bride with flaws of some kind. She asked the social worker – a popular person in the community – to make discrete inquiries. When the girl's family learned about the prospective husband and told her, she turned down the idea immediately and they concurred: "I don't want to marry a vegetable seller. What if he can't sell vegetables someday? What skill does he have?"

Um Fuad with the help of the social worker began to widen the search to include women with more definite disadvantages that would make them willing recipients of her son's attentions. One day the social worker was struck by Riaya, the vivacious and industrious daughter of one of the members. Riaya was in her early twenties and so far unmarried because she had lost an eye in childhood. Um Fuad and the son agreed that the eye was perhaps not so important if Riaya was everything else she was reported to be. Unfortunately, however, on the day Um Fuad went to see her, Riaya was lying in bed looking ill and miserable. Even when Riaya's mother opened a cupboard, as if by accident, to reveal her extensive trousseau, Um Fuad was not to be moved. Though she politely didn't reject the girl immediately, she eventually notified the social worker several weeks later that the girl was not attractive enough for her son. By that time Riaya's family, realizing that the prospects were not good, sent word that they rejected the possibility of their daughter marrying Um Fuad's son. The problem was delicately solved with no one losing face; the social worker simply never told either side of the other's rejection.

The next candidate Um Fuad sought out was a young divorced woman, quiet, attractive, and poor. The social worker was sent to Hoda's mother to make inquiries, but while they toyed with the idea briefly, Hoda's mother and brother felt there might be more suitable candidates. However, Hoda found out about the proposal and secretly expressed to the social worker her willingness to consider the proposal. When approached a second time Hoda's mother used the excuse that a suitor from their home village had requested her hand and said they must see about him first. Recognizing the excuse for what it was Um Fuad let it be known that Hoda would need to bring nothing to the marriage, that Um Fuad would move out of her own room and leave her furniture for the couple. ("I can put a blanket in the corner of the condemned part of our building and sleep there — I need nothing more".) Hoda was all the more eager to accept but her mother was still reluctant. Eventually, problems in getting Hoda's divorce papers dragged on until probably more out of inertia than anything else the negotiations came to a halt. Um Fuad continued her efforts to find an appropriate candidate. Three years later she had still had no success.

Um Fuad had not even paused over the possibility of finding appropriate kin. They were simply not available. A migrant from deep in rural Egypt she had long since lost contact with relatives in her village of origin, and in any case at her age of 70 many contemporaries whom she had known were now dead. In the city she has worked hard to achieve a certain amount of social mobility for her children and now revels in the relative affluence her eldest son's support affords her. (She dresses well — in velvet for her best dress — and always has coffee in her home for visitors.) In choosing brides for her more ambitious sons she is conscious of the personal attributes that enhance their positions. The last son is the problem; given his personal liabilities, it is difficult to find someone she feels meets the high standards of the rest of the family. In his case, she is willing to make compromises but even these compromises seem not to be sufficient to attract candidates.

In general, among all the classes there is a strong preoccupation with matching characteristics between potential mates as closely as possible. Evidence of this preoccupation is found in television serial shows, which spend a great deal of air time debating the issue — in dramatic form — of whether young people should marry suitors wealthier or poorer, older or younger, better or less well-educated than themselves. The common tragic theme in these melodramas is always one of a couple in love who believe they cannot marry because a parent or society feels there is some flaw in how their characteristics match. The following is a plot synopsis of one of these serials, showing also the double standard expected of men and women.

Nabila is a successful engineering graduate working in a government job. Moneim is her upstairs neighbor whom she has loved since they were young. When his father died Moneim left school to work so his sister and two brothers could finish university and become doctors and engineers as their father had wanted. Instead of supporting the family as they became employed, however, the other children bought new clothes or invested money in establishing their own careers, leaving Moneim always responsible for the support of the family. Nabila's parents and brother refused to allow her to marry Moneim, a man, as they put it, without even a high school diploma when she was a university graduate. Otherwise the marriage would have been perfectly suitable since the two came from very similar backgrounds. In fact, at one point the parents were ready to give Nabila to Moneim's brother Rifaat who, like her, was a engineering graduate. In a very moving scene, the parents of Nabila attempt to arrange a marriage for Saleh, Nabila's brother. They admit that the prospective bride does not have a high school diploma but they claim that this is well compensated for by the fact that she owns 10 feddaans (about 10 acres) of land. Nabila's face shows her recognition of the irony, that her brother's bride can have a lower educational status than his partly because she is a woman and partly because she compensates for her deficiency by bringing a large amount of property to the marriage. ("Harvest of Years"—a television serial)

The tragedy of unsatisfactory qualifications is not confined to television drama. It is found frequently in real-life experiences.

Nowal is the fourth in a middle-class family of five sisters. As a child she was a cheerful, relaxed girl whom everyone liked but who did not take her studies seriously. As a consequence she failed her intermediate school exam and after repeated attempts to succeed finally left school. She was fortunate without formal qualifications to find a job that satisfied her family's middle-class requirements — as a teacher in a literacy handicraft program at a welfare center. As the years passed her sisters graduated from the university and the three eldest married three brothers. Nowal did not marry and her father refused to allow the youngest daughter to marry before Nowal, out of concern that his children marry in birth order. It was not that Nowal did not have suitors, but all those who were interested in her possessed less than university degrees and thus her father considered them not appropriate to the family's social level. Those with university degrees were not interested in her because of her low educational level. Nowal is in her late twenties now, a time considered late in Egypt for a girl to marry. Her younger sister feels frustrated that her own marriage has been delayed.

Nowal's father was particularly rigid about her marriage prospects. Most parents in the same circumstances would be willing to make trade-offs, exchanging one weak characteristic in one area for a stronger one in some other area. The following two cases illustrate marriage trade-offs and demonstrate the heavy involvement of family members and mediators when the traits of the partners are unacceptable in some way:

A friend of two lower-middle-class families was moved by the plight of two of their members. One was a young man who had been blinded from birth and had followed the easiest path open to people of his affliction by becoming a religious sheikh. The second, a woman from the other family, had been seriously burnt as a child and suffered disfiguring scars on her face that caused her to remain hidden in her home from embarrassment. The friend took it upon herself to try and arrange a marriage between the young man and woman, neither of whose afflictions would seem significant to the other, given the circumstances. The young man was enthusiastic, happy not only to find a wife, but also to perform what he felt was a charitable act. The marriage was quickly pushed to completion over the weak objections of his parents and the couple lived a generally happy life as four sons appeared in quick succession over the next few years. The man's parents, however, began to involve themselves more in the couple's affairs, finally urging him to seek another wife whom the family could present proudly to their friends. With their urgings he left his wife and children. The family friend who was the original mediator heard of the conflict and paid a visit to the man. She pointed out the good points of his wife—the four sons she had produced and the industry with which she made his home a good place to live—and told the man that it was his business and not that of his parents what kind of relationship he had with his wife. She asked if he was offended by his wife's appearance and, being blind, he of course had to say "no." With the mediator's urgings he returned to his wife and children and insisted that his parents no longer speak of his leaving them again.

One day Mme. Samia heard that the only daughter of a family she was acquainted with had just graduated from the university, and the parents were eager to find an appropriate young man for her to marry. The girl was bright, very shy and rather plain, but she did have the advantage of an apartment already prepared for her marriage and 20,000 £E in the bank which gave her a monthly income of about 200 £E. Mme. Samia felt this was a good opportunity to contact a distant relative and cement a relationship that for other reasons she was interested in strengthening. The young man she had in mind had also recently graduated from the university with high grades and was engaged in doing graduate work toward higher degrees. His family had a very modest income, and he himself had no income, so as a result he had pushed the idea of marriage from his mind until such time as he finished his university studies. Mme. Samia felt that his family would look favorably upon the prospect of such an advantageous marriage, as indeed they did. After meeting the young woman, Muna, only once, Rifat accepted the idea of their marriage, and shortly thereafter they were engaged. Rifat's mother, however, began to have reservations after the engagement when she felt that Muna was not attractive enough for her son. Friends and relatives, however, assured her that this was not important given the otherwise attractive financial features she brought to the marriage.

In this case the parents played the strong and weak points of the bride—her wealth and her lack of physical attractiveness—off against the bridegroom's promise in his career and his straitened economic background, and eventually both sides felt they were equally compensated. Another family less interested in improving their material position might have been reluctant to have their son placed in a position where his wife held the purse strings of the family. They would feel it compromised his masculine role as provider. What is interesting in this example is the way the two most significant bargaining points of men and women (beauty for women and income-earning capacity for men) are weak in these individuals. When men and women excel in these traits, other less agreeable characteristics can be overlooked. Muna and Rifat, therefore, have traded off their most serious defects. Rifat's mother can be excused her concern in wondering whether what is perhaps a temporary defect in her son is not being traded off against a permanent liability in the case of Muna. What appears a cold-blooded attitude is more easily excused when it is realized that, strictly speaking, it is traits and not people being evaluated. The two families barely know each other and certainly have not had time to develop personal attachments. The engagement of the two, which is a fairly strong commitment to marry, occurred barely two months after their first meeting.

The final illustration below demonstrates some of the problems that arise as a result of increasing social mobility in Egypt. It is difficult in this case for the potential spouse to recognize the achieved characteristics of a person who comes from a socially inferior background. These are the words of a lower-class mother:

The children can only help us a little. They have to build their own lives. Besides they are ashamed of this work. Our daughter especially has trouble with what her father does. She works at one of the Ministries and has had a number of men come to her with offers of marriage. But the first question a young man asks now of a perspective bride is "What does your father do?" What can she answer? "My father works as a garage attendant?" She can't. It would embarrass her. This is a generation of government employees. They have been educated, they have diplomas. They look down their noses at anyone who works with his hands. My daughter is in an awkward position. She is in conflict because she doesn't want to have this question put to her. Her schooling is an advantage and a drawback. A prospective bridegroom presented himself to our daughter recently. He is from humble origins like we are. His people are modest like us. He's employed by a bank and is doing a correspondence course to improve his lot. . . . This is probably the only kind of man she can marry. Someone from the same background as us, but who has improved himself like her and has diplomas to match hers. (Atiya 1982: 20)

There are others in contemporary Egypt like this young woman who, for one reason or another, find the usual channels of mate selection inadequate. A study in 1961 of marriage advertisements in newspapers identifies the characteristics of some of these marginal individuals and the qualities they seek in a marriage partner. Both sexes represented in these advertisements were deficient in some way in the qualities considered desirable for a spouse. The women were marginal usually for demographic reasons: they were either older or previously married, a marital status not valued in a bride. The men tended to be marginal for reasons of social mobility. Either they had already achieved a higher social status and as a result were unable to find a bride of the desired status through the conventional channels of family or they hoped to achieve a better position by marrying a wife with financial resources.

Widespread established norms as well as the special requirements of the marginal subjects were reflected in the qualities each sex sought in a spouse. Women wanted husbands who were at least five and up to fifteen and twenty years older, with a college education, a respectable position, and a good income. Physical appearance, personality, and previous marital status were not of great importance. Men wanted wives who were about five years younger, never married, beautiful (tall, slightly plump, and fair-skinned), good-tempered, with money or the ability to earn money. Less important were education, housewifely skills and cultural refinement (Abu-Lughod and Amin 1961:127–36).

In previous generations, and among the urban and rural lower classes still, the tendency has been for men to marry women much younger than themselves. The average age difference between husband and wife in a lower class sample of 176 families was a little more than ten years, yet differences ranged up to forty years (Rugh 1978).

Fictive-Relative Marriage

One of the reasons relative marriage is sought as frequently as it is among the lower social classes is that they do not usually possess strong economic bargaining reserves when contracting stranger marriage. Through relative marriage, they feel they are able to short-cut the selection process by bringing together young people whom they assume have matching characteristics on a number of points simply because they come from the same family. In addition, there is the strong mutuality of interest that should serve to guarantee the stability of the marriage in the otherwise unstable condition of poverty (if that condition is present).

One way that people try to create the semblance of relative marriage when the correct personnel are not available or are disinclined to marry each other is by assigning fictive relationships to well-known trusted "strangers" or by reassigning terms of reference to others to create the semblance of more preferred relationships. Comments like those that follow are common:

> A Cairo-born woman: "I married from my father's relatives, but it was a man who had grown up with me and always called me *bint khalla* (Mother's Sister's Daughter)." [This woman here redefines the relationship to show that she has made as ideal a marriage as possible given the circumstances — the emotional content of the Mother's Sister's Son's marriage is present even if technically the Mother's Sister's Son is not.]
>
> A number of young women in the Bulaq community have married the sons of their mother's best friends. Since friends are normally called *uxt* [sister] and their relations are often assigned the *wagib* expectations of kinship, the marriage of their children is given a qualitatively stronger stamp of approval than strictly stranger marriage engenders.
>
> In one unusual case, a 40-year-old woman was living unmarried with a man younger than herself. Though he was not in fact related to her, she put the best face on the affair by telling her neighbors he was her Mother's Sister's Son, someone she might have prospects of marrying and one with whom in any case, she might have a warm, emotional relationship without necessarily implying immorality.

The illustrations show how, rather than solving the problem of finding more appropriate marriage partners, changing the terms of reference

demonstrates an individual's recognition of what is a more acceptabl
pattern—it shows that the person subscribes to the ideal in theory, if no
in practice. By clothing the relationship in more suitable terms, the hop
is to convince everyone involved that it has the quality of the relationshi
called for.

Vested Interest Marriage

Among those who have strong interests to protect, another commo
form of marriage is one that can be called a "vested interest" marriage
This kind of marriage is frequently used by the well-to-do, the landed
or the politically powerful, though it can be found anywhere when a seri
ous interest is at stake.

As often happens when the values supporting a marriage pattern d
not give clear cut answers, television serials take up the issue. In the fol
lowing example, drawn from the sub-plot of a television serial, "Harves
of Years," Hoda is pictured as a young woman finally seeing the correc
path, after a period of "irrationality" brought about by her love for Ramzy.
Implicit in the story is the unhappiness Hoda will experience if she mar
ries a man of much higher economic class than her own.

> Hoda and Ramzy were students at the university when they met and
> fell in love. Hoda came from a lower-middle-class family with aspira-
> tions to improve their social status through educational channels.
> Ramzy was the son of a man who, with a colleague, owned a factory.
> The family was rich. The dilemma facing the young couple was that
> Ramzy's father had long had a dream that Ramzy would marry the
> only daughter of his friend and colleague at the factory. If he did so,
> then the two men would be able to sign over the ownership of the fac-
> tory to the young couple. Ramzy's father encouraged this arrangement
> by promising also that he would build Ramzy a house and give him
> a car. The material benefits were too much to give up for a marriage
> to someone else, even with one whom he loved as much as he did Hoda.
> One day he broached a plan to Hoda. He would marry her secretly
> and then later marry the other young woman, wait until he received
> the deed to the factory, his house and his car, and then divorce her
> and live thereafter with Hoda. After some thought Hoda rejected the
> idea and cut off her relations with Ramzy.

In real life the arrangements for vested interest marriage can sometimes produce very successful results:

A prominent politician close to President Sadat consolidated his political power as a young man by overcoming the resistance of his family and marrying a relative from another branch of the family that
had been feuding with his branch of the family for a number of years.
As the largest and most powerful family in a particular geographical
area of the Delta, the family had lost its political force through its
continual internal disagreements. The marriage served to symbolize
a new era of consolidation, effectively permitting the young man to
rise to national attention and to continue in a position of prominence
through the presidencies of two men who could not afford to ignore
such an important constituency.

Another example from the lower social classes shows that vested interest marriages are not a monopoly of the upper classes.

Zeinab had been orphaned as a young girl. Her father's brother's family
refused to take her into their household, claiming that they were financially unable to support another child. Since there were no other close
relatives available, Zeinab was admitted to an orphanage. During the
school year she was happy living in the orphanage — she did well in
school and learned sewing skills with the orphanage staff. During holidays most of the children went "home" to close relatives, and Zeinab
similarly was sent off to her father's brother's household. She grew
to fear these holidays in the presence of her bad-tempered, abusive
uncle. As she grew older she became more and more reluctant to take
her holidays away from the institution. On the day she reached her
majority and would have inherited control over her parents' land, her
uncle and his son appeared at the door of the institution and claimed
the right of *ibn amm* [Father's brother's son] to marry her. She was
taken that day from the institution, married, and her cousin gained
effective control over the small plot of land she owned.

Vested interests are not necessarily concerned with material improve-
ment for those initiating the marriage, as this final example from the lower
classes indicates.

Samir is relatively affluent compared to most of his neighbors in Bulaq.
He owns a small shop where he makes and repairs leather goods of
all kinds. He lives with his elderly mother and is her only means of
support. Samir wanted to marry but realized it would be difficult to
find a woman willing to live with his mother and take care of her needs.
As a result he sought a poor woman whom he felt would be pleased

enough with his good income to accept the disadvantages of caring for his mother. As he put it, "A 'higher' one would insist on her own place."

In this case, the prospective husband evaluates his strengths and weaknesses as a marriage prospect and chooses a bride who will satisfy his most important need, to care for his mother. The example indicates the extent to which material resources stand behind personal relations and are thought to determine their quality. A common complaint of married people is that their spouses have used their better status or better economic background to "show off" and make the other spouse feel inferior. The example shows again how much people depend upon structural expectations to realize the kinds of marriages they want.

Another kind of vested interest marriage is less common, but as an unusual type it sheds light on what is "normal." I found several cases of this marriage when studying institutional care in Egypt. Occasionally a young man comes to an institution seeking an orphan to marry precisely because she either has no relatives or because her relatives have more tenuous ties with her. Further examination of the cases usually reveals unusual circumstances: suitors with traumatic experiences in their own families, ones who feel their own weaknesses in marriage bargaining, or ones with unusually strong religious motivations.

The common case in orphanages is for children from unknown parentage to experience difficulty in finding marriage partners outside the institution. Most of them usually marry orphans like themselves. The absence of known background is generally a serious liability in contracting a marriage. If orphans can be considered as individuals with extremely weak bargaining credentials, their plight is more understandable. In one case, a family with scandal in its background experienced difficulty in marrying its daughters. Finally they took a distant relative from an orphanage who was happy enough to marry one of the girls. The other girl of the family never married.

Rationality in Marriage Selection

Love vs. Arranged Marriage

It is difficult to see how a system of selection based so heavily on assessment of objective characteristics can work in a process so complicated and open to human idiosyncracies as marriage. And indeed, "irrational" factors do enter the selection process. In many Egyptian contexts the word *love* is a term invested with connotations of irrationality. And a "love marriage" is considered suspect. It implies that the couple succumbed to personal preference and physical attraction rather than a careful evaluation of personal characteristics.

A social worker, bringing her records up to date, asked her lower-class clients jokingly: "Whom did you marry? Someone from your relatives or your sweetheart?" A reply that the client married a relative implied that she didn't love her husband; a reply that she married her sweetheart implied an immoral relationship not subject to the checks and balances of arranged marriages — a "have you stopped beating your wife" question whichever way it is answered.

A university professor, Dr. Zaky Naquib Mahmud, writing in the newspaper *Akher Sa'a,* presented a view that in its general outlines is relatively well accepted. He says: "love is not the foundation of proper married life, for love is annihilation, one party merging into the other. . . . But marriage is supposed to be primarily for survival, for cooperation between two parties, not for the unification of two souls. Any relationship in which one party loses its identity and is merged into the other is not a social relationship. The family, the *raison d'être* of marriage, needs sincerity through cooperation."[2]

Parents, even those who believe it is best for children to choose their own spouses, are uneasy about love matches until they are reassured that the potential spouse meets the criteria they have set for their child's marriage partner. If there are serious defects most parents can still cut short the relationship, and most children will defer to their parents' wishes.

Fuad is a newly graduated doctor from the university. Several months ago he spent an anxious weekend awaiting a call from the young female doctor he was hoping to become engaged to. These two were deeply in love, according to him. She had travelled back to her family's home in Alexandria to broach the subject of their engagement to her parents. Fuad's anxiety lay in his assessment that his own social and financial background was inferior to that of his intended bride. But he said hopefully, "I should think they would accept me. We are both doctors with a good future ahead of us." The anxiety heightened as the delay increased, and finally when the call came, the answer was ambiguous. They would see him but nothing more definite. Even after meeting the very presentable, handsome, polite, and soft-spoken Dr. Fuad, the family gave no definite answer. And soon thereafter the young woman broke off her relationship with him without any clear explanation.

Obtaining even the most minimal of marriage goals, Egyptians believe, takes an objective detached assessment of the circumstances of the couple, of the outcomes for their kin groups, and an appraisal of the most appropriate mate given the available candidates. The couple themselves are too emotionally involved to provide this detachment. Parents, according to theory, have more experience, want the best for their children, and, therefore, are more capable of providing the advice they need.

Arranged marriage is thus the best defense against "irrationality" in mate selection.[3] Among those social groups where arranged marriages are most common, the rural and urban lower classes, ideal forms of marriage and customs supporting them retain their greatest potency. For example, the custom that the father's brother's son be asked permission if a family intends to marry a girl to someone else is a custom that now tends to survive primarily in rural areas. The converse is also true: where arranged marriage is less common or exists only for public consumption (after mate selection is made by the people concerned), the idealized patterns of relative marriage or sibling marriage have often lost their potency. Under these conditions strict attention to matching the objective characteristics of partners generally also diminishes in favor of permitting individuals to find partners they are temperamentally and philosophically compatible with. Increasingly among the middle classes where these tendencies are strong, young women comment that they will only marry men whose views on certain issues are the same as theirs or ones who can demonstrate a compatible personality. Indeed meetings between the young man and woman who are potential candidates for marriage often sound more like interview sessions the way people describe them.

Aisha had been disappointed in her hopes to marry one of her Mother's sister's sons [they were also her Father's brother's sons] and when the last one was engaged to marry, she accepted the suggestion of her parents that she meet a young man they knew who was seeking a bride. She unenthusiastically acquiesced to an engagement with the young man, but eventually their relationship deteriorated and the engagement was broken. The next time it was much more difficult to find a candidate who was willing to overlook the fact that Aisha had broken a previous engagement. Her Mother's sister, perhaps feeling some sense of conscience, introduced Aisha to a young Egyptian back on holiday from work in the Arab countries. When Aisha met him in the presence of her mother and her aunt they talked at some length. Finally at the end of their meeting she told him quite frankly that she didn't think she could ever love him. Her mother was horrified at this disclosure and attempted to convince Aisha to meet the man again and reconsider. The second time Aisha was somewhat milder and said she liked him a little better but still didn't love him. He was angered by this remark, and though he agreed to see Aisha again at his mother's insistence, he eventually married someone else and they never saw him again.

The idealized system does not break down completely even when children openly choose their own mates. The children themselves are aware of the critical criteria by which marriage partners are chosen and usually monitor their own behavior from this knowledge. The importance of family ties in a child's future constrains him or her from breaking with other family members. Children obtain their information about mate selection not only from their life's experiences but also from watching the barrage of television programs — dramatizations and advice shows — that focus on the subject of mate selection and family life. From sheer weight of time spent on a single subject, marriage emerges on television as the clear winner above all other social issues. Most programs individually depict a clear cut "right way" to select a mate, but overall there is variety, even sometimes contradiction in the answers they provide. In several programs for example, parents were implicitly criticized for choices they made which, though adhering to the structural principles that should guarantee a happy marriage, did not result in such a marriage because they did not weigh carefully enough the "irrational" factors of love and attraction. In other serials, however, the converse was true, and marriages turned out poorly because children did not heed the advice of their parents — they were consumed by irrational motivations. The lack of a clear-cut stand reflects perhaps better than anything the present conflicts over how the process of mate selection should proceed. The goal — a stable and happy family life — remains the same; only the means by which the goal is achieved is subject to debate.

Mediation

Many lower- and middle-class urban families try to prevent "irrational" love factors from entering the selection process by using mediators. They position at least one or more persons between the potential partners to convey messages and negotiate terms. In this way trait matching can be carried on in a more impersonal and face-saving manner. Um Fuad's scrutiny of the one-eyed bride demonstrates this method of operation; preliminary overtures were made by the social worker. In the following example from an élite family we find a similar but more elaborated kind of mediation occurring two decades ago:

Mme. Leila, the daughter of an Al-Azhar sheikh and one-time Cabinet minister, was telling about how she met her husband, Ali. When Leila was about seventeen she and her mother and sisters went to see a film in a respectable theater. A friend of the family, Mahmoud, and a young man, Ali, were sitting in the row behind them. When they turned to greet him, Mahmoud introduced Ali. A few weeks later, Mahmoud's family invited Leila's family to dinner, and again, though she did not speak with him at length, Leila met Ali. Soon, although no one from Leila's family anticipated the move, Ali came to Leila's father to ask if he could marry her. After Ali left without a commitment, the Sheikh called Leila into his study to ask her opinion of the marriage. Thinking quickly she replied that she did not know yet and would like an opportunity to sit with Ali and get to know him better before she accepted his proposal. Her father was impressed with the good sense of his daughter, and though it was the custom of the time to become engaged before meeting at great length with a potential spouse, he agreed to let her mother arrange the meetings while she was present with them. They met several times and Leila agreed to the engagement. She never, however, went out with him until they married. "Now," says Leila, "my daughter of the same age goes out in groups of boys and girls together. We insist upon knowing the names of all the young people in the group to be sure they are from good families, and they must let us know where they are going. We do not permit them to go into private homes unless there are adults present. We hope there is safety in numbers. My daughter reports when young men flirt with her, but so far she has not been seriously interested in anyone. If this should happen we would expect the young man to come to us before he took her out alone."

Even in this élite setting where young people are allowed to become acquainted before marriage, the young man is expected to make his intentions clear before they go out alone.

In Bulaq also when a couple "falls in love" after seeing each other on the street, they do not normally discuss marriage possibilities face to face. Mediators — mother, sisters, or friends — are generally sent out to test the field first.

Most common is for a man to send a female relative out asking other women about a bride for himself, either the one whom he "loves" or another. His decision that he is ready to marry is generally predicated on his circumstances, economic factors normally taking priority over physical or psychological ones. After the initial overtures, more serious negotiations take place between the men of the families. The usual sequence is first to negotiate the terms of the marriage contract, then to hold a formal engagement ceremony after which the couple may visit with each other under specified conditions.

The final marriage ceremony may be held several months or even years later when the bride and groom have fulfilled the necessary parts of the marriage agreement (mainly the collection of furnishings and clothing for the woman and the payment of *mahr* for the man).

Meeting Places

Even with all the efforts to interject people and rituals between the potential bridal couple, urban and rural environments create numerous situations where control by parents cannot be absolute. There are, therefore, many opportunities for young people to observe if not become acquainted with each other. One village boy commented:

> We all know the girls of our village. After all, we played together as kids, and we see them going back and forth on errands as they get older. One favorite place for us to get a glimpse of girls is at the village water source. The girls know that and like to linger there. If we see one we like and think she might be suitable, we ask our parents to try to arrange a marriage, but usually not before we have some sign from the girl that she might be interested.

The extensive role they play in agriculture makes it difficult to control the whereabouts of women at all times.

The urban environment provides similar places where young people can see each other, with the added advantage that except within the immediate neighborhood a certain amount of anonymity exists. In fact the irony of the urban setting is that it provides just the kind of short imagination-provoking encounters that couples can build romantic dreams over, while parents retain enough control to prevent these encounters from lasting long enough to become tediously ordinary. One lower-class woman describes her own experience:

> One day I went to the big vegetable market in Rod el-Faraq to buy mangoes. I said something about the price to the merchant and he insulted me. So I replied, "God forgive you," and he answered in a rude way. So I put away my polite manner and my pretense at meekness and lit into him as I know how to do. I said, "Who do you think you are, you bastard? You low creature, you coward!" And I took my mangoes and left on board a donkey cart. These carts cross the Em-

baba bridge and so I could get off close to home. It seems that a young man standing there watched me through all of this and then followed me home. On the street I met the friend who had come to Lolla's rescue one day. . . . This young man, it seems, then asked her who I was and she pretended I was her sister's daughter and asked him if I had done or said anything to him. He answered that I had not but that he wanted to marry me. So she told him that my father was home on Tuesdays, to come speak to him then. But he wanted to meet my mother first, and one day he appeared at our doorstep. He said to my mother, "I would like to marry this young lady." My mother replied, "Young lady? My boy, you will be struck with a calamity!" But he answered, "I know everything about her and I know her tongue." So my mother asked, "How did you come to know it?" So he told her about the incident at the vegetable market and said that he liked a girl with spunk. (Atiya 1982: 93, 96)

In the end the father rejected this young man because, though he came from a similar lower class background he was better educated and "too rich" for the young woman who, her father said "would always feel out of [her] element" if she married him (Atiya 1982: 96).

The urban places where people meet generally serve to help them preselect a pool of "stranger" candidates of roughly similar backgrounds. People of each socioeconomic level have such places. The lower classes frequent markets and shop in their own native areas of town. The women gather at water taps and pass through the streets bringing water cans back and forth from their homes. The middle classes meet in educational facilities — secondary schools and universities — and the élites meet in private schools and clubs. Holiday spots are informally segregated in the same way. Public gardens are open to everyone but frequented mainly by the lower social classes. There are government-subsidized clubs and resorts for civil servants and fashionable private beach communities where the affluent own homes or apartments. Those who frequent such spots meet others like themselves.

Another important location where matches are made is the work place. B. Ibrahim (1980), in a study of factory women, reported that of the women who married after they began work, 53.3 percent married men working at the same factory. She notes that this method of introducing potential marriage partners has the advantage over traditional kinship channels because it permits contacts between families who will tend to accept the idea of women working. It is a way for women to continue working after marriage. Since the employment of women in formal jobs is not a widespread practice in the lower classes, the work place itself takes on the function of bringing together like-minded people. Though similar figures are not available, there is clear evidence among the middle classes (where unlike the lower classes, there is widespread employment of women) that the work place serves an even more significant role in bringing together potential marriage candidates.

The increasing numbers of Egyptians in recent years who continue their education through the university level have made the campus an important place to meet people and contract "love" marriages. Many middle-class parents accept this fact and expect their children to find marriage partners among either their classmates or, another important group, the siblings of their classmates. The contemporary tendency for men and women of these classes to marry spouses of an age closer to their own can probably also be attributed to the particular age range of candidates available on the campus. The following is an example of one young woman's experience.

> I met Mostafa at the university when he joined our group of boys and girls that used to hang around together. As a group we often would gather together to have tea or just to talk. Though it is not generally accepted that a boy and a girl be seen often alone together unless they are engaged, it is all right for boys and girls to be friends in groups. Several times when we all were together I would be sitting and talking with Mostafa, but I was not aware that he was interested in me until one day when he appeared outside the place where I work to ask for an appointment to meet me. Since that time he occasionally escorts me home from work or from the club. I still am supposed to go out in a group, and my parents always want to know exactly where I am and all the people I am with.
>
> I was afraid at first to tell my parents that there was a growing interest between myself and Mostafa, but soon I told my mother. We are very close and I never keep anything from her. I knew she would help me tell my father when the time came. He is very strict and I feared if a meeting between him and Mostafa didn't go well, I would be forbidden to see him further. It is better in these cases not to tell parents too much too early because it relieves them of a lot of worry. Mostafa is very conservative in his background like my father, and anyone who knew him would know that he could not behave in a way that would hurt his or my reputation.
>
> Mostafa and I considered making all our plans for marriage first: finding an apartment or perhaps as he is thinking now, finding a job overseas, and then telling my parents and having the wedding shortly thereafter to shorten the time during which problems might arise. But we discovered that our plans could not so quickly be car-

ried out, and my mother felt it was better for me to tell my father since it would be far worse if he found out by himself. We tried to pick a good time for Mostafa to come and see my father. We were lucky and the two struck it off well. They both found they were interested in sports and so discussed that subject most of the time in that first meeting.

In this case, the university provides the setting where young people meet, but it does not exempt them from fairly stringent controls (see Chapter 9). What has changed is the mechanism by which the "stranger" is introduced into the household of the young woman's father. The mother retains her traditional role as initial mediator, but this time mediates between her already involved daughter and sweetheart, and the father who is still expected to support the forms of arranged marriage by assessing the suitability of the bridegroom.

Among the middle classes and élites there is evidence that relative marriage persisted as a common form until the present generation of young people. Until the 1952 revolution and the extension of education to the masses of Egypt's population, there was little to interfere with the family as a key socializing institution. Those who received private educations did so in carefully sex-segregated institutions, along with their sisters or brothers, cousins, and well-screened others of the same social classes. Leisure-time socializing took place in the family courtyards or apartments of relatives. Parents exerted much stronger controls over whom their children met than they do now. Middle-aged and older people of those classes almost universally comment on how restricted their access to the opposite sex was, beyond those individuals of the extended family group with whom almost their whole time was spent.

Family genealogies of these classes are filled with kin and sibling marriages up until about a generation ago when, in an impressive reversal, stranger marriages replaced them in the vast majority of cases. This phenomenon to a large extent reflects the changing degree of parental control among these social classes. Young people now have greater freedom of movement, rationalized as noted by the increasing importance of extended education. Controls now are vested less in overt mechanisms such as confinement and protection (seen in chaperonage and veiling) and more in internalized "nice-girl" constructs (see Chapter 9) which individuals implement to a large extent by themselves.

As often happens when changing conditions produce a modification of behavioral pattern, people begin to invest the new behavior with a "morality" that makes it seem a positive development. One middle-class mother commented:

My eldest son was welcome in my sister's house until she heard he
was about to marry a colleague from the university. She was disappointed that he was not to marry her daughter, Muna, and made it
clear that her house was no longer so open to him. Then she concentrated her efforts on my youngest son. He realized what she wanted
but explained to me that he and Muna had grown up together in such
close contact that he felt she was a sister to him. He was unable to
think of her as a wife, though he loved her as a sister.

This young man says he considers the relationship with his cousin
as like one of siblings and, therefore, marriage to her would be similar
to violating an incest taboo. For him too much close contact has stifled
sexual attraction. In a parallel example inhabitants of kibbutzim in Israel
mention the unusually low marriage rates among cohorts of children who
are brought up together. One of the advantages of seclusionary practices
that has often been ignored is the effect those practices have in heighten-
ing sexual attraction between closely related people. Given the ideal of
relative marriage, separation of those involved helps make realization of
the ideal more palatable.

In Saudi Arabia, where father's brother's daughter marriage and
large extended residential family groupings are much more common than
in Egypt, this necessity becomes more important. By confining the females to certain parts of the house and the males to another, cousins retain much of the attractiveness of strangers even when in close physical
proximity.

A more sophisticated but erroneous argument from a highly educated male observer gives a scientific twist to the rationale behind a shift
in preference sometimes seen among lower-class urbanites from patrilateral
to matrilateral relative marriage.

Almost no one marries a relative these days among the educated
classes. We have learned that such marriages can produce weak children, physically and mentally. It is mainly among the ignorant peasants that this custom is still continued. Those who still prefer relative
marriage are tending to marry more on the mother's side for genetic
reasons to reduce the negative biological effects. [When asked why
that was better biologically he said the following:] In the process of
conception, the man places the seed which becomes the baby in the
mother. She is only a receptacle that nourishes the baby, but otherwise does not contribute to the baby's genetic background. It is the
same as producing a child by a stranger woman, from the genetic point
of view.

One man was "proving" the same point with the following story: "There was a man I know who had a violent argument with his sister's husband. Afterward in an attempt to hurt the sister's husband, he killed his son, who of course was also his sister's son. This proves that there is no blood passing between mother and son, for the man could never have killed his own blood relative."

These comments, inaccurate as they may be from a biological standpoint,[4] reflect the deep-seated sense of patrilineal origins that continues in contemporary Egypt. These are the *asab* or the backbone of family descent links. In the light of its strong reinforcement it is not difficult to see how the emphasis on patrilineality has persisted even beyond the time when in certain contexts conditions are no longer as conducive to its persistence. The principle is too deeply embedded in moral and other rationales to withstand too rapid a change. It is not unusual for a middle-class respondent to rationalize a change process in "scientific" terms in this way without basically modifying the traditional premise upon which the behavior is built. He retains the value while recasting the ideological support structure and the ultimate behavioral outcome. The truth in what this respondent states is that there is a sharp decline in the number of young people of the urban educated classes who marry close relatives these days. Those who do, one might add, probably come from families who are able to maintain relatively strict control over their children's activities and feel the desire to solidify their family group through the same devices their own parents used.

Arranged marriage, common enough still among the middle classes and very common among the lower classes, provides a useful function in the contemporary Egyptian scene. First, it acts as a compensatory mechanism in communities where social controls are strongest against males and females intermingling, by providing a means by which mate selection can take place. In those segments of the population where controls are eased for one reason or another the practice is found less frequently, partly because other means exist for becoming acquainted. Second, arranged marriage is one of several options available when needed for families of all classes and styles of life. In a single family it may be used for some children and not for others. If, for example, young people are bashful or their advantages do not immediately attract suitors, arranged marriages are a face-saving way of assuring them partners. In the example of the not-so-attractive rich girl, her father unabashedly started the interview with the mediator by pointing out her financial assets. In this way, marriage is assured to a very high percentage of Egyptian men and women. Arranged marriage becomes just one in an arsenal of marriage strategies, the effectiveness of which is determined by the extent to which those involved have judged its appropriateness to a particular set of conditions. However, some young women face the problem that parents still exert strong controls on their daughters but feel themselves "too modern" to arrange their marriages. With neither the opportunities to meet young men nor mechanisms to circumvent the difficulty, these young women are doomed (in the Egyptian view) to a life of spinsterhood. It may be as much a dilemma for the parents as the children since most parents feel an obligation to help their children find suitable marriages.

The Influence of Context on Patterns of Relative Marriage

Whether marriage takes place in a rural or urban context affects the expression of preferences and the kinds of marriages people actually contract. Consider these comments made by lower-class women born and married in rural areas of Upper Egypt, a part of the country considered more provincial: "What do you expect? Of course I married my father's brother's son. I'm from the village, aren't I?" "Father's brother's son, of course. I'm from Upper Egypt, we all marry like that there." Or expressing the same expectation in a negative example, "Well, I did marry my mother's sister's son, but it was because my father's brother's son was too young for me." And note these comments by Cairo-born lower-class women: "People here in Cairo would prefer to marry their daughters to mother's sister's sons if they could, but often in the city it is difficult to get children to do what parents want." "I married from my father's relatives, but it was to a man who had grown up with me and called me *bint khalla* [mother's sister's daughter]." "I married my father's brother's son instead of my mother's sister's son because he came from the village and told my parents he wanted to marry me. Of course by the tradition of the village, he feels he has the right to marry me."

The preferences expressed by rural women about ideal marriage patterns are stated in a much stronger way than those expressed by urban lower-class women. Rural women view the father's brother's son pattern as the expected one while their city sisters feel that mother's sister's son marriage is to be preferred but often difficult to achieve. The city women's ambivalence stems partly from their own close acquaintance with rural customs, either as a result of their coming from rural areas themselves or because many of their neighbors have come from these areas. When they prefer patterns that contradict the rural ideals they demonstrate that they are aware of what constitutes an advantageous marriage in the lower-class city environment. Their ambivalence about kin marriage stems also from a recognition that intervening factors are more likely to prevent the realization of any kind of preferred marriage in the city. The most significant of these factors are the wider range of marriage opportunities in urban environments, the absence of appropriate kin members, and the greater difficulty a parent finds in gaining the concurrence of a child who may have developed other interests.

Does the desire to contract different kinds of marriage in urban and rural environments show up in the statistics of actual marriages contracted? Among a sample of Bulaq households (see Rugh 1978) in which the responses of 340 husbands and wives[5] were recorded, 45 percent (152) married strangers, 45 percent (152) married a relative from the father's side of the family, and 10 percent (35) married from the mother's side of the family. Overall, marriage to a relative was favored over marriage to a stranger, and marriage to paternal relatives was strongly preferred over marriage to maternal ones.

When the tabulations were disaggregated by the birth places of the respondents in rural and urban locations, a new pattern emerges. Among those from the rural areas 66 percent (150) married a relative, and 34 percent (78) married a stranger. The reverse ratio is the case for the urban area (38 and 74 cases, respectively). In the rural area relative marriage took the following forms: 75 percent (113) married father's brother's children, 11 percent (16) married father's sister's children, 3 percent (5) married mother's sister's children, and 11 percent (16) married mother's brother's children. In the urban areas relative marriage included 53 percent (20) who married their father's brother's children, 8 percent (3) who married their father's sister's children, 32 percent (12) who married their mother's sister's children, and 8 percent (3) who married their mother's brother's children.

Those marrying from the rural area, therefore, showed an extremely strong preference for father's brother's son marriage, while the preference was much weaker for the same kind of relative marriage in the urban area. Moreover, in the urban area marriage to mother's sister's children had gained significantly, rising to ten times[6] the ratio it had sustained in the countryside. Marriage to the children of cross-sex siblings of parents stays at a relatively stable level both with relation to which parent is being considered and with relation to urban and rural contexts. This suggests that these marriages have little of significance to recommend them beyond their generalized value as relative marriage.

The trend toward sister's children marriage in the city becomes even stronger among the young preparing to marry. At the time of the survey, of those preparing to marry relatives (12 cases)[7] ten were marrying mother's sister's children and two father's brother's children. The one couple marrying in the father's brother's children pattern was explained by neighbors as occurring because the young woman concerned had been caught in a brothel and her father's brother's son was prepared to marry her for the sake of the family reputation. Subsequently the engagement was broken off by the young man.

Why do these differences in patterns appear in urban and rural areas? We can suggest a possible answer to this question by summarizing points that will be discussed more fully in Chapter 12. We shall see that family is a more potent organizing force in rural than in urban areas. Membership in family units is significant in the countryside not only for political and economic reasons but also as a way of giving individuals an identity. Maintaining broad networks of personnel in extended kin groups requires an emphasis on jural aspects of relations, meaning in the widest terms, maintaining the general commitment to fulfilling the obligations of membership. This includes being ready to mobilize forces in the interests of the family group and also on a daily basis to maintain the standards by which the family will be publicly known. It means also developing a highly defined authority pattern with the leadership of the units well marked — in the village they ask who your father is, or looking to broader networks, who the head male of your branch of the family is. In marriage the family attempts to keep its boundaries intact by not releasing girls out to produce new members for other groups and conversely by not letting the obtrusive stranger in to "sabotage" the works from inside. People express these ideals obliquely when they say it is a shame for a man to marry outside his father's family if there are appropriate girls of marriageable age available within the family. A girl who marries out is said to have denied her father's family. Extra reinforcement is also given to family endogenous marriage by the stipulation that the father's brother's son has the first right to marry his father's brother's daughter. No other man can take her without his permission.

Given these special conditions existing in the rural environment it becomes clear why brother's children marriage meets the requirements most efficiently. In brief (see Chapter 7) the young man and young woman carry the same patrilineal blood lines; they jointly owe their obligations to the same male members of the extended family. They have grown up together and have shared the family secrets; they are committed to preserving the family image and supporting the same family members. The young bride fits into her husband's household without disruption. The authority lines are preserved, and families are unified in a way that no other marriage pattern can achieve. Work groups, political units, emotionally supportive households remain intact. Women sustain a weak position in terms of authority, but this is irrelevant in terms of what the family accomplishes in the organization of the village.

The urban context and requirements differ markedly from those existing in the countryside. There is the reduced significance of family as an identifier in the city's mélange of strangers. Among the lower classes, without substantial property to inherit, with labor and wages individualized and less reliance placed on family productive units,[8] with families larger than husband, wife, and children physically dispersed in separate dwellings if not in separate areas of town,[9] and with the reduced importance of family name, the significance of jural ties among relatives is diminished. Furthermore, the straitened economic conditions of many of the lower classes encourages them to maintain affective ties with a number of relations as a safety net for emergencies, while at the same time resisting overcommitment financially to helping others out. It is as important to retain a hold over kin who feel obligations to one as it is to keep from becoming financially inundated by those to whom one owes obligations. The balance is a delicate one. Solidifying jural ties by marriage on the father's side of the family can sometimes over-tip the balance by "doubling" the sense of *wagib* obligation.

In lower-class circumstances the small and large services women exchange become an added resource to the family, one that produces collectible debts if the favor is given, and one that adds materially in goods if received. Errands are run, babies watched, household tasks of cooking and cleaning shared, and special life cycle events celebrated mainly with the help of women. Marriage to maternal relatives, particularly to a mother's sister's son, strengthens the opportunities for the exchange of services in these resource-starved households. At the same time it does not overly reinforce exchanges of an obligation resource-drawing nature. The bride's mother is pleased that the new mother-in-law (her sister) encourages relations between herself and her daughter. The three women willingly help each other and because of women's stronger affective ties, they are more likely to endure long term unbalanced *maruf* exchanges with the stronger individuals helping the weaker if that becomes necessary. In this way a married daughter, for example, may secretly help her impoverished mother with money from her own household account and not expect anything in return. In these marriages also girls move into a stronger relationship with the warm "loving" households of their maternal aunt, a plus that has to be considered in light of the city's impersonal anonymity among strangers. Husbands are happy because their women are occupied a good deal of the time with maternal relatives and thus not as open to the advances of strangers. Mothers too actively seek such marriages for their children for practical and strategic reasons that are more compelling in urban environments. Such marriages strengthen a mother's position in relation to her own husband and increase the likelihood that holidays and other family events will be spent with own rather than husband's kin.

Since families are everywhere vulnerable through their girls, parents want to secure good stable marriages for them as early as possible. One of the greatest burdens a lower-class urban family may be forced to bear is the return of a married daughter with or without children to the family home again, temporarily or permanently requiring support. This circumstance is much less likely to happen as a result of marital discord, according to theory, when the marriage occurs with a relative; it is even less likely to occur, also according to theory, when the relatives are sister's children with their emotional feeling for each other but without the other financial support entanglements that can cause tensions in the economically insecure families of the lower classes. These are some of the rationales expressed for the tendency to view sister's children marriage as ideal in lower-class urban settings. That people are unable to realize these "perfect" marriages very often attests to the complexity of the selection process in urban areas and the greater likelihood that other factors may intervene.

In summary, marriage provides the opportunities for families and their members to strengthen certain ties at the expense of or even the exclusion of other ties. There is a wide variety of strategies open for people to manipulate. To characterize the Egyptian system by only a select number of these (as scholars do when they describe the system solely as patrilineal) does a disservice to the full potentiality that exists in marriage choices. Individuals, as we have seen, draw on a complex of marriage patterns that are considered ideal and which have certain expected outcomes. Their particular choices reflect specific environmental and familial priorities. The tension to conform to the ideals of society and to present one's family members as model recipients of other people's choices helps to make the marriage selection process one of the most conservative influences in Egyptian society, reinforcing other social norms and values.

9

Solidarity

"The man able to control a woman allows her to participate"
—Arab proverb

IN THE last chapter marriage was shown as a major proving ground for tests of solidarity for the family, both in its internal and external social relations. First, the need to marry imposes behavioral controls on people that are partly self-inflicted and partly imposed through social norms and sanctions. These controls reduce erratic anti-social, anti-group activities. Second, the process of partner selection and marriage preparation provides the opportunity for family members to demonstrate their support for one another. Third, the act of marriage provides a graceful, approved way of redefining the strength of allegiances and the groups to whom they are owed. But marriage also contains high-risk factors, as was noted, that may cause some primary allegiances to weaken or in other ways to be disrupted. Practically, it is such fears that cause the institution of marriage to be surrounded by so many normative supports prescribing approved procedures.

Within the family, other controls exist to promote the harmony of group interactions. Some appear in the guise of ideals, values, and prescribed norms that serve as guides in the normal course of daily life. Even when people do not comply fully with these prescriptions, they usually publicly present themselves as doing so, since serious violations are likely to evoke negative sanctions, and even minor violations tend to diminish the social rewards that accompany approved behavior. Other controls are found in agreed-upon modes for family interaction and in set procedures for resolving group conflicts. This chapter is concerned with the kinds of

149

controls that promote harmonious behavior both within the family unit
and in its relations with external individuals and groups. The forms these
controls take are shaped in large part by the desired end of group solidarity and the belief that ultimately responsibility to group should weigh
more heavily than individual rights.

FAMILY INTERACTION

The event was a seven-day party in celebration of the birth of a son
in a middle-class family. Each person [relatives of the mother and father
and some work colleagues of the mother] who came was greeted with
kisses and individual attention, even down to the tiniest baby. If anyone was quiet for a while, he or she was drawn into conversation again,
regardless of age. The conversations included comments about events
that took place on the way to the visit, about events of importance
to those assembled, news about persons who were not present. The
remarks were normally personal, and the topics rarely touched upon
esoteric matters beyond the immediate experience of the people present. The host and hostess were active in directing the conversation,
asking the critical questions that would bring out each person in turn.
There were no long soliloquies except when a story was told about
a sequence of events that everyone could enjoy; more common was
rapid-fire comment around the group. The time passed quickly, and
the conversation was light and full of jokes. Meanwhile, there was the
constant movement of people going and coming, bringing drinks and
taking the empty glasses away. It was not easy to distinguish the hosts
from the guests; everyone helped out. Age groups were not segregated
in different locations nor did they assume special functions at the party.
Everyone was included in all aspects of the activity.

The interaction of people in groups in Egypt often demonstrates a
high degree of sophisticated skill in handling sensitive human relations.
Within the family some fairly consistent patterns emerge. Though individuals are assigned relative positions within the family based on age, sex
and other status characteristics, each person's position also carries with
it a value in itself that gives it independent importance within the group.
Thus a baby does not have to grow up to adulthood in order to have a
full measure of importance in the family. A baby is a valued asset within
the family already and is recognized as deserving certain kinds of attentions that will allow its personality to develop to its full capacity. For this
reason, people draw babies into their family groups immediately, almost

from the moment of birth, making sure they feel a sense of participation, and seeing that their demands are not frustrated. Egyptians see a baby's demands as his or her way of participating. Egyptians view the satisfaction of a baby's demands as a way of allowing the baby to feel his or her own personality within the group. By being indulged small babies are first shown their rights within the group. Children later learn their responsibilities by being asked to assume tasks in the household. In both cases the membership of a baby and a child in the family is affirmed.

The "seven-day" party is a way of dramatically demonstrating the importance of the baby to the group and the family's desire to see that the baby will develop the requisite personality traits to deal with adult life. These messages of fertility, wisdom, courage, and faith are conveyed through the symbols of seeds, knives, grain sifters, banging pots, and lighted candles.

The "seven-day" party, like other family gatherings, also serves the more general purpose of developing solid family relationships. Each individual is brought out and encouraged to participate in his or her own way — by conversation, by serving others, by any kind of social response. In this way the person develops a social personality that at times puts that person at the center of attention and sometimes requires that he or she be audience. Activities are kept at a level that everyone can enjoy. Children are not asked to go to a separate room while their elders talk. The party in effect becomes itself the occasion where each member establishes his or her importance to the group and the group's importance to him or her. From these family gatherings over the years young children gradually develop a sense of group identity.

Role differences are not highly emphasized in this particular social event — men and women are not segregated, distressed children may be calmed by mothers, fathers, or other children interchangeably, the young and the old respond equally to one another, and visitors help hosts in the kitchen. The activity demonstrates several important facets of family group membership — that each person's part is important, that to some degree their support of each other is interchangeable, and that the normal distinctions that separate people in public life are deemphasized if not suspended altogether in this special circumstance of a family gathering.

Paradoxically, many families promote internal harmony by opposite techniques, by specifically assigning responsibilities and orders of succession to certain family members and not others, or to others only in their turn. The segregation of sex roles that was discussed earlier is one of these techniques. Little girls do not expect to engage in the same activities as little boys just as women do not expect to assume the roles and responsibilities of men. In this way a great deal of interdependence is created and competition reduced between family members expected to perform the same duties. Expectations are strong that family members will behave according to appropriate role models; only a few marginal individuals resent the limitations these norms place on their lives.

Hierarchies within families achieve much the same kind of division of responsibility and interdependence. Elder males and females of the household receive deference and are accorded decision-making roles in the household within the spheres of their influence. Older children take care of younger ones and in return occupy positions of greater respect and authority among the siblings; boys protect girls, fathers command, and mothers obey.

With respect to important life events such as marriage, the family may demand strict sequential order by which the group resources and support are made available. Children may be married one by one from eldest to youngest; if an older sister fails to marry she may hold up the marriages of younger sisters (see the example of Nowal, Chapter 6). Other families may also pair a brother and sister, requiring that the brother wait until his sister marries before he does. This means that any resources he may accumulate must be made available to his sister before pursuing his own marriage plans. If a predominance of girls exists in the family, all the boys may be asked to wait until all the girls are married before they marry. All these practices serve to cut down the competition for restricted resources within families, and for this reason they tend to be found more often among families where limited resources are a significant factor — among the poor or the middle lower classes. For these classes the rationale in support of such behaviors is still the generally held belief, true for all classes, that individuals will restrain their own needs when the needs of the group require it.

Another way the family demonstrates its unity is through substitutional practices — by developing concepts of the appropriateness of substituting personnel within the family. If a mother is missing, for example, it is her mother or her sister who are considered the persons most likely to substitute adequately in caring for young children. Similarly, a mature son is required to provide economic support for his mother, younger brothers, and sisters if a father-husband is missing. So firmly is the pattern established among the lower classes that until recently a self-perpetuating cycle was often created that was difficult to break. Men marrying women much younger than themselves died earlier than their wives by natural attrition while young children still remained in the home. Elder sons were pressed into providing the main support for such households. This, of

A mother in traditional dress sits proudly with her educated children in the European-style reception room of a transitional middle-class family.

course, meant that these sons put off marrying until an older age and then, by marrying young women, created the same demographic imbalances in the next generation. Each generation, as a result, was required to compensate for the disparities created in the preceding one. Again a unity of group was established, this time appearing whole only through the passage of time and with the acceptance of substitutional processes.

Families commonly establish a sense of unity by group activities and through a sense of group responsibility. Few activities are seen as isolated tasks to be performed by a single person. Family members work together on household tasks or they sit together in designated gathering rooms to enjoy their leisure together. Children do school homework in the midst of the group, studying with older and younger siblings or with the help of their parents. Families usually go visiting together as a family or by dividing themselves in sex-segregated clusters. Middle-class young children who go to visit friends usually go with brothers or sisters accompanying them, whether or not there are other children of suitable age and sex in the homes they are visiting. Egyptians, in other words, do not see the ne-

This woman shopkeeper will be able to pass her means of livelihood on to her son.

cessity of pairing their children with friends of the same age and sex as we in the West do. Children are first and foremost sisters and brothers with strong common interests; only secondarily do they cultivate interests of their own outside families, and if these interests interfere with family activities they must be dropped.

Similarly, children are not usually encouraged to have a strong sense of individual property. They share rooms with siblings, and in restricted environments, at best, they may occupy only a position in a bed or on the floor with other children. It is not uncommon in poor households for them to sleep where they find themselves, at whatever time they happen to feel sleepy. Other kinds of property, clothing, appliances, toys, etc. are shared in the same way without a strong sense of personal ownership. In fact, politeness training usually stresses sharing as a value above others. If a thing can be shared, as for example sweets, children are encouraged to give first to others before taking themselves. The tiniest children are often given the task of offering sweets to guests to help them learn the habit.

The above practices, insignificant in themselves, add up to a conceptual frame that emphasizes unity and the reduction of competition among individual members of the family. Together with other similarly intentioned practices they form a consistent organizational framework for the conduct of family life.

CONTROLS ON MALE-FEMALE RELATIONSHIPS

Simply stated, the control of male-female relationships has the effect of reducing potentially disruptive behavior that might arise from unregulated competition for marriage partners. In the last two chapters we saw the importance of marriage as a social institution in Egyptian society and we looked at the controls on access to females during the marriage selection process. Also important are the more general controls that restrict male-female interaction. Ostensibly the controls are exerted on women by male members of their households. In reality, though, much of the regulation is self-imposed or imposed by women on each other. Men too impose or find imposed upon themselves limits upon their behavior with regard to women. The discussion here, however, is devoted mainly to controls on women because within the family these controls are most vital to maintaining family reputation. By the greater latitude their roles allow, men usually can violate approved behaviors without jeopardizing the interests of the group in any significant way.

One scholar has suggested that there are three basic strategies in the world used to regulate and control the behavior of women: first, confinement, which restricts a woman to the vicinity of her household and proscribes much independent movement outside; second, protection, by designated protectors who accompany a woman out into areas where her virtue may be comprised; and third, normative restrictions, such as are found in the "nice-girl" standards of a society (Fox 1977:805). If one adds to these strategies the physiological control of clitoridectomy, the basic patterns of control in Egypt are represented.

The majority of Egyptians do not have the economic means to sustain, even if they wanted to, the extreme forms of female control that have been carried out in places like Saudi Arabia, where women actually do remain much of the time confined to their homes in special quarters. Such forms of restriction, when carried out humanely, require large gardens, high walls, and the resources to maintain extra personnel to act as chaperones. Confinement and protection as strategies in their purest forms are, therefore, more an ideal of an irreproachable morality than a contemplated reality in the crowded conditions of lower-class Bulaq or middle-class Shubra.

Controls on women's behaviors in Bulaq and Shubra form realistic compromises with these "ideal" forms. Confinement in Bulaq, for example, is represented in the tendency for women to wear black modesty coverings the moment they step over their thresholds into the public world. It is seen in the belief that it is more honorable for women to remain in the home than work and found in the separation of male and female worlds: in classrooms after elementary school, in different areas for leisure activity, in separate purchasing lines for goods in stores or tickets at bus stations. The "ideal" however is also often compromised in the press of male and female bodies on public transportation systems. Protection similarly requires what rarely exists in Bulaq—the surpluses to afford guardians. Nevertheless tensions to strain toward the ideal still exist. "Proper" women try to move in public places accompanied by an adult friend or relative or, when these are not available, they take a child along to indicate the fact that they are respectably married women. A lone woman moves briskly and carries with her some evidence of her destination, a shopping basket or a pot of food to indicate that her errand has a pressing purpose. A Bulaq woman never walks alone for the sake of the walk. Shubra women tend to use similar symbols to demonstrate their virtuous intent. They may don a scarf if required to go out at night to give an added touch of respectability. In general middle-class women are given greater leeway in the amount of time they spend in public since it is expected their business will require them to be out in the streets more. In their districts shopping areas may be further away, their need for a variety of goods is considered greater, and it is well known that many work. Titles, like *doctora,* lend a respectability to single, educated women out on the street. They widen the personal horizons of mobility for those who bear them simply by drawing a respectable frame around the activity.

Perhaps closest to the practice of chaperonage is the custom that is instituted when a young man and woman are engaged and he comes to visit her in her home. The couple is considered particularly vulnerable to moral indiscretion at this time, and their legal attachment is not so great that the relationship cannot be dissolved. Someone usually remains with the courting couple or nearby to assure that nothing improper happens. As one mother noted: "If this young man doesn't marry her nobody else will if they think he has even so much as kissed her."

Middle-class engaged couples are often allowed to go out walking together; élites may meet each other at clubs. The watchword, however, is *public;* the couple should remain in the open and not be thought of as frequenting private places unless, of course, it is her home and her parents are present.

A young man, whose mother was my "sister," wanted to bring his fiancée to meet me for my approval. He suggested that we meet for soft drinks at a casino with tables overlooking the Nile. We had an enjoyable two hours talking together, and as we parted I suggested they come to have tea with me in my home in a few days so we could become better acquainted. There was an uncomfortable silence, and then the young man explained that before they were married the woman's parents would not permit her to go to a private home with him, for fear of eliciting gossip about their relationship. Soon after their marriage they paid a visit to me in my home.

In Bulaq terms the kind of control that comes from internalized norms, what it means to be a "nice girl," is cheaper. Most of the vestiges of "confinement" and "protection" have in fact been reduced already to this kind of control as the examples above indicate. The advantages are that control is primarily self-imposed and internalized, extends over the lifetime of the individual, covers behaviors beyond those purely related to male-female contacts, and extends to all elements of the population, not just to those who can afford the costly forms of protection and confinement. (Fox 1977: 805–11). Girls in Bulaq and Shubra are willing to shoulder the responsibility of self-control because they are interested in the rewards that accrue to those who are reputed to be "nice girls." The main reward is the possibility of marrying well, but other rewards include society's approval, especially the approval of one's own family. Wayward behavior of a female household member jeopardizes not only her own chances of marriage but those of other family members, so the inducement to good behavior is a long-term one, first as a prospective marriage partner oneself and later as the relative or mother of one.

Women recognize that the normative controls they impose on themselves give them a different responsibility from that of men. One woman noted this when she criticized another woman who refused to live with her husband because she discovered that he was having an affair with another woman:

> I think women must close their eyes when their husbands go with other women. If they don't say anything and pretend they don't know about it, their husbands will eventually come back to them. [I asked, "Will men close their eyes when women do the same?"] Women who are good can't do things like that. They can't because men would never understand, and, besides, their neighbors and relatives — everyone — will know and criticize them. Women have their children to look after, and they must always think first of them.

"Nice-girl" constructs are characterized in Egypt by their stress on public image. The self-controls people internalize are ones that usually stress how to present oneself to the world rather than how to satisfy purely personal moral standards. What is not known publicly is often not considered an important moral indiscretion since it does not carry with it the sanctions people fear. Even when other family members know about the indiscretion, their common interest in preventing publicity will usually reduce or negate the sanctions they might otherwise apply. On the other hand, publicly known indiscretion forces the hand of other family members to publicly display their sanctions against the offending member. It follows also that what is thought publicly to be an indiscretion but was in reality not one can have just as serious repercussions as one that is:

> In Bulaq, all the neighbors talked about Amina, one of the daughters of the widow Um Samir. She had tried several times to get work as a shop girl, but each time she was fired because she came late or did not show up at all for work. The neighbors felt it was because she

was seeing men during the time when she should have been working. Eventually Amina got engaged to a young man from a nearby quarter, but when he inquired further into her background he learned what the gossips were saying and immediately cut off the engagement. For a long time there were no suitors, but finally Um Samir let it be known in a distant quarter through relatives that Amina was free; the relatives could be relied upon to be discreet. The neighbors chuckled at the young man who came forward but who was unwise enough not to look carefully into his wife's background, and wondered what would happen on the wedding night when he would find out. Um Samir, according to a nearby neighbor, rushed out with Amina to a doctor who specializes in hymen repair. On the wedding night, it was said, there was a great deal of tension in the family, but either the doctor had done a good job or through the bridegroom's inexperience, Amina's lapses in behavior were not discovered.

The neighbors in this case were kind enough to keep silent about their suspicions since they were not directly involved. In a smaller community, however, the secret would have been known to all. In Amina's case the impersonal conditions of city life were what made a second chance possible. Some people in Bulaq argue that it was having no male presence in the household that created the problem in the first place, and they comment that in the village one of the relatives would have taken over that role of protecting the widow and her children.

Although symbolic display of modesty is an important aspect of a "nice-girl" image in all the classes, norms with respect to modesty differ significantly between classes. One of the most easily observed is dress which conveys meaning at a glance. The lower classes wear calf- or ankle-length dresses and hair coverings that are usually black except in children and young women. Adult women wearing flowered prints normally cover them with a black overdress when they appear in public areas. Lower-class women cover their arms (especially the upper arms), the body, and any but the smallest expanse of leg or hair. The breast may be exposed when nursing a baby. This still leaves a great deal of room for personal idiosyncracies of dress — differences in cut, style, material, and the extent to which the garment is draped to reveal the shape underneath. The "nice girl" not only must follow dress conventions but must show by her deportment and bearing that her intentions are honorable.

Middle-class dress norms allow greater expanses of leg and arm to be displayed, to the knee and to the mid-arm, and they usually accept a fully uncovered head. The more tightly fitting clothing of these classes reveals the figure more fully. The major exception to these general dress patterns of the middle class is the adoption of the new Islamic dress (to be discussed in more detail in Chapter 11). This dress takes many of the modesty requirements of lower-class dress and weaves them into a new outfit that is unmistakably different. Whereas the lower-class woman wears her dress primarily because it is customary, the middle-class woman chooses Islamic dress from motives that are more self-consciously pious.

In short, normative restrictions that are self-imposed recognize that the world of women consists of appropriate places to go, approved kinds of transportation, legitimate purposes, the right kinds of dress, and appropriate companions, all determined by the person's station in life and her general circumstances. To violate these principles risks social sanctions. To project the image of a respectable "nice girl" brings society's approval and perhaps, as hoped for, a good husband.

A final form of control exercised widely in Bulaq is the practice of clitoridectomy. It is considered locally to be a highly successful means of controlling the otherwise "unrestrained" sexuality thought characteristic of women. As one lower-class man described the necessity of clitoridectomy: "In the cold countries of the north where the blood runs more slowly you do not have the need for this operation. But here in the warm countries we are more emotional and less restrained. Without this operation there is no telling what our women might do. For sure, one man would not be enough to satisfy them."

The convenience of a one-time, cheap operation has probably done much to continue the practice of clitoridectomy despite the ban by government officials and the refusal of responsible medical practitioners to perform the operation. Clitoridectomy still remains almost universal among the lower classes. According to a Women's International News bulletin published in 1979 and purporting to have statistics compiled from the literature, ten million women in Egypt (about 50 percent of women) have been subjected to excision operations. All segments of the population except those in the urban, educated upper and middle classes practice the custom. In general, it probably accomplishes its purpose as much because of the psychological mind set it creates as from the physiological effects that are produced. There is debate among doctors about the effects of clitoridectomy on sexual response. Some women also have doubts about the extent to which their sexuality is reduced by the operation, but they rarely discuss feelings of sexual frustration openly. Sexual topics themselves are not taboo, but talk of women's unsatisfied sexual needs might create the very image of her that the practice of clitoridectomy is designed to control. One circumcised woman, however, commented that her husband had been made impotent by the death of their son. Though she says she can get along without sex and now lives only for her children, she confesses to a feeling of nervousness and irritability from time to time. But to avoid hurting the feelings of her husband she refrains from telling him about her "unquiet" moments.

Numerous beliefs surround clitoridectomy. Some believe that the operation is required to cut out the masculine qualities in a woman, that without it she cannot marry and will in fact grow a penis like a man. Others emphasize the cosmetic effects of removing what is considered ugly in appearance.

Within the middle classes, the practice of clitoridectomy has now become very rare, though a number of older women underwent the operation several decades ago. A middle-class woman relates how quickly the practice changed among the middle classes in the conservative towns of Upper Egypt:

> When it came time for my first daughter to be circumcised in Upper Egypt, I was not very much for it; but my mother and friends and relatives said that it should be done to her or she might not be able to marry. I tried to have a doctor do it for both my son and daughter at the same time, but even then it was banned for girls and he refused. So I found a simple village woman who seemed clean. She took 5 £E and just cut off the clitoris without anesthesia. My daughter screamed and bled for a long time. She grew sick and pale, and it was a long time before she recovered. That was thirty years ago when she was about three or four years old. Seven years later it came the turn of my second daughter, but by that time all the same people were saying that the operation shouldn't be made on girls. It changed that quickly! People were also saying that men didn't want to marry women after that operation because it makes the wives not want to sleep with their husbands. It's true! My eldest daughter never wants her husband for that reason, and he blames us for having had that operation done. In my generation in Upper Egypt we were all done!

Controls on the behavior of women still remain reasonably strong in Egyptian society. The National Centre for Social Research interviewed a small sample (50) of young men and women between the ages of 18 and 30 and discovered that 60 percent of parents do not want their daughters to have friendships with those of the opposite sex. Of the young men, 38 percent declared that their fathers supported their relations with girls. The study concludes (perhaps on the basis of other data) that parents are more reluctant for girls to have friendships with males than parents are for sons to have relations with females (*Egyptian Gazette,* May 27, 1980). This coincides with comments made to me by one young middle-class Egyptian woman:

> My father always wants to know where I am, what I am doing, and whom I am with. I only see my fiancé at planned meetings when my parents are present. Sometimes he knows my brother is out late but simply says, "Well, he must be with Leila," though they are not even engaged. Parents are like that; they will trust the behavior of a son but are afraid of a stranger man who might do something to the daughter that would spoil her chances to marry. Even if he didn't do something to her, people might think he did. With a son's girl friends, they feel it is up to her parents to control what she does.

This young woman feels a strong sense of guilt because she spoke to her fiancé and got to know him as the brother of her school friend before he went to her father asking for permission to see her. She is not so concerned with the morality of the act itself as she is with violation of the trust her father has in her to proceed according to the appropriate conventions.

SANCTIONS

Controls are exerted on people who violate social norms by a number of means. The next illustration is a "trouble" case, where a young girl has violated nice-girl norms and created a problem for everyone concerned. The situation is complicated by the fact that those involved are Christian with the possibility of divorce virtually excluded. The case has been chosen because of the wide range of sanctions applied to the errant member of the community.

> During visits in Bulaq one day, A. [the mediator in this case] and I learned that a young woman, Suna, aged 15, had been married a month before and was now having difficulties with her husband and parents-in-law. As Suna's mother described the problems, the source of conflict lay in the harsh treatment and heavy work inflicted upon Suna. We offered to visit Suna and see what the situation was. At the house we were greeted warmly by Suna and after a few pleasantries got down to the task of finding out about Suna's problem. The story slowly came out. Suna had not realized the full ramifications of marriage. To her the main point had been to obtain new clothing and furnishings and

a room which was her own. She wrinkled her nose with disgust when she talked about the sexual demands of her husband. Her mother-in-law interjected angrily, "Why did you get married then?" We confirmed that part of the problem was also the large amount of housework that fell on Suna as the new daughter-in-law. She was expected to do all the laundry and most of the cleaning for a household composed of her mother-in-law, father-in-law, an old grandmother of her husband, and four of his unmarried brothers.

After listening to a catalogue of ills on both sides, with sympathy in each case to establish her impartiality, A. finally turned to Suna and said, "My daughter, you must do what your husband wants of you whether you like it or not. That is why you are married. Do you want him to go out on the street for such things? No! You are young and beautiful, and he loves you, and he wants you. You must keep yourself clean and beautiful for him; do as he wants, and then he will love you and be good to you. Look, this is true for all women. I am old, but I go to my husband when he wants me." Then she turned to the mother-in-law and told her that Suna was only a girl and that she needed a mother more than a mother-in-law: "Treat her as if she is your daughter, teach her to be a good wife and help her in the housework. It is too much for a young girl to do all alone."

We promised Suna also that we would come again to visit if she behaved. Two months later we visited Suna again, stepping immediately into her own room so that she would feel we had come especially to see her. She reported that things were better now though the problems were still present. The work was still difficult and her husband's demands still an irritation, but she was submitting to both situations passively. We congratulated the mother-in-law on the happy resolution of the problem. "Will you come again?" begged Suna. We agreed with the same stipulation that she behave.

A month later we found Suna back in the home of her mother. She complained that her husband had beaten her, and the work had become intolerable. He had brought her to visit her mother and then had left her with taxi fare to go home. We caught up on the events that had precipitated the present crisis, and learned among other things that Suna was pregnant but had not notified her husband of this fact. A. was aghast: "Suna, don't you know that if you don't go back now he will say it is not his child, and besides what will people say if your baby is not born in the house of its father?" Suna and her mother began to look more solemn. [By this time the mother in her fury over the treatment of her daughter had become a willing ally in Suna's departure.] The mother began to tell Suna what a foolish girl she was and how she would have to improve her behavior as a wife. She particularly emphasized the fact that the only way to keep a husband happy was to sleep with him whenever he wanted. She claimed that in all her years of marriage she had never run away even when her husband beat her. She pulled some exotic nightgowns out of her wardrobe and noted that under the transparent one she "wore nothing at all." She showed us other dresses that indicated she "takes care of herself" and explained how she uses eye make-up to make herself more beautiful to her husband. She said, "We have these two rooms, and my husband and I sleep here all alone while the children are outside in the other room," and she looked at us meaningfully. "You," she said to her daughter, "must be good to your husband because we are Christians, and there is no divorce for us."

Over the next few weeks we went to Suna again. Some gestures toward reconciliation had begun through the offices of an intermediary (who it appears was telling both sides that they needed to hold off somewhat longer until the other side was more anxious to resolve the difficulty). Suna's mother was exerting even stronger pressure. A. remarked that Suna looked like a tramp in her dirty dress. "My mother won't let me borrow a dress, and I left all of mine in the other house. I have only the one that I came in," she said sulkily. In an aside to me A. said, "Well, that proves anyway that her mother wants her to go back." Again they scolded Suna for not being a good wife and not wanting her husband. "It's a sin to be like that!" retorted the mother and she proceeded to make her point with the following story.

"There was a woman in our village who was a very excellent woman in every way except that she refused to sleep with her husband. One day she died, and shortly thereafter her daughter had a dream that she was up in the place where decisions are made about whether people go to heaven or hell. She looked out a window in one direction and she saw a woman with an iron stake driven in one ear and out the other. The daugher was told that the woman had been one who in life had listened too much to the gossip of neighbors. Off in another direction was a woman who in her lifetime went with many men; she was being bitten by a dog directly in the part of her body where she had done the bad things. Then the daughter heard her mother's voice telling her not to open the window on the other side. She was anxious to see her mother, however, and disobeyed her. Looking out the window, she saw her mother burning in hell. So you see," said the narrator, "it doesn't matter how good you are in other things; if you won't sleep with your husband this is what you can expect."

Eventually with the agreement of Suna's father we returned to the home of Suna's husband to effect a reconciliation. We found the mother-in-law slopping around with dirty water on the floor, dirty dishes and food on the table, and a pile of laundry filling the corner of the room. "You see what Suna has left for me to do?" she asked angrily. "You will take her back, then?" asked A. "Yes, of course."

Then the recriminations began. Suna had done some inexcusable things, most of which we had not heard about. Her husband had thrown a knife at her, and she had picked it up and thrown it back at him. It missed but broke in the door. Suna had also leaned out the window several times and had spoken to strangers in the street. "What will the neighbors think?" said the mother-in-law primly. Once Suna had ridiculed her mother-in-law saying she was skinny and had no bosoms, then had stripped to the waist and done a shimmy-shake to show off her own attributes. To make her husband jealous Suna had kissed her brothers-in-law in his presence. And then, of course, there was the same old problem that she always caused about not sleeping with her husband. "She has given us so many problems! The next time I bring a girl for one of my sons I shall take a girl from among our relatives. At least then I won't have so many problems. I brought Suna especially to do the housework for me, but even that she resists doing."

A. was angry then. "It is shameful to get a young girl like that to do all the work for so many people. She can't do it all alone. You must help her, and the two of you do it together. She is pregnant now, and it will be too much for her. Did you know that she was pregnant?"

"No," and her face relaxed into a gleeful, if toothless grin. "Of course we want her back!" All the animosity melted for a moment.

But before long she resumed her attack: "'Woman is a man's shoe'—she's there to do what he wants. You know that saying from Upper Egypt; it's true. Suna must obey and do what her husband wants."

Again, A. spoke sharply with her: "Women must not be considered like that; they are people, not animals, and Suna is only a child. You must help her to learn as you would a daughter. It's finished— will you send someone to get her now?" The mother-in-law went to look for her husband, but he said he had work to do then and would go to get Suna in the evening. "Fine," we said and left.

A. sighed, "There is no end to that problem; Suna is foolish, and the mother is hardheaded and wants a daughter-in-law only for work. Suna tells her own mother everything and more, until her mother becomes angry with the mother-in-law, who then ends by forbidding Suna to see her mother any more. If Suna were cleverer, she would keep them on good terms, and she would try harder to help her mother-in-law. She can't do more than she can do, and they would see soon enough that they have to help her."

In almost every line of this case is a statement about what is considered appropriate behavior for certain members of the household. There are also striking examples of the double standard that judges men and women. Suna's husband may throw a knife at her and as long as no damage is inflicted, his behavior is not seriously criticized; but there is a great deal of protest when Suna throws the knife back. Suna is considered "forward" because she speaks to strangers walking by in the street, yet her husband is "expected" to go out on the street if Suna does not keep him satisfied at home.

Suna's case is atypical in certain ways. Not many young wives so seriously violate "nice-girl" norms or are so resistant to the kinds of sanctions imposed on Suna. All manner of sanctions were employed by those interested in reuniting the couple: general disapproval was expressed; ideal models (of the mother's and meditator's appropriate sexual responses to their husbands) were held up to Suna; illustrative stories were related to her; she was scolded and ridiculed; her husband used force; her mother refused her clean clothes so she would not feel her retreat to the parental home was a permanent solution; mediators attempted to reconcile the couple. The urgency in this case — what probably compelled Suna to return — was the impossibility of divorce. Everyone was motivated to exert as much effort as possible toward a reconciliation. If they were willing to accept the costs, a Muslim family under similar circumstances might well have cut its losses at an earlier stage by starting divorce procedures. The possibility of that occurring, however, would probably have acted as a strong deterrent on the willful behavior of the wife who as a divorced woman would have few opportunities to marry again.

CONFLICT RESOLUTION

A commonly articulated view emphasizes the positive aspects of harmonious relations between primary group members, whether families, friends, colleagues, or any other intensely interacting circle of people. People feel a compulsion to resolve their disagreements within these groups whenever possible, and even strangers are usually ready to step in to help resolve the public confrontations of others. The peace maker is a respected personality in Egyptian society. The lower classes particularly fear the evil eye and curses directed by those who hold a grudge. The density of population in lower-class areas provides conditions where animosities can develop more easily. Superficial observation suggests that relationships are often more unstable in these areas, moving from animosity to friendship and back in short time spans. But still even these classes, like those of the middle classes who live more separate lives, show considerable concern for mending their fences, particularly with close family members, as rapidly as possible. Whether the reconciliation is genuine is not as important as public acknowledgement that a reconciliation has taken place. This is not to say that animosities do not fester between people for long periods of time. But a person who allows this state of affairs to continue realizes the insecurity and risks that are involved.

One scholar has characterized Egyptian lower-class society as one based primarily on the animosities and conflicts she has observed there (Wikan 1980). She points out that some of the most intense of these occur within the family itself. It is important, of course, not to neglect the continuous fluctuations in personal relationships by over-emphasis on the tension to comply with cultural ideals. On the other hand, it is possible to be misled into over-emphasizing the instability in a social group because of continuous bickering and confrontation. For one thing, emotional reactions tend to be more exposed in Egyptian as compared to Western society, and particularly in lower-class society the lack of privacy makes it difficult to conceal strong feelings. Such outbursts as occur usually do not have long-term destabilizing effects. Conflict may even force a kind of solidarity upon those involved as they seek out supporters, usually along the lines of those structurally obligated to support them. Contenders still attempt to present an image of themselves conforming in as ideal a way as possible to group norms and values, and attempt to show how their opponents have violated these same principles. Conflicts are not exempted from the cultural ideals of the society; they often give people the opportunity to associate themselves publicly with them. In this way, the cultural principles become reinforced and those involved reaffirm their allegiance to them.

In the Egyptian case, the fabric of life requires that people constantly are involved in assessing their relationships with others, in strengthening some, in developing others, in storing up reciprocal obligations, in letting some lapse, in mobilizing others, and in other ways keeping their networks operational. Conflicts are as much a way of activating and assessing relationships as are pleasant exchanges. Flare-ups permit bad feelings to be aired and dissipated rather than allowing them to simmer and create tensions in the relationship.

People resolve conflicts in basically similar ways. The following example comes from the "seven-day" party described above. A dispute developed during the party that provided a glimpse of how a family treats a recalcitrant member:

> One family came to the party in a taxi whose driver refused to come any closer than several blocks away. His excuse was that his car might

be damaged in the uneven and crowded streets. A daughter of fourteen felt she had been asked to walk too far and complained that her feet hurt. She volubly blamed her mother for not having urged the driver to come all the way. Her mother and sisters in turn loudly criticized her for being so difficult in an unavoidable situation. They took their case to the hostess, the girl's mother's sister, describing how impossible the girl was even under the best of circumstances. The rift in the family became so heated that it began to seem irreconcilable. But after a short period of time the girl unconcernedly got up and decided to light the candles in the flower arrangement bought especially for the event. The hostess asked her not to light the candles yet, but the girl persisted. Mother and hostess shrugged their shoulders as if to say, "See how difficult she is," and everyone laughed including the girl herself. A few minutes later the girl went to look at the new baby, and the hostess put an arm around her, giving her an affectionate hug and kiss and allowing her to hold the baby. Later a sister told her to come see something in another room. The mother, too, gave her a hug as she passed by. The argument was clearly over, and everyone involved made some gesture to demonstrate that normal relations had been restored with the offending member.

In this example, several features of conflicts become apparent. First, all the parties recognize the importance of a period for "letting off steam"; they do not rush the course of the argument, nor do they tone down the force of their comments. Second, there seems to be an unconscious understanding that what is said in anger will not be considered the immutable feelings of people, that family members will not desert each other no matter how trying the circumstances. Third, people recognize the need to reinstate the offending member in the group again as soon as possible with some kind of concrete evidence that the reinstatement has occurred.

The steps for settling a fully elaborated dispute frequently follow a characteristic pattern. If one of the disputants comes or sends a mediator to settle the problem, the first step is one that acknowledges the intent of both parties to enter into negotiations toward conciliation. This may be implied at a very minimum by an initial exchange of courtesies. A second step may see a revival of the conflict with each side again airing its most extreme complaints. Step three moves to an explication of each person's own misbehavior. In step four, a gesture of compromise is offered by one of the disputants and in turn is followed by a generous concession from the other side. Finally a period of calm, perhaps with tea drinking, restores relationships to a semblance of their previous normality. This process may be modified, as in the family case above, by abbreviating the steps or, as in the case of Suna, by expanding and elaborating them until they become discrete episodes separated by spans of time and by intervening mediators. What is essential, however, is the end-result — the resolution of the conflict — and this usually requires concessions from all parties rather than the determination of absolute blame in any one party. People recognize that there are always extenuating circumstances important enough to force a person to initiate a dispute. Whether the process of reconciliation is lengthened or shortened, however, the skeletal pattern remains much the same whether those involved are nations, strangers, acquaintances, or relatives.

The function of such procedures is to resolve in as short a time and in as concrete a fashion as possible, tensions that weaken important social groups. In the example above, family unity was restored; in the case of Suna, the marriage was patched up. The groups affected can be as large as religious communities or even nations. In most cases permanent rifts escalating from superficial disagreements could produce unspeakable catastrophes for the individuals concerned. Having a stylized pattern for reconciliation smooths the way and allows the parties concerned to recognize the point at which the breach has been healed by conventionally approved behaviors.

TENSION REDUCTION

General frustrations and tensions that arise from seemingly unsolvable problems find expected if not always approved channels of expression in the family. Many of these modes of expression are commonly found worldwide. A man, for example, who feels oppressed by his boss may feel some sense of relief by shouting or beating his wife. The wife, as we noted in an earlier chapter, who cannot or is unwilling to comply with her required role behaviors may lapse into a "spirit possession" or, as defined elsewhere in the world, into varying degrees of psychological disorder. One Egyptian psychiatrist intends to study the high incidence of diarrheal infection in infants from the perspective of maternal neglect which he believes stems from a woman's unconscious resentment of her position in society. Another common channel for tension release is found in institutionalized and informal religion. (This will be discussed at greater length in Chapter 11.) Perhaps the most common of frustration outlets is the resort to chronic disease and sporadic acute illness. Almost any doctor will report a high incidence of vague, hard-to-identify pains and other symptoms. Doctors universally include tonics, vitamin supplements, and other general medications in their prescriptions to their patients to satisfy the need for some kind of evidence of sympathy-evoking illness. The way these tension outlets are handled and channelled tend to be culturally influenced. In Egypt, an oppressive frustration affecting an individual is usually perceived as coming from a force outside that person: as a justified response to a wrong suffered at the hands of another person; from some undeniable condition that causes the anger; from evil forces, curses or infection that cause sickness; from demons that invade and possess a person. The cause can be natural or supernatural. The person is not held responsible for the sickness, the possession, or the anger. People generally, in fact, feel sympathy for the afflicted person. He is not considered lacking in personal control, for example, nor is his character considered impaired by the invasion. He may have permitted his condition to become weakened in some way so the invasion occurred, but he is not responsible for the invasion itself.

When the person is affected by such forces, he seeks and receives consolation from others, usually those in his family group. He does not withdraw or seek to solve the problem alone. There is almost always some aspect of his behavioral response designed to draw the attention of the group whether it is a simple trip to the doctor and a return with medications, exaggerated illness symptoms, an outburst of anger in a family gathering, or an acute episode of devil possession. The group responds by gathering at the bedside so the person is not alone, offering support to calm the anger, or going with the person to group spirit-placation ceremonies (see Chapter 11).

Intolerable tensions that have no possible solutions within the group sometimes can be referred to other institutions especially designed for that purpose. The first two illustrations involve a secular "seer" (*mandal*) who has the superhuman power to see forward or backward in time as well as into the minds of others, thereby making it possible for him to resolve the problems of those who need some piece of information they do not possess. This power makes him suspect among many Egyptians, who, like other Middle Easterners, feel it is somewhat presumptuous to assume powers which only God should possess. The first illustration shows the kind of family case brought to a seer; the second shows how he tries to solve a problem.

One of the teachers from the Bulaq Social Center was having problems with a man to whom she was engaged. Some people felt that he might be making problems in order to try and break the engagement; others thought that his difficulties with her family were real and their fault

instead of his. T. was in a quandary to know if he really loved her
or not. T. heard about a seer in another town who, it was said, could
take an item of a person's belongings and be able to tell how the person feels or what events will happen to him or her in the future. He
could remove curses from a person or place them on someone if the
client so desired. T. decided to take a picture of her friend to see if
the man could help her know what was in his mind. She was also prepared to pay to have a curse removed if that turned out to be the problem. When T. asked for time off to go to the seer, the woman in charge
of teachers said to me: "I don't really believe that someone can have
power like that over another because if that were the case. he could
make himself king. But T. wants to do something, and she can't just
sit here doing nothing, so I will let her have time off to go." T., in
the end, did not use the services of the seer, and in a few weeks her
relationship had improved with her fiancé.

A. and I had been selling donated clothes to those girls in the
handicraft classes whose families were more prosperous. We were hoping to use the money to buy a knitting machine, so we could employ
one of the poorer girls. As the piasters came in, we filled an empty
tennis ball can kept in a cupboard of the office. We had slowly accu-
mulated 7 £E in this way. One day A. found the cupboard door ajar
and the money gone. She went from one classroom to another to ask
if anyone knew about the money. The teachers suggested that the girls
be searched, but still there was no money to be found. Later a group
of students, worried by her anxiety, came and offered to collect enough
money to go see Hag S., the *mandal,* to find out what happened to
the money. A. agreed, and soon they had collected the 50 p. fee.

A delegation of girls set out to Hag S. and explained the problem to him. He selected one of the smaller girls and told her to come
look in his mirror while the other girls watched from across the room.
"What do you see in the mirror?" he asked her. "I see a king standing
in front of me." "Greet the king," he told her, showing her how to
nod and salute touching her hand to her forehead. "Now what is he
doing?" "He is returning my greeting." "Look again," said Hag S., "you
will learn now about the money. What do you see happening now?"
"Now I see the office . . . , the two long windows on either side of
the cupboard, and inside the cupboard the long thin box where the
money was kept. Someone is taking the money from the cupboard."
"Do you see who it is?" "Yes, it is Hoda!" she said, pointing at the
mischievous girl student on the other side of the room. "No, it wasn't
me," Hoda protested loudly. "Look again," said the Hag. "No, it is
not Hoda; it is a woman all dressed in black." "What does she look

like? Do you recognize her?" "She is short and fat with a fair skin." "Will you know her if you see her again?" "Yes, I think so."

The Hag told them as they walked out the door that they would know the woman who did it because she would have "a yellow face and be shaking all over." On the next Wednesday morning, the young girl stood in front of the women who had assembled for the religious meeting and tried to recognize the one she had seen in the mirror. But it was no use, and she finally admitted that she could not recognize the person who had taken the money.

Despite the Hag's mirror, A. was not convinced that one of the older women was guilty. The students were in classrooms near the office and had better opportunities to slip in and take the money. So when the girl failed to identify the woman she had seen, A. went from one classroom to another and told the girls, "The money was God's money. Anyone who uses it will be known to God. There will be a curse on the person who uses it for herself."

Another category of secular specialist is one who places or removes curses for people. People attribute certain of their frustrations and problems to curses placed by ill-intentioned others. When symptoms do not respond to other treatments or are clearly of the kind that need the special arts of the magician, many people readily seek their help. The gamut of specialists of this type runs from part-time practitioners with special gifts to full-time practitioners who use complicated magical techniques. The most common of these is the neighbor or relative known for her skill in the art of curses. She knows how to write papers with magical formulae, a mother's name, or religious verses, and either soaks them in water or burns the paper using the water and ashes later to sprinkle where the victim or affected person walks. There are numerous variations—putting doctored items in food or drinks, burying bags with special magical items inside, performing rituals over the possessions of the victim, his nail parings or hair. Some of the variety is seen in the following excerpts from newspapers:

> A sheikha (sorceress) was arrested . . . for obtaining money under false pretenses. (She) sold trinkets and lucky charms to people from her flat to cure illnesses and solve marital problems, a police spokesman said. (*Egyptian Gazette,* March 21, 1980)

> A dark closed room, heavy with the smell of incense; a young woman listening to spirits promising charms from the heart of crocodiles or from the halls of deserted tombs; the sound of screaming and roaring to frighten away curses . . . (El-Hassani) and his assistant . . .

promised spinsters that "for a fee" they could work charms to make them irresistable to any man. They also helped divorced women to return to their husbands and cured the sick of chronic diseases. (*Egyptian Gazette,* March 9, 1980)

"Sheikh Shafei's novel method of healing used long strings of magic worry beads which were wound around the afflicted. We were astonished to find 20 almost naked women inside tied together with a 100 meter long string of worry beads," said a police spokesman. (*Egyptian Mail,* August 30, 1981)

Spiritual healing and seekers after magic cures are extremely common among the lower classes, and they are frequent enough also among the middle classes. As the newspaper articles indicate, officials are on the lookout for fraudulent practitioners of the curing arts, but sometimes they can be convinced of the validity of the practitioners if there is some evidence of special power. The following case caused considerable controversy when it appeared in the courts:

When a court ordered a defendant to prove his claim that he could use spirits and jinns to cure the sick . . . [he] made correct diagnoses of the ailments afflicting a random five people in the courtroom, including lawyers and the recorder, and issued the appropriate prescriptions for their treatment. "I am practicing these acts under el-Hajjah's [a woman demon's] instructions." The court will resume the hearing after receiving the report . . . about the man's mental condition and the truth of his alleged connection with spirits. (*Egyptian Gazette,* April 17, 1980)

Later the case was dropped because of his correct diagnoses in the courtroom, but the controversy continued. An authority on religion at Al-Azhar University made a formal judgment (*fatwa*) in which he stated that man cannot control or dominate jinns, and to claim to do so is sacrilegious to Islam. Other authorities joined the discussion. A professor of theology at Cairo University denounced him as a charlatan taking advantage of the credulous and criticized the court for encouraging such practices by its vindication of the accused. A dean of law was more charitable arguing that in many "civilized" countries it is known that some diseases can be cured by spiritual treatment, but, he adds, that this does not mean jinns are being harnessed by man. Others echoed the first comments, expressing sharp differences with the court action and the beliefs that supported it. The head of the Medical Association called on the prosecutor-general to take action to curb the spread of such beliefs (*Egyptian Gazette,* May 2, 1980).

Shortly after these negative reactions, a further wave of more supportive comment appeared in the newspapers. An editorial in the Gazette asked, "In so far as our 'jinni' doctor is concerned, does it matter essentially if he describes his healing power in superstitious terms as long as he can produce a cure?" (*Egyptian Gazette,* May 5, 1980). Another Arabic weekly, *Akhbar el-Yoom,* organized a symposium on spiritual medicine in which a number of professors made statements in support of certain kinds of spiritual healing, along with a few others who did not. "The symposium ended," according to news accounts, "without agreeing on a scientific and spiritual assessment of the phenomenon from an Egyptian point of view" (*Egyptian Gazette,* May 17, 1981). It is important to note the mixed feelings of highly educated Egyptians in the controversy over the matter of spiritual healing. Though there is no doubt that the practice is widespread (and in certain cases with undeniably good results), its superstitious, traditional folk-cultural connection makes it a sensitive subject with those Egyptians wanting to see their country as a modern state basing its medicine on scientifically proven remedies.

This chapter has been concerned with the practices employed by people to reduce the tensions within their primary social groups, in particular within the family. These practices include organizational devices that reduce competition between members of families, that control moral behavior which may have negative effects upon the family group, that resolve conflicts between members in significant groups. They include also the kinds of sanctions that people command to encourage compliance with vital norms and the accepted channels that exist to release tensions with either a long-term basis or no other means of clear-cut resolution. It should be clear by now that the devices used to protect family are not always foolproof. In certain circumstances, they may even serve to make a situation worse, as when norms are too strictly interpreted or penalties too severely imposed. In general however they provide a satisfactory way to resolve difficulties that occur in family groups.

10

Disruption

"The bad woman goes back to her father's house" — Arab proverb

THIS CHAPTER is concerned with the major disruptions in the family
that result from marital discord, death, and the effects of poverty.
It looks also at the institutions — homes for the aged and orphanages —
that appear to reflect a breakdown in some of the functions families have
traditionally performed for their members.

THE DISSOLUTION OF MARRIAGE

Divorce and Separation

Separation of married couples does not show up in official statistics in
an adequate way, and therefore the extent of its occurrence is hard to estimate. Divorce, to a certain extent, may be considered an extreme, more
final case of separation. Observation of Bulaq families over an extended
period suggests that temporary separation is not uncommon and leads more
often to reconciliation than divorce. Thus separations are much more numerous than actual divorces and may not require more than temporary
rearrangements of living quarters and/or adjustment of income sources.
Reconciliation is usually marked in a concrete way by formal negotiations
with the help of family members (see the case of Suna in Chapter 9), concessions by one or both sides, or by gifts to entice the runaway member,
usually the wife, back to the family home.

Divorce in Egypt basically takes two forms, depending on whether a man or a woman initiates the divorce proceedings. The first is by far the easiest and most common and explains why women usually see themselves at a disadvantage in the matter of divorce. To be specific, a Muslim husband may, if he will, dissolve a marriage contract without the intervention of a court simply by repudiating his wife three times (*talaq*). The right of divorce by this means can be delegated to the wife by her husband when it is so designated in the marriage contract. A wife by contrast must go to court to ask for a dissolution of the marriage contract by judicial decree (*taltiq*). While her husband is not limited by conditions when he seeks divorce, she can only petition for divorce on the grounds that her husband failed to support her, has a serious defect or ailment,[1] has a deleterious moral or social effect on his wife, is absent for a long period, or is imprisoned. Two other means of effecting divorce are, first, by mutual consent, where a woman may pay a certain amount to her husband to compensate him for his expenses, and, second, annulment of a marriage which has been contracted in violation of prohibitions. The first means reflects the strong underlying material basis for relationships which is the last to unite a couple when layers of affective relationship have disappeared. By the reform provisions of Article 5-b, 1979, a man must now register a divorce and the wife must be informed of the action. For her, the divorce only becomes effective from the date she has knowledge of it.

The difficulty a wife faces in trying to effect a divorce is great when compared with the ease by which a man divorces his wife. There is no question that this difference has caused hardship in a number of cases — witness the very popular film, *I Want a Solution,* that dramatizes the real-life story of an Egyptian woman's struggle to win her release from an unhappy marriage. In this instance she goes through a protracted court case to no avail, since her husband finds it convenient to keep her hanging rather than to release her. At one point her husband activates the *bayt al taa* provision, by which a wife who leaves her husband can be forced to return home by the police. After this film was produced, improvements in court procedures were instituted, including the abolishment of the *bayt al taa* compulsion by a ministerial order issued on February 13, 1967.

Newspapers relate the sometimes extreme means women or their concerned relatives use to dissolve unhappy marriages. Below are two such cases:

> A laborer . . . was arrested yesterday for murdering his nephew when the latter refused to grant his wife (the laborer's daughter) a divorce after they had been separated for a whole year. (*Egyptian Gazette,* August 28, 1979)

Police yesterday arrested a housewife . . . who went to security authorities . . . with a fictitious story about three men whom she said had raped her. . . . She then asked [her husband] to divorce her to avoid any offense to his honour. . . . Investigations revealed that the wife wanted a divorce so as to get rid of her husband from whom she could not beget a child. She had a love affair with a neighbor who had promised to marry her if she got a divorce. (*Egyptian Gazette,* November 25, 1979)

The divorce rate in Egypt is relatively high. In 1970, 68,810 divorces were recorded in the official census during the same period that 325,828 marriages were contracted (CAPMAS 1970). The ratio of divorce to marriage in that year was therefore 21 percent, or about one divorce for every five marriages. The rate of divorce was about 2 per thousand of the population and marriage about 10 per thousand.

The preliminary census reports for 1976 (CAPMAS) claimed that the percentage of the divorced and widowed population (not disaggregated) decreased to 9.4 percent of the total population of marriage age (starting from age 16 for females and 18 for males) from 12.5 percent in the 1960 census. There are clearly a number of disparate factors involved in the decrease. The CAPMAS report, without giving figures, credits the decrease in the totals to conditions favoring fewer divorces: lower mortality rates, the decrease in age differences between spouses, and increased opportunities for persons who have lost their spouses to remarry. A later release from CAPMAS in 1980[2] suggested that Egyptians shun marriage and divorce during times of economic crisis.[3] Figures also reveal significant differences in the sex distribution of those who are divorced and widowed. In 1976, these included 2.6 percent of males and 15.6 percent of females of marriageable age, a decrease from 3.5 percent and 20.4 percent respectively in 1960.

Field research[4] of a sample of 600 urban and 300 rural families in three governorates and 200 divorcées in two governorates examined some of the factors affecting divorce. The findings can be summarized briefly. Most divorces were initiated by the husband but 33 percent were initiated by wives. Rates of divorce are higher in urban areas and lowest in the provincial governorates considered the most conservative. The highest rates occurred among industrial and agricultural workers. Rates decline with the increase in level of education. In the population as a whole 95 percent of divorces occurred among those who were illiterate. The causes of divorce in rank order according to female respondents were polygamy, conflicts with the husband's family, and financial causes. For men the chief causes were incompatibility or lack of harmony and conflicts with in-laws. Only a small number (7 percent) mentioned sterility (Azer 1979: 75).

Statistics of the sample seemed to indicate a smaller than usual number of children in the divorced families and official divorce statistics tend to confirm the correlation with small family size. The study showed that 63.3 percent of the sample had no more than three children at the time of divorce; 61 percent in rural areas and 47 percent in urban areas had no children at the time of divorce.

Other statistics, however, show that the largest percentage of divorces occurs in the age bracket of less than twenty-five years (Hill 1979: 86). If divorce is indeed related to length of time married and a disproportionately higher rate of divorce occurs in the early as opposed to the later years of marriage, then family size may carry less weight than the study assumes. In practical terms, though, the belief women articulate that larger numbers of children discourage divorce most certainly has an overall effect on population demography. While divorce may cut down on an individual woman's fertility, the fear of divorce may increase the birth rate of women who remain married.

The disruption of a family by divorce raises the issues of, first, who maintains custody of the children and, second, how long a man is obligated to provide financial support for a woman and her children. The law is explicit on these two related concerns. Mothers are considered the appropriate parents for nurturing children until they reach the ages of ten for boys and twelve for girls. After this age a judge can order that a boy remain with his mother until he is fifteen years and the girl until she marries if it is in her best interests. It is a mother's right as well as her duty to care for children until this customary age. Fathers have the full responsibility for financial maintenance of their children, for boys while they are minors (less than twenty-five years) and girls as long as they remain unmarried, are widowed, or divorced. The obligation to maintain children devolves on male next-of-kin, preferably the father's father or brother, if the father is unable to perform this duty. When children reach the appropriate age, the father assumes the responsibility for their further secular and religious education, the latter according to his own denominational preference.

As far as the wife is concerned, she is entitled to an alimony for the duration of one year, which covers also the length of the period of *idda*, the time when she is forbidden to marry, in order to ascertain whether she is pregnant with a child by her former husband. The duration of *idda* is about three months or until a pregnancy is terminated. During the *idda* period, the woman is entitled not only to alimony, but to other rights of a legal wife, including inheritance. Theoretically also a husband should pay his former wife an amount that compensates her for the period she nurses her children.

The study of divorcées cited above notes that the source of income most commonly (67.7 percent of sample) utilized by both urban and rural divorced women was aid from their own families. Next their own work (20.1 percent) was listed as an important source of income, and third, for rural women, children's work (Azer 1979: 77). The results of this study point up concrete reasons why a woman would want to keep her relationships in her parental home strong. Practically, they provide her with the long-term economic security that marriage may not. Her security in marriage lasts only as long as the marriage contract itself.

Women can provide for their own economic security before divorce occurs by two other means. However, many feel these actions reveal a cynical and distrustful frame of mind and refrain from taking such precautions for fear of creating bad feelings. The first is to amass a quantity of gifts from the husband, usually in the form of gold jewelry. Even in the lower classes a great deal of gold is exchanged in this way to become the individual property of a woman. The second means is an optional but formal way to secure a set sum upon divorce. Included at the time of marriage in the negotiations over the obligatory gift paid by the husband to his wife, a portion can be designated as payable at the time of death or divorce. Parents of a bride who insist on this provision give her a means of recourse if her husband divorces her but, as noted, it is a sensitive subject that most do not want to broach at the time of marriage. Some parents in the lower classes prefer in any case to have the lump sum of the husband's obligatory gift before marriage in order to help in the purchase of the bride's furnishings which remain her property whether her husband dies or divorces her.

Reform provisions in 1979 gave an important boost to the support requirements of women when, in Article 4, the divorced wife who assumes custody of her child was entitled to occupy the rented marital home unless the husband prepares another suitable domicile for her. This right continues until the period of custody ends. Under the conditions of the present housing shortage in Egypt this new provision added substantially to the strength of the woman's economic position in divorce and provided one more economic deterrent to divorce itself.

Though questions of child custody, maintenance, and alimony are well spelled out under Islamic law, the practical results of divorce often vary considerably from what theory indicates, sometimes because the individuals concerned abrogate their responsibilities and sometimes through direct perversions of the law. Formal officialdom in any case often does not come into divorce proceedings except to register actions that come out of a dissolution worked out by private individuals. Men and women of all classes more often than not are drawn along by the agreements made for them by relatives, intermediaries, and lawyers.

Women of the lower classes are more apt to use the formal court system than the upper classes simply because they often have no other practicable alternative when they are forced to seek their rights. Divorce for the upper classes usually involves property and money, and these families are not inclined to leave to the vagaries of the judicial system such important matters as property settlement (Hill 1979: 92).

In reality few women in lower-class Bulaq who are divorced receive either alimony or child support payments from their husbands except sporadically or through coercion from the courts. Also few men in Bulaq claim official custody of their children even when they are of legal age to be remanded into the custody of their fathers. Either the fathers have no way of caring for the children or they are remarried, and their new wives are not anxious to entertain the presence of children from a previous marriage. Occasionally a father seeks the return of a teenage son to help in his work.

In the classes where property of even the most limited kind is involved children are a valued economic asset. Since they cannot be deprived of their legitimate share of the father's or mother's inheritance, influence over them means influence over the property should one or the other parent die. Even without inheritance parents benefit economically from their children's support if relations between parents and children are good. Resources and conditions in these classes also make it easier to afford the costs of legal expenses (if custody of children is challenged) and appropriate facilities for the care of children. For these and other reasons, parents of the middle and upper classes are much more likely to claim the custody of children.

The following case, related by the grandfather of the child concerned, demonstrates that abuses of the laws as they stand are not uncommon:

> Our daughter married a man who asked for her hand. We didn't know much about his personality before the marriage though he came from a good family and seemed to have good prospects in the legal profession. His temperament revealed itself soon after their marriage — he was often away from home and seemed totally disinterested in his wife. When their son was a year and a half old, he left abruptly, without notifying his wife, to work in Libya. During the years he was away

he didn't communicate with his wife or pay for her or her son's support. Our daughter came back to live with us and we helped her to raise the child. Finally when the boy was eight years old the father returned and seized him one day on his way home from school. At first we didn't know where he was taken but eventually we found out where the father held him. We were prevented from making any contact with the child. In the two and a half years since that happened we have tried everything to get the boy back, but even though the circumstances made it appear that we should win the court case, we always lose and have to appeal again and again. According to the law, if the father does not support the child while it is in the care of its mother, he has no right to claim the child later. Also the boy was only eight when the father took him so he should have remained with the mother. Even with the passage of the new laws [extending the age when a mother is given custody] the situation has not changed for us. Laws are only paper to frame and hang on the wall.

One time when our grown son tried to go reason with the man, he tried to shoot him and we realized the lengths he might go to keep the child from us. He might have claimed self-defense. I go constantly to the court as my daughter's *wakil* [representative] to preserve her from the shame of appearing in public. She is so distressed by the situation now that her outbursts might jeopardize the proceedings. We are very discouraged about the case at the moment; we are only hoping to have the opportunity to get visitation rights so we can at least let the boy know we care about him. But so far the courts have not given us these rights. When he gets older we hope they will not be able to control his movements as easily and we will surely get a chance to see him, but by then his mind will be so poisoned against us that he may not want to see us. Why is the court so partial in this case? Because the father is a judge himself and the other judges help him, but there are other cases like this where it is money that influences the decision.

It is impossible to confirm all the details of this case independently but enough are known to be true to ascertain that in this custody case, a gross misuse of the legal process is taking place. What appear to be straightforward legal requirements concerning divorce, alimony, child support, and child custody are in reality not air-tight legal principles; they still give plenty of room for manipulation. A main difficulty is that the endless bureaucratic steps involved in court cases are fraught with opportunities for the miscarriage of justice — a messenger induced to serve papers to the wrong address, perjured witnesses, etc. Among the middle and upper classes what usually happens in divorce is that premarital family groupings reassert their early force, and loyalty to them commands a higher morality than loyalty to abstract notions of justice and fair play. The child, no longer a member of its own family unit, becomes a pawn in the struggle of other family groupings claiming their own priorital rights.

This is probably also true in the case of many lower-class families. But an intensive study of sixteen lower-class divorcées who had resorted to court actions did not show strong support from their premarital families. According to this study, family did not serve as a primary reference group for either rural or urban divorcées. Relations in the family were primarily materialistic with a great deal of suspicion involved on both sides about what financial demands might be made by the other party. Some families demanded to have furnishings back or compensation for them; some wanted payment for any services they performed. If parents, however, were able to support their divorced daughter, she was usually forbidden to engage in "dishonorable" work (that is, any work outside the home). The study concludes reasonably that family relations in the lower classes seem to be affected heavily by the level of poverty (Zaalouk 1975: 94). One might also add in clarification that cases that come before the courts (except divorces initiated by women which must by definition go through court channels) often do so because family mechanisms to support the causes of their members have broken down. This does not necessarily imply that personal relationships themselves are any the less strong among lower-class family members not suffering the severe effects of poverty.

Death

An earlier chapter noted the demographic disparities created by older men marrying younger women. This practice along with the difference in life expectancies of males (51.6) and females (53.8) (Nyrop 1976: 73) has resulted in a significantly high population of widowed women. Recent trends toward marriage of persons closer in age to one another should eventually serve to decrease the disparities. Numbers of widowed persons in Egypt as a whole are usually included with divorce statistics (see above).

Structural Changes

In practical terms women have more to lose by death in a family than men. Women are closely tied to family relationships for their emotional, social, and psychological needs as well as for their financial support. The death of a male family member, father or husband, usually results in subtle changes in the status of a woman who receives much of her own status through the position of related men. Such a death in a lower- or middle-class household usually requires that the female members of the household reorganize their lives in major ways: by forcing them to become dependent relatives in other households or alternatively by developing new ways to support themselves in still independent households. Both of these possibilities carry with them lower prestige when compared with the position of a wife in her own household where, as one person noted, "she is like a queen."

The death of a related woman also has practical consequences for other women. Her death may remove a helping hand in the work of the household. If she leaves responsibilities, children and husband, then the remaining women feel obligated to take over her duties. Islamic law states that it is the right of small children to have their mother's care and in the event of her death to have the next best substitute, her mother or another closely related female if the maternal grandmother is not available.

> Um K. (65) and her husband S. (79) are an elderly couple who live with a mentally disturbed son (43) in a single ground-floor room. A widowed daughter with six children lives on the same floor in a back room. Another son is in the army. The father, S., earned money by selling material door-to-door until recently when his leg was broken by the mentally disturbed son in a fit of rage. The old man's leg is better now but he limps badly, and it is difficult for him to work long hours.
>
> Most of the family's income comes from private charities and neighborhood help. The situation was already desperate when another daughter of Um K. died, leaving three young children in the care of their father, a worker in a spinning factory. He quickly disposed of the children in the home of their grandmother, Um K., announcing that he planned to remarry again soon and that the children would be a liability to his chances of marrying well. Occasionally he offers Um K. small amounts of money, but for the most part the burden of the children's support has fallen to the elderly couple, while all the actual care of the children has been taken over by Um K. herself.

Men's lives are not so totally family centered; they have outlets in the coffee shops and with work mates and friends. The death of male members of the household may increase a man's obligations to support female members of a household, but at the same time it may also diminish the competition of males for authority within the household. The death of a female also has different practical implications for the remaining men in the household who can more readily replace the services of a wife or mother with another woman relative or new wife who can cook and clean for them. Older men, however, sometimes suffer more serious dislocations (see below).

The psychological impact of death should not be minimized for males or females; but leaving that aside, females are usually structurally more affected by death than males. The recognition of this greater loss to women is consistent with the way women support each other at the death of a family member with a great deal of time and emotion and through the symbols of dress.

For the first week after a death, women friends and relatives sit almost continuously with the bereaved woman. Formal visits are required on the seventh day, fortieth day, and year anniversay after the death. Women wear all black, and the bereaved herself may continue to wear black for the rest of her life if the death was that of her husband. Neighbors serve bitter coffee to the mourners, and many will not bake sweets for a whole year if someone in the building has lost a close relative. Men by contrast make much shorter visits to pay their respects, and their clothing normally does not specifically reflect the state of mourning.

The emphasis placed on women mourning with other women symbolizes their role as supporters of others in society. To mourn well is to demonstrate that a person fits the supportive role well. Condolence ceremonies also provide the opportunities for others to demonstrate their willingness to support and allows the bereaved to assess their relationships to determine where future help may be sought.

Inheritance

The legal apparatus stimulated into action by death involves most importantly the provisions for inheritance. Both Christians and Muslims in Egypt follow the inheritance provisions of Islamic law. While the lower classes rarely have much property to bequeath (and consequently have fewer economic bonds to tie generations together), middle-class and upper-class families are both united and divided by the consequences of property apportionment.

The legal stipulations of property division, like those for divorce appear straightforward and exhaustive, yet there are enough areas which permit flexibility and enough of a margin for judicial interpretation so that quarrels are a common feature of the inheritance process. The law stipulates that property must be distributed in quotas to those holding a particular relationship to the deceased as prescribed by Koranic law, with the exception of one-third of the property that may be disposed of by a testamentary will. In Egypt Article 37 of the Law of Testamentary Dispositions of 1946 made it possible for a man to bequeath the one-third of his estate to another who was already an heir to his property. Previously this was only possible with the consent of the other heirs. This article effectively favored the nuclear family against the rights of more distant relatives both by increasing the amounts its members could receive and by reducing the amount that was left for others to inherit.

The stipulated ratios for property division are complicated and contingent on the numbers and kinds of personnel present within the circle of relatives of the deceased. Some of the general guide lines that pertain are that an entitled quota holder receive his prescribed share, and then any remainder should go to the nearest agnate of whatever distance. If no agnates exist then the quota-sharers will divide the remainder among them. Where there are no quota-sharers or agnates, then other relatives are entitled to inherit by a system of priorities (Anderson 1976: 149).

As a general rule, a widow receives one-fourth of the estate if there are no children; if there are children she receives one-eighth. If there is a daughter she receives one-half of a father's estate; if more than one, they share two-thirds of the property. If there are sons and daughters, the daughters receive one-half the share of a son in recognition of the greater support requirements that devolve on men. When even one son exists, the entire property can go to him if no other member of the immediate family exists. The presence of a son, therefore, becomes important in preventing property from reverting to siblings or parents of the deceased. By law, property also does not cross religious lines, a strong encouragement for families to reconcile religious differences by conversion. Children are expected to follow the religious choice of their father. Mothers are, therefore, usually the ones who find it most expedient to convert although in the process they may find themselves cut off from inheriting property of their own parents. These kinds of difficulties do much to encourage marriage within the individual's own religious community.

Even when the division of property seems straightforward family members can contest the arrangements if they feel they have received unfair treatment. It is not uncommon for parents to make gifts to their children or incur special expenses on their behalf during their lifetimes. When that happens other quota-holders can claim that the inheritance as a whole has been reduced and their rightful portion denied them. Much depends, therefore, on the good will of the quota-holders when property is divided in any way that might be construed as unfair to any of the claimants. A common kind of case is the following:

> Gamal and his three brothers grew up in a small village in the Delta where their father was a small landowning peasant. All the boys were sent to the village school. Of the four Gamal was the only one who

distinguished himself as a student, and he was always at the top of the class. After intermediate school there was no local school for Gamal to attend, and the family began to incur the expenses of transportation to and from a larger town about a half hour away. Along with the necessary supplies and special clothing appropriate to the level of a student, the expenses mounted over the years, particularly when Gamal finished secondary school and became eligible for university in Cairo. Then it became necessary for him to pay the expenses of food and lodging as well. Gamal's father was hard put to find the money for all these expenses and worried about concentrating so much of the family funds in the future of one child. But the thought of the prestige an educated son would bring to the family determined him to find a solution. Eventually he called his sons together and sought their agreement on his plan to sell off the portion of the family land that would have been Gamal's share. Under this arrangement Gamal would give up his claim not only to the land but also to his share of the family home. Eventually the father died and Gamal finished his studies and became a professor in an Egyptian university. He frequently visits the village and stays in his father's house as the guest of his brothers who are now all married and still living together in the family home. One works in a factory in a neighboring town and the others work what remains of the family property. They have all maintained the agreement with their father to count Gamal's share of the land as already given.

The newspapers report another similar case with a more unpleasant outcome:

A man . . . has been arrested on a charge of killing his mother . . . in a dispute over his father's will. . . . He allegedly told police he had failed to persuade his mother to help him obtain his father's entire estate. "I am the only illiterate son. . . . My brothers are being educated to take nice jobs. I told my mother that I deserve the appropriation of the whole legacy. I am a farmer and I should seize the few feddans [acres] left by my father. The estate was equally divided among us. Later I even failed to make my mother concede her share in the legacy for me alone. She strongly refused saying that it is incompatible with Islamic law." (*Egyptian Gazette,* April 19, 1980)

Even more complicated problems can arise out of jointly owned urban property, where sale is contingent on the agreement of the owners. Difficulties arise when some of the inheritors prefer to retain the property and others wish cash from the sale of the property. A later chapter examines the effects of joint property ownership on contemporary family life, but it is enough to say for the moment that inheritance, like many things, serves generally to unite already close families even more strongly and provides the grounds for discord where relations are already strained and the potential for cleavages already exists.

POLYGAMY

In Egypt it is possible for a Muslim man to marry four wives provided he is able to treat the wives equally. This matter of equal treatment, however, is left to the man's conscience rather than to judicial review. In the twenty years between 1950 and 1970 the average ratio of polygamous marriages to marriage contracts by five-year periods has gradually decreased (with the exception of a much lower figure of 7.39 between 1960-64), from 8.96 in 1950-54 to 8.08 in 1965-69 (CAPMAS 1972). In 1970 there was a ratio of 7.45 (CAPMAS 1970) polygamous marriages. About 95 percent of those who contract polygamous marriage are either illiterate or minimally literate without intermediate or higher degrees.

The subject of polygamy is introduced here in a chapter on "family disruption," primarily because the effects of polygamy are often disruptive to family life. Observation of lower-class urban families where a man takes a second wife indicates that this practice is often corrupted to other than its intended sense of providing humane and equal treatment under special circumstances. Many men marry again as a simple way of getting rid of one wife while taking another, thereby avoiding certain kinds of legal or economic complications that come as a result of divorce. Until recently the man could simply leave the first wife and take up residence with another, either secretly or openly, and avoid paying any alimony or delayed *mahr* installments in the marriage contract.

In 1979 long-awaited reforms in personal-status laws made it impossible for a man to marry again without a written statement of his marital status. Now the registrar must inform any current wives by registered mail of the new marriage. If the husband marries another without the wife's consent she has a right to demand a judicial divorce from her husband. This prevents the kind of limbo many wives found themselves in, neither able to marry again nor to live as married women with their husbands. The reforms do not, however, restrict in any significant way the right of a man to marry up to four wives. Like divorce, the institution of polygamy, whether practised or not, serves to create a tension within Muslim households between husband and wife. Both know that there is potential for cleavages between them, and the wife particularly feels vulnerable by her limited rights in divorce and polygamy.

POVERTY

Poverty, where real economic deprivation is present, can have a significant impact on how the drama of family life is played out. In poor families it is still meaningful to talk of the cultural ideals and values by which behavior is motivated, but not without noting that choices and preferences are limited by the possibilities that exist. Poverty affects the composition of households, the carrying out of norms, the fulfillment of obligations, the quality of family relationships, the ability to deal with crisis, and the alliances it is necessary to make in order to survive.

Poverty is not necessarily a constant for lower-class families. Many lower-class families have found affluence through work in other Arab countries or through increasingly better paid skilled labor inside the country. They are lower-class families because of social rather than economic criteria. Other families are affected by poverty only sporadically or cyclically as a consequence of circumstances of the moment.

Factors which exacerbate poverty in urban areas are obvious: too many children in a family with a disproportionately small income; the difficulty of participating in social insurance and pension schemes; the inability, disinclination or absence of children to support the aged; physical incapacitation; compulsory military induction; medical problems; death of wage earners; inflation and rising expenditures.

What many who study these problems do not take note of is the extent to which the natural cycle of the family with its changes in personnel tends to create the conditions for periodic economic crisis in families living on subsistence incomes. The critical points for families are the periods when there are many young children in the household, when children reach the marriageable age and drain families of their needed resources, and when wage-earning husbands, because of their shorter life expectancy and higher age at marriage, die leaving a widow to support children (see Rugh 1979). The most favorable periods are just after marriage when income is sufficient; later when older children bring in additional income and are not yet ready to extract expenses from the household for marriage; when children are away and married but before the wage-earner is retired. In this

way a family that under the best of conditions is self-sufficient is affected
by poverty when circumstances periodically converge to create a strain on
the family finances.

The effects of poverty are variable and usually not predictable. They
are also not easily measured or easily removed from other factors affecting an event. It is obvious that the ability to buy is restricted, and where
this ability relates to family life it becomes important. Housing and household composition are two areas where restricted income has an impact.
A poor person does not have the latitude to choose between a number
of neighborhoods, a range of dwelling places, or several kinds of architectural lay-outs. He may even not have much option concerning with whom
he lives. He lives in run-down neighborhoods, finding rooms through relatives and other contacts. He keeps the space where he lives multi-functional,
his furniture convertible to many uses, and lives with those who feel the
most compulsion to take him in. This means in terms of family composition that he lives ideally in small units of immediate family members where
close proximity to others either does not offend sex taboos or can be rationalized by exigencies of the moment. The following case is unusual but
shows the difficulty the poor face in realizing even minimal standards of
privacy:

> Um A. had been widowed for a number of years and lived with her
> only child, a grown son. His income was sufficient to support the two
> of them. As he reached his late twenties, however, he began to think
> of marriage, but it was difficult for him to amass enough money to
> afford a new home for his bride and support his mother at the same
> time. Housing was becoming difficult to find and prices were escalat-
> ing rapidly. After a frustrating period of trying to figure out a solu-
> tion, he found a bride who was willing to move into the one small
> room he shared with his mother. When the couple wanted to be alone,
> Um A. discreetly visited her neighbor Sitt D., an elderly woman liv-
> ing alone after the recent death of her sister, to drink tea and some-
> times sleep the night. When the new bride did not become pregnant
> immediately the neighbors joked about their lack of opportunities,
> but eventually she did produce a boy that joined them in their cramped
> quarters.

The composition of households among poor families normally includes father, mother, and unmarried children, but it is not unusual to
find households with individuals related in much more tenuous ways as
the following illustration shows:

The unskilled older laborer has difficulty making ends meet with today's rising prices and demand for skilled labor.

Um B. had been a widow for a long time, supporting her two daughters on what she could earn washing clothes and cleaning in homes. Though all her neighbors knew she engaged in this kind of work, she never talked openly about it, and out of respect for her feelings, the neighbors refrained from talking about it in front of her. Her eldest daughter, B., eventually married and went to live in her husband's house. After a number of years they produced three children. Eventually B. and her husband quarreled and one day he simply walked out and was not heard from again. B. was unable to pay the rent for her room and soon returned with her children to the single room occupied by her mother and sister. Um B. was forced under the circumstances to try to support six people. Increasingly the younger sister had to interrupt her schooling to help her mother. Expenses soon overpowered the women and Um B. was unable to pay the rent of the room. One day she moved out with all her belongings. "Look," said a neighbor, pushing at the shutter of her old room, "the pile of clothes she slept on is gone. The owner took the room back and is going to use it for a storeroom." Um B. sought help from the parents of her daughter's husband, a kindly old couple, Abu Fahmi and Um Fahmi, who themselves only occupied a small room on the edge of Bulaq. They were unhappy with their son's behavior in deserting his wife and children and felt responsible for helping them. Abu F. was retired and living on a small income whose source he refused to divulge. He invited the six members of Um B.'s household to join them in their already crowded dwelling where for sleeping space there existed only one bed. The newcomers slept on the ground. Now Um B. and her unmarried daughter wash clothes for a living while the married daughter B. works as a servant. B.'s children are all in school.

In this instance Abu Fahmi has a *wagib* obligation to help his grandchildren financially in the absence of their father, but in Bulaq an elderly man of such limited means would be excused if he did not fulfill such an obligation. Abu Fahmi happens to be a man of conscience and sympathy and goes beyond his obligation by inviting the unrelated Um B. and her other daughter to join them as well. "What can I do," he says, "let them live in the street?"

The illustration above demonstrates another fact of poverty, that in a society which values keeping social ties active and ready for immediate and future needs, the poverty of some creates a ripple effect that has an impact on many. People expect to help those whom they know have difficulties, realizing the general ineffectiveness of impersonal private or government institutions for such purposes. The self-sufficient classes can sometimes afford what the lower classes cannot, to absorb the deficits of poorer family members in order to preserve the larger family's joint standing in the community. What pulls one down pulls the rest down, just as when one family member falls upon unexpected resources of influence or money all expect to gain. Inside the committed circle of relationships a leveling effect is created to the degree at least that an acceptable minimum standard is reached for all members. Outside the committed circle a zero-sum game applies. Then the gain of whomever is perceived as the other group is seen as a loss for the immediate group. The key is in identifying where the sense of commitment lies in any given instance. The much-used Arabic expression:

> I and my brothers against my cousins,
> I and my cousins against my tribe, and
> I and my tribe against the world,

demonstrates very well the shifting nature of allegiances.

In the following example Um Saad tries to create a more lasting bond with her daughter's husband, against the interests of her own daughter and in violation of a series of usually accepted norms:

> Um Saad's husband died and left her a penniless widow. She had no near relations except a married daughter who lived in one room in Bulaq with her husband and two children. Um Saad could not afford the rent of her own room so soon had to move out. With nowhere else to go she asked and received reluctant permission to move in with her daughter's family in their one cramped room. With their privacy invaded the daughter and her husband began to have violent quarrels, at first with Um Saad backing her daughter, and then anxious that she might be thrown out, turning more and more to side with the daughter's husband. The husband complained that his wife was a terrible housewife and mother and neglected him and the children. The wife complained that he never gave her enough money to buy food. Um Saad began to encourage his anger at her daughter, and even started to encourage him to make sexual advances at Um Saad herself. The two finally took up a more serious sexual relationship, flaunting it in the face of the daughter. In a weak moment, the husband was convinced by Um Saad to formally register them as married to "stop the talk around the neighborhood."
>
> Despite the illegality of marrying both a woman and her daughter at the same time, the husband somehow formalized the relationship "for the sake of his conscience," as he put it to outsiders. Eventually there was a falling out between Um Saad and the husband and

a reconciliation between him and the daughter. They sent Um Saad out on the street one day and refused to let her return. None of the neighbors would let her stay with them, and she eventually found an elderly woman acquaintance living alone who let her stay with her. Um Saad tried piecework to support herself for awhile but her eyesight was not good enough to do close embroidery, so she turned to selling produce on a street corner instead. Two years later, the daughter disappeared, and shortly thereafter the husband died of natural causes. The children have now been placed in orphanages.

There is no guarantee, of course, that Um Saad's behavior contradicting social norms — asking help from a daughter's husband, competing with the daughter for the husband's sexual favors, turning to a mere acquaintance for lodging, and selling produce publicly — is all necessarily a consequence of her impoverished condition. These are effects that cannot be measured precisely. But there is little doubt that compelling need invests her actions with a sense of urgency. Her desire to make her relationship with her daughter's husband "legal" shows she does not disregard community norms altogether.

The poor use the most tenuous bonds of intimacy to solve their problems, demonstrating in some cases better than other class groups the range of possible relationships that can be drawn upon. In general the behavior of the poor tends to reveal less of their actual preferences and more of the practical realities that are forced upon them by their social and economic conditions. If norms are upset and values seemingly disregarded, it is because both assume not only the decision to conform but also the latitude to carry out the decision.

Primary family members may, for example, have real difficulty when they are poor in meeting their obligations to other family members. In the following case, the brothers of the woman concerned attempted to meet their obligations to her, but only with a great deal of hardship on their part:

Sitt W. had been married for about ten years when her husband left her because of his doubts about her "being a real woman." People assumed he referred to the fact that she had had no children, but a doctor's examination revealed that she had been born with only the vestige of a vaginal canal. Despite efforts to reunite the couple and a painful operation in a government hospital to correct her defect with plastic surgery, the husband remained adamant in his insistence that he would not take his wife back. Since her parents were dead, Sitt W. was forced to fall back on her two married brothers for places to stay and for support which, despite court orders, her husband refused to give her. Sitt W. alternated between the homes of her brothers staying just long enough in one before going to the next so that their relationship did not break down completely. Each brother lived with his wife and children in cramped quarters where the presence of Sitt W. deprived husband and wife of any personal privacy. And though the expenses she required were not great, nevertheless they added to budgets already stretched thin. Eventually Sitt W. found a distant relative who was a widow and moved in with her. Both receive small amounts from their relatives and are often offered food by neighbors who have extra themselves. Sitt W. refuses offers to find employment for her because she says it is not considered proper in her family for women to work. As long as her brothers provide her with a minimal amount she is able to maintain this prohibition.

With poverty comes pressures to increase family income. Usual norms about esteemed, respectable work break down rapidly, and men accept any work for which they can get paid. The norms in lower-class neighborhoods discourage women from seeking outside employment, but economic imperatives may force some of them to do so. It is almost a general rule of thumb that women do not work in lower-class neighborhoods unless they feel compelled to do so for economic reasons or have achieved a level of education where they can find respectable work in government employment. They may, however, contribute significant amounts to income by their incidental work of raising poultry, selling produce from their villages of origin, or doing simple sewing for neighbors—all work that does not interfere substantially with what they consider their natural responsibilities in the household.

Poverty sets special limits on the ability to carry out male and female role expectations. The burden of increasing the family income normally falls on men—fathers and sons—as appropriate to their male roles. When a family is poor, the man is, by definition, not succeeding in his main function of support which, because it is so sex-related, means in most cases a reduction in his masculine self-esteem. Women have no trouble fulfilling their expected roles. Even in poor households it is still possible to produce numerous children, run a household well, and be a good wife. Women from poor families may in fact have fewer demands placed on them as a result of small living quarters, few possessions, and limited food preparation. They are not normally expected to assume a man's duties of contributing income.

Poverty tends to reduce the time children are permitted to pursue the activities of childhood—education and play—and throws them more quickly into the responsibilities of adulthood—earning money.

Um M. is a widow whose husband, a street cleaner, was killed by a car on his way to work. By a miscarriage of justice she did not receive the pension she was entitled to as the wife of a government employee. Um M. has six sons between the ages of 6 and 15. Those who were in school at the time of the accident were studious children receiving good to excellent marks. Um M. withdrew them all from school and set them to work to earn income. In 1977 the eldest earned 50 p. [about 75 cents] a week helping a small shopowner. Two other younger boys earned 35 p. and 30 p. in similar jobs while a fourth earned 25 p. in a scrap iron shop. The employers see these jobs as "training" positions and pay the boys accordingly. Together they earn 8 £E [$12] a month, an income that pays for rent and daily bread and not much else. Even were their prospects to change, it is too late now for the boys to return to school.

This case illustrates how short-term decisions forced upon families result in irrevocable long-term implications. By leaving school, Um M.'s boys lost their opportunity to prepare for higher-status work requiring advanced education. They also lost the chance to move up the social ladder into the educated middle classes.

INSTITUTIONS FOR SUBSTITUTE CARE

Institutions for the orphaned and the aged provide a test case for the durability of family relations in Egypt. At first glance they appear to indicate a breakdown of family structures in a society where families are normally expected to take care of even their most distant members. Close examination of these institutions, however, shows, at the same time, the resilience of family institutions and the devastating effect that poverty has on the ability of families to carry out their obligations. Poverty alone is not normally a sufficient cause for abandoning family responsibilities but coupled with a crisis, it can become critical.

Orphans

In the sense of "children without relatives who have the moral obligation to care for them," few orphans exist in Egyptian society. There are almost always relatives who should assume this responsibility. The institutional definition for the term orphan has assumed a broader meaning: "children who for one reason or another require substitute care outside of the family." The following illustration shows how children of one family came to be institutionalized:

> Nadya is a young woman in her late twenties. People remember her as a shy, striking, blond, blue-eyed beauty who used to walk over the Ramses railroad station bridge every morning on her way to work at a cigarette packing plant in Gezirat il Badran. It was during one of these walks that she attracted the attention of a handsome temperamental horse and buggy driver named Ibrahim. They soon married and moved to an apartment near Nadya's work. Before long there were three children, a girl and two boys. Increasingly Ibrahim's violent temper turned their marriage sour—the neighbors report that he continually beat Nadya with or without reason. Nadya spent six months during part of this period in a hospital being treated for a case of tuberculosis that she was told occurred partly as a result of her work in the cigarette factory. At the end of the hospital period she was given release papers and told to come regularly for medication to keep the active stages of her disease from recurring. Meanwhile, during one of Nadya's visits to her mother when her youngest son was three months old, Ibrahim refused to let her return home, telling her that he had divorced her. Nadya remained in the building of her parents where she found a small dark ground-floor room about one yard wide by three yards long, for which she paid 5£E rent. There she received the news that Ibrahim had died and along with him any hope that she might receive financial aid to bring up her children. Nevertheless she managed for about two years to live on the few piasters her father was able to give her to buy food. Slowly, however, her health deteriorated and she began vomiting blood again. She appealed to various charitable agencies to help and they were able to find places in two orphanages for her three children so that she could return to the hospital again.

Nadya says that when she becomes well again she wants to work and establish a better home for the children. Her prospects of accomplishing this goal are small, however, given her limited skills, the difficulty in finding the kind of home and food necessary to improve her health, and income enough to give the children even a few of the benefits they derive from the orphanage.

Orphanages have existed in Egypt since the last decade of the nineteenth century. Previously ad hoc methods predominated—abandoning children at mosques or selling them in public places (Lane 1954, orig. 1860:

200). From the start, the reasons for such abandonment were almost always illegitimacy or poverty of the kin, coupled with a crisis such as the death of parents or the loss of the main wage earner. In a study of eight orphanages carried out in 1981, interviews with administrators revealed three major categories of admissions: (1) abandoned newborns, assumed to be illegitimate; (2) foundling children up to about the age of four, thought to be abandoned by parents for reasons of poverty; and (3) children brought by relatives, social agencies, or neighbors because of a critical inability to care for them (Rugh 1982).

The histories of many children in institutions are unknown for obvious reasons, but in one institution where the backgrounds were all known because of the requirement that the children be Christian, the facts bear out the generalization that families abrogate their responsibilities to children usually only where a significant crisis is coupled with poverty. In this institution, among the cases where sufficient information is known (38 out of 42), all cases report poverty as a contributory factor in the institutionalization of the child. By far the most common immediate cause for admission (28) was the loss of the male wage earner in the family by death, desertion, mental illness, or imprisonment. The loss of maternal care was stated as an immediate cause in five cases; both parents were absent in three cases, and where both parents were present (six cases), poverty was given by the majority (five cases) as a reason for putting their children in institutions. The remaining case involved a physically incapacitated father, so, strictly speaking, it was his inability to earn a wage that caused the final institutionalization of the children.

Disguised in the data on institutionalized children is another factor that sheds light on family processes: the expectation of widowed spouses that they will be unable to remarry if they have a number of dependent children.

Um I. lives alone under conditions of extreme poverty. Her three daughters, however, married well and live in self-sufficient households. One with seven children knocked over a kerosene stove shortly after the birth of the seventh child, and her clothing was consumed in flames. She died a day later in the hospital. Relatives and neighbors helped with the care of the children for a short time, and Um I. herself would have taken them were it not for her tiny room and her total lack of resources. It is not unknown for men to forget their children after a period of time. The father of the children soon began to think of marrying again. As the women put it, "A man can't live alone without a woman to take care of his needs." In preparation for the event, he con-

tacted orphanages and placed all seven of the children in ones that
corresponded with their ages and sex. Soon he remarried and began
producing offspring with the second wife.

Institutions are aware of this way of "getting rid" of children, but
there is little they can do to prevent it when the families have incomes that
make them unable to support two families (that is, the first set of children
and the new set being created). The practice of sending children away is
one used more by men than women. A woman is still expected to stay with
her children and not marry again. If she does marry, she usually feels some
embarrassment over asking her new husband to support her children by
another man. In one instance, in a well-to-do middle-class family, the
woman worked to be able to say she paid the expenses of her son by her
first husband.

These cases illustrate the extent to which family units are created and
sustained by children. When new units are being created, it is a burden
to the new spouse to have to deal with the remnants of the old unit. Children of the two units will always be expected to compete with each other
in the household, and the mother who is present will support her own offspring against the others. It is interesting in this respect that many times
when a man both wants to remarry and keep his children he recognizes
his liabilities and chooses for a wife one who for some reason has not been
selected before — because of a physical defect or because her family is extremely poor. In this way he hopes her gratitude for the marriage proposal
will compensate for the burdens of raising his children.

Adoption is not the answer for most institutionalized children in
Egypt. Islamic inheritance laws prohibit formal legal adoption of children
that would give the child the name of a family and a legal share in the
division of property. Substitutes for adoption, such as formal foster home
care or attempts by private individuals to raise a child that comes under
their protection, eventually face the problem of the ad hoc relationship
between "parent" and child. Occasionally families develop a legal relationship by claiming falsely that one of the parents has fathered or mothered
the child concerned. This fiction is then written into the child's registra-
tion papers, and the child is considered legally theirs. Others circumvent
the problem of inheritance by giving monetary gifts to their "adopted"
children or assigning up to one-third of their property to the child (a be-
quest that is legal under Islamic laws). Occasionally a couple applies for
permanent foster care of a child and attempts to pass the child off to
neighbors as their own. Other children, particularly those in institutions,
grow up with their status as orphans publicly known. Officials of orphan-

ages, however, often prefer to obscure some facts, such as their illegitimate origins, from the children. Most are told they are foundlings, abandoned by parents who were too poor to care for them.

Orphans create a contradiction in a family-oriented society like Egypt.
Parents who abandon illegitimate children are reacting to the extreme moral
opprobrium that accompanies unlicensed sexual unions. By abandoning
the children, parents deny them the family name and life that is being so
zealously protected. In the abstract people sympathize with orphans, but
in daily life they are reluctant to marry them or to become closely associated with them. People assume that where there is no clear evidence of
parents, there is an illegitimate liaison involved, and they generalize the
moral contagion of illegitimacy to other family members, including the
child itself.

Orphans are an extreme case in Egyptian society. They are either victims of sanctions that protect the family unit from moral excursions outside its legitimatizing framework or they are victims of circumstances where
the family is no longer able to function in a normal way, usually because
of economic insufficiency.

Institutionalized Elderly

The elderly in Egyptian society normally continue to maintain a close
relationship with their children as they grow older. The way the relationship is played out, however, may change significantly over the years. In
the early years of their children's marriages, the parents may help out a
great deal with child care and material gifts (see Chapter 6). As time goes
on the father either retires with or without a pension or if working for
himself may let his children slowly take over his business while he remains
titular head until advanced age or death. In this last case, the evolution
to dependency is gradual and less traumatic for the elderly—it may in fact
not be consciously recognized by family members who still see the patriarch as the head of the clan.

By contrast when parents retire abruptly from full-time work, the
form the relationship between parent and child takes is often dependent
to a large extent on the solvency of the older people. Large numbers from
among the middle classes retire with pensions that are minimally sufficient to support them. Many in urban areas are also accustomed to occupying independent apartments. In general where both spouses are still
alive and enjoy good health and there is sufficient income, the elderly remain in separate dwellings from their children. It is usually only when one

spouse dies and the other feels the lack of company, support, or care that the other provided that other measures such as moving in with children are considered.

Even when the remaining spouse lives alone, children feel the obligation to have close and frequent contacts. Usually it is widowed women who live alone, and it is their daughters who take over the task of keeping up the contact:

> Muna's mother lives alone in her own home. Her resources make it possible to hire help for the difficult task of keeping up such a large building. Usually, however, she is in the midst of hiring or firing maids who never meet her standards. Though she lives fairly far from Muna, Muna drives out to see her two times a week, and the whole family visits on Friday. In between, the women talk a great deal together on the telephone. Their discussions are concerned mainly with servant problems and a catalog of the mother's physical complaints. Muna listens dutifully and with sympathy. As the children become older they complain about the compulsory visits to their grandmother. Muna's husband also complains mildly but accepts the fact that Muna is obligated to see her mother often.

> Fattin has an almost ideal situation with her mother. The widow lives in an apartment just across the street from her daughter. Since the birth of the eldest of Fattin's three children, their grandmother has come every day to care for the children while Fattin and her husband are away at work. Though she sometimes stays overnight if they are going to be out late, the widow still maintains her separate home.

Though custom frowns upon a woman's parents being supported by her husband, emotional attachments often intervene in the case of women to reverse what is customary:

> Faiza is a working woman, away from home much of the day. Her children are grown and she does not need to worry about child care. Her eighty-year-old mother is probably closest to Faiza, but lives instead with another daughter who still has children at home and grandchildren that she cares for. The old woman enjoys the activity around the house and takes part in simple tasks. She would enjoy spending more time with her son, but from visits in the past she knows that she does not get along well with her daughter-in-law. Rather than ag-

gravate the relationship she keeps her visits short. As a result she is
unhappy that she is not very close to her son's children.

Lower-class families are more likely to have members of the older
generations living with them. The arrangements tend to be made on the
basis of strong affective relationships rather than strictly according to structural obligation.

> Nowal is an industrious woman who, with her piecework sewing, usu-
> ally makes more money in a month than her husband. She has a num-
> ber of children still at home including a daughter who has graduated
> from the university and is waiting to be called for a government job.
> Despite the cramped quarters of their home, Nowal's elderly father
> and her mother-in-law have come to live with the family.

The fairly good financial situation of this lower-class family contributes
to its attraction for these elderly people as well as increasing the pressures
on the family itself to help less fortunate relatives.

Institutionalization of the elderly has until recently been a last resort for only a few of the elderly. The old names for homes for the aged
in Egypt, "orphanages for the elderly" and "homes for beggars" reveals
the extremities of the clients who used them, implying the absence of families to take care of them. By the end of 1981 there were a total of thirty-
four homes for the elderly registered with the Ministry of Social Affairs,
catering to more than sixteen hundred clients.

A study of five institutions for the aged and one day care program
for the aged revealed some of the factors involved in the institutionalization or non-institutionalization of the aged (Rugh 1982). The study showed
that there were two distinct types of institutions. The first was a better-
quality institution where residents drawn primarily from the middle classes
paid their own fees (or had them paid by relatives). The second was a low
quality service institution with residents drawn from mostly the lower classes
and in many cases unable to pay the fee. Those in this last institution were
mostly in some critical state of financial insufficiency, physical incapac-
ity, or abandonment by their families.

Two case histories indicate the nature of these two kinds of clientele:

> Mme. N. is a well-to-do widow in her eighties who has been accus-
> tomed to living in her own large apartment even after the death of
> her husband a number of years ago. She has three children, now grown

— one married and living with her husband who is working in a distant Arab country, the second, a married woman with children working for her living, and the third, a son, with the custody of two teen-aged children who has recently moved back into the home of his mother. Mme. N.'s home has all of a sudden become full of activity again, and she, at her age, is finding it difficult to cope with all the responsibility. Her daughter stops in after work every day to bring her necessities from the store and to help her with some of the housework, but she can do only a limited amount because of her own household responsibilities. Efforts to find a maid have all failed because the old woman's standards are too exacting for modern young girls "who want to sit around all day and get paid like a minister." Recently, Mme. N. went to visit a friend of hers in a private well-kept home for the elderly and was impressed by the high standards of the service. She was particularly pleased by the fact that one could choose a residential wing by price range and thus need associate regularly only with those of a similar class background. She is thinking of leaving her home to her son and moving into the institution as a solution to her problem. There she feels she will not be a burden to her daughter and can escape from the noise and responsibility of her grandchildren. And when she needs nursing care, as is increasingly the case, she will have it close at hand. In the institution she will have her own room but looks forward to a social life with others her own age.

Mme N. is considering an institution as a choice between alternatives and she can easily afford admission. What she considers as her problems are not serious enough to force her admission to the institution. In the following case, illustrative of the clients in the second kind of institution, choices are much more circumscribed:

Sitt Zeinab and her elderly husband, 'Amm Abdu live together in a fairly spacious but poorly furnished room. He is a porter of goods in the wholesale market, but his old age makes it increasingly difficult to compete with physically stronger young men for the jobs that come along. The great tragedy of Sitt Zeinab's and Amm Abdu's lives is that they never produced any children to satisfy the financial needs of their declining years. If there had been children Amm Abdu would have ceased working long before. Recently Sitt Zeinab suffered a stroke that has paralyzed her left side and left her in such weak health that she is unable to walk or even feed herself. Amm Abdu feels extremely impatient with her condition, trying to force her to get up and stir around the house. In his frustration, he has resorted to beating her at times. As a man, he is not used to playing the role of nurse, and feels cheated of the service he used to receive from his wife. He has been heard to grumble that a woman in Sitt Zeinab's condition is worth nothing once she no longer can fulfill her function. She is a burden that he feels he can no longer bear and wants to have her admitted to an old people's home.

The study of institutions reinforces some of the factors revealed in the cases above. If one compares an institution of lower-class, more destitute clients (1) with an institution of middle-class paying clients (2) and a "day care" program where the clients reside in private households (3), one finds a graded scale of certain factors. Moving from 1 to 3 one finds ever-increasing levels of income suggesting that the higher the income the more likely that the person will live outside an institution. Second, the more intact and less disrupted the family by death or dissension the more likely that an individual will live outside the institution, or if within the institution that generalized obligations for visiting and support by other relatives will be realized. Third, the higher the ratio of those who have children, especially still unmarried children, the more likely that the clients will remain outside the institution. All these factors suggest once again that where circumstances permit normal family functions to be performed, they will be performed. Where circumstances, for example, deprive old people of children (who are their resource), or those children are poor themselves or the old people are poor, crotchety, or possibly incapacitated, then family support networks break down.

What is new in institutions for the aged in Egypt is their occasional use as a residence of choice among the middle classes. Conditions of urban living and discrete separate residences of nuclear families have become a value that people are willing to pay money for in order to preserve. High-quality institutions provide a consistent alternative for conscientious children, who may be living abroad or occupied full time by outside employment, to provide for their parents the kinds of physical and financial support that the elderly need. In this case the obligations of family are fulfilled in a way that satisfactorily suits the new circumstances of urban living. And by "spending money" on the care of the elderly, a positive image is preserved in what would otherwise be considered a reprehensible way for a family to act toward its elderly.

In this chapter we have looked at family disruption and its consequences. Theoretically when such disruptions occur, other circles of family reassert their influence over the individuals and provide the kinds of support needed. This is expected and normally turns out to be the case. It is usually only when poverty becomes a critical factor that one finds total breakdown of family support systems and the need to resort to impersonal institutions to fill the gap. The exception is a few homes for the aged, specializing in alternative care that can be still construed in some cases to meet the essentials of family obligation.

11

Religion

"He who sees no good in his own religion will not see it in the religion
of others"—Arab proverb

RELIGION is such a pervasive factor in Egyptian life that it is impossible to discuss family life without noting its significant influence.
In earlier chapters we noted the stability that religious legal principles provide for family practices, lending them an air of moral absoluteness that
would not be possible were the laws considered secularly inspired We noted
also the remarkable resistance to erosion that family laws more than any
other legal area of the sharia have sustained. In this chapter we will look
at recent reforms in the laws guiding family behavior, at differences in
Christian and Muslim family life, and at the institutions that evolve to solve
the separate kinds of family problems of the two religious communities.

MUSLIM AND CHRISTIAN COMMUNITY

Community Boundary

The Islamic invasion, as we noted before, found Egypt an almost exclusively Christian country with deep and continuous roots far back into its
Pharaonic past. At the last complete census (1976), Christians numbered
only 6.3 percent of the Egyptian population. Nevertheless, Christians form
a strong, publicly visible community even while conscious of their minor-

ity status in the vast sea of Muslims surrounding them. Stressing the differences between the two communities runs the risk of overlooking the vast areas of similarities the two religious communities share, but it is necessary in order to show the very real differences family life patterns sustain from the impact of the two communities' ideological and circumstantial conditions.

Religion in Egypt is not something that affects only a minor portion of a person's life. Because of the separate legal provisions governing personal status, an individual must from birth identify with a religious denomination or by default he will be assigned to the Muslim community as the religion of the state. The boundaries of religious community are imposed by these different sets of personal-status laws, by the restriction against inheritance passing across religious boundaries, and by the efforts the communities themselves exert to prevent their members from converting to another denomination or contracting marriages that would alienate them from their own communities.

It is easier to talk of the Christian community and the means Christians use to mark the boundaries of their communities. As a minority population they have a stronger consciousness of themselves as a unity contraposed against a larger population. Muslims feel and act more as though they were the universe themselves which, indeed, to all intents and purposes in the circles where they interact, they normally are. The layers of Christian consciousness move from identifying first with family, then to religious community, and only last to nation. The first two overlap and reinforce each other since family almost always also means only members of the Christian religion. There is significance in this middle-level allegiance that serves to create bonds between even strangers at a level less than that of nation. Muslims have a conscious identification with other Muslims usually only outside their country when confronted with other denominations, or when they relate as members of an Islamic grouping that sees itself as different in some way from the bulk of Muslims in Egypt. This does not mean that Muslims are not concerned with their religion; rather it means that they are not as concerned as Christians with setting their community off against others. Most Muslims in Egypt feel they *are* the community.

Christians feel the pressure to keep both family and community intact and to refrain from incurring the negative attention of external communities like the Muslims. For them, strong families with few rearrangements of personnel mean communities with fewer disruptions. Communities with fewer disruptions are less likely to invite the incursions of other groups. For these reasons Christians exert their strongest efforts toward preserving families intact and providing ways for potentially devisive behavior to be channelled into harmless outlets.

Different sub-groups of Egyptian Christians approach these goals in different ways. For example, in rural villages where the tendency for newlyweds to settle near their relatives sets up whole sections of villages that are homogeneously Christian, boundaries are more easily closed and relations with Muslims more easily confined to formal, ceremonial visits and other friendly but less intimate relations than those normally required of neighbors.

By contrast, in an urban lower-class neighborhood like Bulaq that is predominantly Muslim, Christians live dispersed among Muslim neighbors. They demonstrate their desire to reside with co-religionists statistically by their greater ratios in districts of Bulaq closest to what was known at one time to have been the almost exclusively Christian area of Shubra. Christians who have settled in Bulaq have almost surely felt the attraction of low-cost rentals that at an initial period of settlement took priority over their desire to live in a predominantly Christian community. They are not unaware of the vulnerability that comes from their physical dispersion among Muslims and set the boundaries of community in ways appropriate to their circumstances (for details see Rugh 1978).

Christian families in Bulaq have ways of integrating their members more tightly into the group. For example, they are probably more likely to try to marry a relative because of their wariness of strangers and because of the reduced pool of potential Christian mates in their immediate surroundings. They develop a more conservative policy toward women working and women's movement in public areas than do Muslims of the same background. They also tend to control their children's movements in public more than Muslims. An administrator in a welfare nursery school commented that it was very difficult to get Christians to bring their children to a local Christian-sponsored nursery school even though the school was intended to upgrade educational standards for lower-class Christian families.

Along with this reluctance of lower-class Christian parents to let children out to mingle freely in public areas goes their own tendency when faced with a crisis to prefer to seek help from private church, as opposed to government, institutions. For Christians the church is usually the most embracing organization they pay allegiance to. Muslims may feel a relationship with the institutions of both their religion and the state, but Christians equate the latter with Islam and believe they do not receive equal treatment in those quarters.

In the upper-middle and upper classes, conditions are such that extensive extra-kin relationships may be actively sought, regardless of religious background, for economic and political reasons, and as a result the importance of religious affiliation in developing close relationships diminishes, retaining significance mostly as a factor in marriage selection. In recent years the breakdown of urban neighborhoods that at one time were much more homogeneously ethnic, religious, or regional into distinct areas segregated by similar life style, level of economic affluence, and other social factors has done much to reinforce these latter influences among the middle and upper classes. Unlike their lower-class co-religionists who keep their women at home, middle-class Christian families attempting to carve an indispensable economic role for themselves have been the first to send women to work. Such an act is easily rationalized by a community that finds it desirable at times to set different value standards than those of the national majority. One observer comments:

> Women belonging to the religious minorities in the Middle East enjoyed a freer social life and higher educational standards than their Muslim counterparts; they learnt foreign languages in parochial schools and were able to take advantage of commercial institutes established for the benefit of the European communities. The combination of these factors gave Christian and Jewish girls an early monopoly of most secretarial and other clerical positions in the private sector. (Youssef 1971: 437)

While it is therefore impossible to generalize for Christians of all classes concerning the specific behavioral manifestations of family life, nevertheless it is possible to say that even contradictory behavior is often generated from what is a base of common goals, the solidarity of the family, and the unity of the religious community.

MUSLIM–CHRISTIAN FAMILY STRUCTURE

A significant difference in family structure of Christian and Muslim households results from the implications of their separate personal-status codes and their separate views of family life. For Christians, the family unit of husband and wife is strengthened by the practical difficulty of obtaining a divorce, a prohibition deriving from the underlying perception of marriage as the joining of two persons into one. It is unusual for the Christian family unit to be dissolved for reasons other than death or because children grow up and form their own households. Strong community pressure dictates against separation for any other reasons. Married children usually attempt to live as near to parents as they possibly can.

When tension arises in the Christian lower or middle-class family, it frequently occurs between parent and child (particularly the son).[1] Christian parents exert strong controls over their children to assure that they not face temptations to convert or to marry outside the Christian community. These fears tend to deter efforts to encourage children to pursue their own interests as they approach adulthood. Christian sons, like Muslim sons, are expected to stay long in the family and help out with the support of the parents if that is needed. They are also expected to keep up a close emotional relationship with parents after marriages. These expectations tend to put pressures on sons who may be desirous of creating their own family units.

Muslim personal-status law does not support the family as a unit to the extent that Christian law and custom does. Marriage under Islam is a contract between two people who retain their individual names, property, and complementary rights and obligations toward one another. Marriage is the contractual joining of two persons who for practical purposes only become a unity upon the birth of a child. Christians from the start conceive of marriage as creating a union of persons into an indissoluble whole that is only further augmented by children.

The ability of the Muslim man to divorce his wife fairly easily and to take custody of children after their early years creates a permanent tension between married couples. Women, in particular, who do not have the same unrestricted rights as men, feel the insecurity of their position. In the lower classes one can see that insecurity visibly expressed in the way that Muslim women in general take better care of their appearances and are more concerned with how they carry out their functions as housewives and mothers. As a lower-class Christian said: "Because divorce is so difficult in our religion, we Christian women tend to neglect our duties in the household. We don't recognize the importance of sex to our men the way the Muslim women do. We neglect our appearance, wear shabby clothes, don't eat well to become sleek and beautiful as they do, leave our houses dirty and untidy. You can see these differences between them and us."

Muslim women have more reason to keep up their connections with their own natal families in the knowledge that these relationships are more to be depended upon in the long run than those of husband and wife. A Muslim woman also has an interest in keeping her relations with her children warm. They support her in arguments with her husband, and if she is divorced her son is legally responsible for her material support as long as he lives. Children cement a marital relation when it is good but may aggravate it when it is bad. In the Muslim household the child becomes a pawn in the relations between the spouses while in the Christian family the child is the focus of the parents' struggle with the outside, threatening world.

Muslim women in the lower classes with an eye to the future are more likely to learn skills and work to accumulate money, so they will not be left without anything to fall back on. They are considered in those communities to be sharper, better able to drive a bargain, more clever at selling and taking advantage of opportunities. In Muslim households the property of husband and wife is carefully distinguished. Household furnishings, her own gold, and personal property belong to the woman. The man, unless he has inherited or amassed property, has only his own personal clothing and small belongings. A Christian noted, "When a Muslim husband gives his wife gold jewelry, it is a sign that he loves her very much. It means that the relationship is secure or otherwise he would not take out of his own pocket to put into hers."

The difference in how the husband-wife relationship is viewed by Muslim and Christian is indicated by the different patterns of investment in marriage. In both Christian and Muslim lower-class marriages about the same amount is spent on the gold engagement gift, the engagement party, and wedding expenses (in 1978 about 50£E or $75 for each). What differs is the amount that goes toward buying the furnishings. The Muslim bridegroom pays about 150£E as a *mahr* (bridal price) to the parents of the girl, and they in turn use this money along with about 300£E of their own money to buy all the furnishings of the bride. There is an emphasis on buying the best they can afford in furnishings, china, and clothing so the girl will have a secure property base. The Christian bridegroom on his side, rather than paying a lump sum, buys some of the furnishings, and the china, and pots and pans, while the bride's family buys other furnishings (usually the bedroom furnishings), clothes and bedding. In other words, Christian brides and grooms contribute about equally (150£E each) to what will be their common property and neither is as insistent upon the very best that is available realizing that what is paid now takes away from what will be available later. Many lower-class Christian women, for example, settle for everyday dishes rather than expensive china sets.

The Muslim woman's family, therefore, invests more in marriage than her husband does (if the apartment expenses are excluded). She also receives more if the marriage is dissolved. All the furnishings that come to a couple at the time of marriage are registered in her name and become her property if there is a divorce. The difference in price paid (about 100£E) for Muslim and Christian marriage reflects, besides the matter of a woman's property, a difference Christians feel exists generally in the two communities concerning financial matters. Muslims feel the importance of spending lavishly and generously while Christians tend to conserve their funds. One Christian said: "The Muslims live by the motto, 'Spend generously all you have from your pocket and the money will come back to you with interest.' Christians follow the motto, 'Save the white coin [piaster, like a penny] for the dark day.'"

Divorce is a particularly sensitive issue in both communities. Muslim women frequently mention how fortunate Christian women are to have such strong restrictions on divorce in their communities. Muslim women recognize their own weak position in the household when compared with their husbands. Christian men, on the other hand, compare themselves with Muslim men and see the advantage of the weapon of divorce in maintaining control over their women. The ultimate weapon a Christian husband has is to threaten to become a Muslim and divorce his wife.

From its measures against divorce it appears that Christianity views the stability of community as resting in the stability of marriages. From the theoretical view Islam's easier divorce possibilities and provisions for multiple marriages put the emphasis elsewhere. Community strength under Islam, it would seem, is protected by creating all the right conditions for increasing the numbers of community members. Polygamy theoretically keeps more women productive.

One study notes that the average number of children born to polygamous husbands in rural areas was 6.6 children and in urban areas 5.4 children while a total sample of married couples averaged only 4.18 children (Azer 1979: 72–73). The study concludes that polygamous marriages result in more births. It would be more accurate to say that polygamous husbands have more children. From these statistics one suspects that wives are less fertile than if they were married to non-polygamous men.

Prohibitions against Muslim women marrying non-Muslim men keeps child bearers within the community. The rule that children follow the religion of their father means that when a man marries a Christian or a Jewish woman, a practice readily accepted by Islam, the children of the union will remain Muslim. The relative ease with which men divorce and remarry means also the possibility to keep up and sustain an active sex life with interested partners and, at the same time, gives more opportunities for divorced and widowed women to marry again. These implications, whether consciously intended or not, serve as a means by which the Islamic community can strengthen and augment its numbers.

Christian legal structures with no prohibitory provisions (only customary ones) against marrying outside the community, no polygamous possibilities, and strict limitations on divorce freeze the community into a *status quo* where no new members are taken in, where incompatible people sometimes live together because they have no other alternatives, and where, more than that, they are vulnerable to the incursions of outsiders. Christians rely on social sanctions, perhaps as much if not more than legal sanctions, to control and stabilize their community. In other words, Christians fear the effects of social ostracism, should they contravene community norms, more than they fear the legal penalties which are slight if not nonexistent. The most serious social sanctions, virtual expulsion from home and religious community, are reserved for what is considered the most serious violation, conversion to Islam, whether for practical reasons (economic, marriage, or divorce) or out of religious conviction.

RELIGIOUS INSTITUTIONS FOR CONFLICT RESOLUTION

Individuals of both religious groups are naturally prone to many of the same kinds of tensions that arise in the conduct of everyday life. They also tend to express their frustrations in similar culturally accepted if not always approved kinds of ways — through general sickness complaints, quarrels and not uncommonly, through spirit possession. Differences when they occur between Muslims and Christians tend to occur in a different source of acute conflict within the family. As mentioned above, in the Muslim family the tension arises between husband and wife and consists of a long-term tension with potential acute periods any time that disruption in the marriage is considered possible. The "cure" consists of long-term reduction of the level of tension since a final resolution is not possible by the very nature of the condition. With Christians the source of the problem is less clear-cut. It is more likely to involve conflicts of parents with their children, but it may also involve anxiety over husband-wife relations with respect to possible long-term unhappiness in the relationship. In either instance the "cure" for the Christian is a more clear-cut need to resolve the problem as quickly as possible.

Happily there is a neat fit between these separate kinds of "cures" and the ideology of the two religions which is clearest in the matter of spirit possession. Spirit possession is a convenient ailment with ambiguous symptoms. It can be blamed for causing a person to act in irresponsible, irrational ways, for causing a person to abrogate certain role responsibilities, and for causing real physical and psychological illness. The spirit can remain as long as the person needs it, or it can disappear abruptly. The spirit (*ifrit* or plural *afarit*), enters the human being when he or she is vulnerable — in the dark, in the toilet, after childbirth, etc. The symptoms are usually alarming enough — swooning, fits, irrational speech and behavior, even sometimes attempts at self-destruction — to attract the special attention of friends and relatives who usually gather around to give special support to the possessed individual. These supporters look at "true"[2] spirit possession as an affliction beyond the control of the victim. If the possession is a mild one, the concern of the supporters may be all that is needed to effect a "cure." If it is not, then the person may be taken to one of the practitioners who deal with the problem. Muslim and Christian possessions, according to respondents who have seen numerous cases, tend to evoke different symptoms. Muslim spirits are generally jealous and demanding, continually wanting the victim to wear special clothes and jewelry and wanting to hear special tunes so the spirit, in the guise of the victim's body, can dance and enjoy itself. Skeptics of the genuineness of a particular possession comment that such demands have the added effect of keeping a possessed woman's husband "always paying and paying so he can't afford to even think of another woman."

Christian spirits, it is said, tend to cause mainly physical and psychological illness in the people they possess. The victim may not be certain whether the complaint is produced by the spirit or by purely natural causes, and so may be attending ridding ceremonies as a means of testing this, as only one of several remedies to be tried.

Since spirits appear in both the Bible and the Koran, there are authoritative texts about their character and their treatment. In Islam it is written in the Koran that spirits are not necessarily incompatible with religious life. Some spirits are righteous and others are contrary (from Sura LXXII: 11). It is therefore not necessary always to rid a person of the spirits. Some may require expulsion while others may require only placation to keep them from causing problems to their host. Another Sura (LV: 15) astutely recognizes spirits as typifying "the hidden forces and capacities of men." And yet another (Sura LXXII: 6) warns people against using spirits as an excuse for their own weakness.

Christianity views spirits in a very different light. According to this view persons become possessed only when they are weak in their faith. Devil possession is antithetical to a religious life, and people must be rid of devils in order to be restored to good standing within the Christian church. Placating devils is like flirting with evil. The cure is to restore the person's faith so that there will be no room for the evil of the spirits. The authority for this view comes from the Biblical passages where Jesus casts out demons from possessed people (Luke 11: 19, 20). In one (Luke 11: 20) he remarks that he is enabled to cast out demons through God's power while in another (I Peter 5: 89) the Bible warns that devils can be resisted if the faith is firm.

The theology corresponds well with the two kinds of tensions in Christian and Muslim families: the kind that needs abrupt cure and the kind that needs long-term placation. It is therefore not surprising to find the institutions, formal and informal, that cater to such ills emphasizing two separate kinds of treatment. Muslims favor the placation ceremonies of communal *zars* and the Christians the exorcism sessions of specialist priests. The church forbids Christians from participating in the *zar*, preferring that they attend church sessions. Formal Islam generally ignores the methods people use to solve their spirit possession problems. As a result Christians do not participate significantly in the *zar* in Bulaq while Muslims frequently take advantage of the final ridding process of the church if their problems are acute enough. The only alternative ridding process for the Muslim is a costly special *zar* that is ordered especially for one or more individuals.

The Zar

A local *zar* in Bulaq attracts perhaps 100 onlookers and participants one night a week. It is run by a self-confident middle-aged woman who rents a double room and organizes a few players of drums, tambourines, and castanets to set the dance rhythms. Each person who enters the rooms pays a small amount which is augmented by a contribution when a person dances or desires a special rhythm. Most of the possessed individuals bring along a coterie of helpers to give them moral support between and physical support at the end of the exhausting dances. Though the band may consist of a few male members, the dancers and onlookers are always women in this *zar.* These *zar* dances are intended as placation exercises, and no formal attempts are made to rid a person of her spirit. The same group that sponsors the weekly *zar,* however, also puts on expensive marathon sessions of several days for private individuals that include animal sacrifice and more explicit attempts to exorcize the offending spirit.

In general, it is possible to characterize the *zar* as a place where some of the restraints of correct society are dropped. One of the main points of the *zar* may in fact be to allow free expression of the kinds of inappropriate behavior that normally must be suppressed in a restricted area where it does not spill out and cause problems for the everyday life of the community. It is most unusual in Egyptian society, for example, to see such free relations between stranger men (musicians) and women, or to see women dancing seductively in thin and form-revealing clothing. It is also uncommon to find the kind of unharnessed public revelation of sexual fantasy that is frequently found in the discussions of women about relationships with their spirits. Even if the specific frustrations of individuals are not wholly resolved by this kind of psychological release, the sheer physical exhaustion of the strenuous dancing is often enough to give the participants at least temporary relief. This exhaustion is similar to that men find in the rhythmic chanting and swaying of the *zikr,* a common religious observance of lower-class urban and rural men. For the women who participate in the *zar* the support of sympathetic helpers gives the added solace of group sympathy to their problems.

The Exorcism

Christians, and a large number of possessed Muslims, turn to the free ridding ceremonies priests perform in churches for the cure of cases where exorcism of the spirit is required. Three times a week in a chapel near Bulaq, a well-known priest conducts ceremonies to exorcize malevolent spirits from possessed persons. He uses holy symbols extensively to revive the faith of the possessed. One of the most potent signs of faith, a crucial dividing issue between Christian and Muslim ideology, is acknowledgement of the divinity of Jesus Christ. With Muslim possessed, the priest relies on more palatable symbols like crosses, pictures, oil, and special Biblical verses. In a rough and usually emotional confrontation he grasps the hair of the victim, swathes the mouth or face with holy oil, dazzles the eyes with a cross, and demands to speak with the spirit. He is usually successful in ousting the spirit by pronouncing holy words or by sending the victim to touch a picture of a saint of the Virgin Mary at the front of the church. These contacts make the spirit "burn up." But often the possessed have more than one spirit or fear the return of an exorcized one, and return week after week to strengthen their resistance.

One illustration will suffice to demonstrate how devil possession gives the individual a culturally accepted means of showing culturally disapproved behavior. In this case a young woman, Gamiila, became possessed after the birth of her first child. Her spirit in his "jealousy" refused to allow her to have intercourse with her husband. She was brought protectively to the exorcizing priest by her husband and sister to see if the offending spirit could be removed. In a series of confrontations with the spirit, however, the priest was unable to budge him, and the woman retained her affliction. Nevertheless by their solicitous efforts on her behalf it was clear that the family still sympathized with her and would continue to support her.

If this case is compared with that of Suna, the runaway wife in Chapter 9, it becomes clear how spirit possession is a much more satisfactory way for a person to frame his/her misbehavior than simply to indulge in the misbehavior directly.

In both cases, the wives refuse intercourse with their husbands. Suna runs home to her mother; Gamiila stays with her husband and blames an oppressive spirit for keeping her from intercourse. Suna aggravates everyone and brings down a multitude of sanctions on her head; Gamiila is still loved by everyone, and treated all the more supportively because of her affliction. Suna eventually must submit, but she does so leaving behind a residue of distrust and blame on her reputation. Gamiila can string out her possession a long while, but when she decides to end it, she will remain absolved from all blame, and her relationships with others may even be stronger as a result of the crisis they have suffered together. The difference lies in what people see as behavior that is generated out of the individual herself and behavior that is imposed on her from the outside.

Faith Healing

Another group of informal practitioners, faith healers, use the symbols of Christianity to effect general solutions to a range of problems.

Sayyida Antoinette is representative of one of these quasi-religious specialists in Bulaq who uses the power of holy symbols to solve a client's problems. Her appeal has several aspects. She offers a range of alternative healing modes, one that is not too expensive by Bulaq standards, and may provide a last resort when other methods fail. She is a local personage with a reputation in the area for curing all manner of problems. It is safe for both men and women to go to her without eliciting negative comment because she is so respectable an individual in the community. Because of her special power, which comes through the seeping holy oil from her pictures of the Virgin Mary and St. George, the community sees her as someone marked for healing.

The advantage of Sayyida A.'s ministrations over those of certain other healers is that she can tailor her treatment to the individual. In the following case, where the root cause of the problem is a conflict between

Christian parents and daughter, going to Sayyida A. allows the parents to take action where there appears to be no other path they can take.

> S. was in her early twenties, and her parents were becoming desperate to find her a husband. She had been engaged before to a young man that her parents had forced upon her and whom she didn't like. Eventually their relationship deteriorated, and the engagement was broken. But for a long time S. lived under the onus of this broken engagement, and no one was interested in asking for her hand. Finally, a very presentable candidate appeared, but S. was somewhat hesitant to accept another young man that her parents recommended. When S. met the man, she told him very frankly that she didn't love him. Her mother, who was sitting there at the time, was horrified. After remonstrating with S. when the man was gone, she finally got S. to agree to meet him again and reconsider his potential as a husband.
>
> So the mother arranged for them to meet again, and this time S. said she liked him maybe "50 percent." He was angered by this, but at the pleadings of her mother agreed to stop and see S. when he returned from a visit to his village. S.'s parents knew that there was another bridal candidate lined up in the village and they, of course, feared S. would lose this good opportunity. So while he was in his village, S.'s mother went to Sayyida A. to consult with her on how to make her daughter more tractable so that if the man returned S. would accept him. Sayyida A. prayed with her and gave her some holy oil to sprinkle on the doorstep of the house and all the doorsills inside so that S. would become more tractable as she walked over them. In the end Sayyida A.'s cure was never tested, for the man married in his village and never returned to see S. S. had refused in any case to go see Sayyida A., so it could be argued that the full effect of her capabilities had not been tested.

The contrast between Sayyida A. and the seer (discussed in Chapter 9) is a contrast between one who deals with temporarily errant individuals and satanic forces that must be dispelled and one who challenges the power of God by looking into the future and influencing the thoughts of other people. The first retains the aura of respectability, being still compatible with what at the local level is taken to be Christian doctrine. The other is anathema to both Islam and Christianity alike, though both formal religious organs may studiously ignore such practices.

Though spirit possession and faith healing have been illustrated here by mainly lower-class examples, the phenomenon is not confined to these

classes only. Frequently middle-class individuals resort to such practitioners also. Those who are more "scientifically" minded have little opportunity to relieve their psychological frustrations in an explicit way through
consultation with specialists since psychiatry is still in the formative stages
in Egypt. They must either project their discomforts into other kinds of
neurotic behavior or concretize them into physical illnesses that can be
treated.

CONTEMPORARY DIRECTIONS

Both Christian and Muslim communities in Egypt have experienced a religious resurgence in recent years, the Christians at least partly as a result
of what they see as the growing menace of Islam. As witnessed historically, the church appears to revive its dynamism particularly during periods
when it feels exposed to what it sees as physical or psychological persecu-
tion. Recent signs of resurgence appeared in the 70s and early 80s in a new
emphasis on monasticism and retreats; an increased incidence of reported
miracles, particularly around the early 70s when there were numerous sight-
ings of the Virgin at Zeitoun; a greater willingness to show public disapproval of incidents affecting Christians through fasting, public statements,
and soliciting international support. This activity of the church culminated
in the banishment of Pope Shenuda to a monastery in the Wadi Natroun
and the imprisonment of a number of Coptic bishops and priests by President Sadat in the summer of 1981 at the same time that he was taking
strong measures against Islamic and other dissident groups.

From the late 60s the resurgence of Islam brought new forces to bear,
first on the college campuses and later on broader areas of the society.
Islam, however, tended to remain split between a number of groups with
very different means and ends. Broadly speaking, at least four stand out:
(1) the progressively liberal who sought to modernize society according to
international standards; (2) the formal religious structure of the Al-Azhar
establishment that for the most part was obligated to the government for
its positions and political power; (3) Islamic fundamentalists seeking
through peaceful means to establish an Islamic society; (4) and Islamic
militants dedicated to the rooting out of non-Islamic corrupting influences
even if it meant using the force of arms. The significance of the militant
threat only became fully realized when a small number of them succeeded
in assassinating President Sadat in October of 1981.

While these political developments were emerging, a number of other developments with more direct influence on the family were also taking place — promoted by the various religious denominations according to their own objectives.

Christian Entrenchment

The contemporary concerns of Christianity and Islam diverge in ways similar to the divergences of their institutions, family structures, and ideologies. Many arise out of the implications of what people see as their special vulnerabilities. Christianity, for example, recognizes its vulnerability as coming from the increasing strength of Islam and the potential for Muslim institutions to absorb areas of controls previously reserved for Christians. Their active efforts have been directed at closing ranks, at preserving what areas they already control, and at keeping at bay what they perceive as the potential Islamic breach of their community boundaries. A key area of importance is the domain of family; if Christians can raise children loyal to the religion, find good Christian spouses for them, and the children live happily ever after, the essential boundaries of Christian community have been maintained. The Christians see the preservation of their own personal-status laws as crucial to this process and one of the most effective means of maintaining the distinction between Christian and Muslim communities.

It was to be expected then that the Christian community reacted apprehensively to talk of making the Muslim sharia the basis of the law of Egypt and extending its jurisdiction to areas broader than that of simple, personal-status provisions.

By 1979 a general committee composed of, among others, the speaker of the People's Assembly, the Grand Sheikh of Al-Azhar, and the Minister of Waqfs, and a number of subcommittees were meeting to formulate laws closer to the original sharia model in broad areas outside of the personal-status provisions. Dr. Abu Taleb, the speaker, announced on December 5, 1979 that the laws on the procedures for litigation were almost ready but that the committee for commercial dealings was expected to take some time before finally presenting their draft suggestions. Dr. Abu Taleb hastened to add that the committees intended to assure that the new laws would in no way conflict with other religions (*Egyptian Gazette*, December 6, 1979).

Christians had been reassured before by other mosque authorities, government officials, and Muslim intellectuals but were not convinced that their institutions were secure. In recent years, particularly, they have experienced an erosion of their institutions through nationalization of their schools and hospitals. Further, a reorganization of the court system in 1956 that shifted judicial hearings from religious to civil national courts tended to blur the edges of personal status separateness. What were being abolished, said the Christians, were the communal non-Muslim courts since the Muslim sharia judges would simply shift to the new national courts and judge personal status cases of both Muslims and non-Muslims alike, still, however, according to their separate personal-status laws. In two instances, where the parties concerned were affiliated with different Christian denominations or when one of the parties had adopted Islam, the courts were able to apply Muslim sharia laws even in the cases of Christians.

Upon the publication of the new law abolishing the sharia courts, the leaders of all the Christian communities gathered together and unanimously adopted a memorandum which they presented to President Nasser on October 3, 1955. They asserted that the new legislation threatened "the very existence of Christianity in Egypt by legally authorizing fraudulent maneuvers in religious matters."[3]

Much later in the spring of 1978 the following case, reported here from newspaper accounts, heightened the concern of Christians who continued to criticize the potential of new legislation to raise havoc with their careful mechanisms for controlling the break-up of families. The newspaper account is entitled provocatively: "Christians may marry four wives." The case concerns a judge's ruling in the case of a Christian man who was being accused by his first wife of contracting a bigamous marriage with another woman. The first wife asked that the second marriage be repealed on the grounds that the Christian religion entitles a man to only one wife. The judge, however, upheld the contention of the deputy public prosecutor that the law of the land be applied to all personal status disputes. Since the law of the land was Islamic law, the judge was ruling in favor of the validity of the second marriage (*Egyptian Gazette,* April 7, 1978, p. 3).

Strictly speaking, the judge, ruling under the provision that those of separate denominational background follow Islamic law, was not exceeding the requirements of the law in this case. It is unclear whether it was the publicity surrounding the case and the way it was reported that provoked such controversy or whether the church felt this a flagrant attempt in the new climate of Islamic resurgence to take advantage of legal provisions in order to strike at the heart of Christian insecurity. What resulted was that the several denominations of Christianity met together to form a united front against this form of slippage within their legal structure. In August of 1980, two years later, a special committee completed the first unified bill of personal status applicable to Christians of all sects in Egypt. With more than a hundred articles, the bill contained provisions concerning engagement, marriage, divorce, and other matters. Divorce was forbidden for Catholics but permitted among non-Catholics in the case of adultery and for six other reasons tantamount to adultery. (*Al-Ahram,* August 26, 1980). By May of 1981 the Cabinet was preparing to discuss and approve the Christian Personal Status bill in its final draft (*Al-Ahram,* May 2, 1981).

While Christianity was building its defenses against breakdown of the family and directing much of its attention to the potential intrusion of Islam, the Muslim community was reappraising the modern direction of family institutions as a whole and finding them wanting in many respects.

Islamic Reappraisal

There were at least two directions that Islamic thinking took, directions that for the sake of brevity are called here "progressive" and "fundamentalist." The progressives, many of whom have a great deal of experience in international forums, were looking at the disjunctions of the legal codes with the changes that had occurred in modern life and were attempting to institute legal reforms that would bring the provisions more in line with these realities. The "fundamentalists" on their side were disenchanted with what they saw as a basic modern moral collapse and the inability of any modern ideology to show a way to the solution of society's ills. Both took a long, hard look at family and both imagined a separate direction to the problems that faced the institution.

Progressives

The progressives focused their attentions on reforms in the sharia laws of personal status that would be more fitting under contemporary conditions. Since most of the contemplated reforms involved women, many observers spoke of them as reflecting feminist inclinations. In fact, however, they were not, in the mode of Western feminism, designed to bring women equality under the law. Instead they were designed to give women a more secure place within the family unit. In most essential public areas, such as the right to vote, the right to own and disperse property, and the right to equal pay, women legally already have the same rights as men in Egypt. In fact the argument can be made that women are "too equal" under the law, with so many protections and special benefits that it may work to their detriment in private hiring. Where women felt vulnerable was in the household, where at the whim of a man they might be cast out with little economic security and little regard paid to their years of homemaking service. It was in this area that the progressives hoped to bolster the woman's position.

To talk of modern reforms in the personal-status laws it is necessary to return to the early decades of this century in order to show the full extent of the difficulty reformers faced. Earlier we spoke of the remarkable stability of family law when compared with the major changes in other civil and commercial jurisdictions of Islamic law. While other areas of law could be transformed in comprehensive ways each minor modification of the personal-status laws took years of persuasion and preparation.

Most writers credit religious reformers of the turn of the century with preparing the groundwork for changes that are only recently being realized. Foremost among those calling for reforms in the family law were Muhammed Shakri, Qasim Amin, and Muhammed Abdu. In the several centuries before their advent, little movement had taken place in these areas of the sharia law.

A law concerning capital homicide enacted in 1880 set a precedent for some flexibility in the school of interpretation the Egyptian jurists could use in divorce proceedings. On this basis a commission was set up in 1914 to choose provisions more suitable to the age from the four schools of Islamic jurisprudence (not just the Hanafi which previously served exclusively as a base for the Egyptian personal-status laws), but opposition forced the government to shelve the findings of the commission until the end of World War I. The first real reform came with Law No. 25 in 1920, derived from the Malki school of jurisprudence. It concerned the conditions under which a wife might separate from her husband (if he did not support her or had certain defects) or be declared divorced (if the defects prevented the resumption of marriage or if the man was missing for four years).

Those calling for reforms, however, were not satisfied with the modest gains of the 1920 law. The Union of Egyptian Women continued to demand a reconsideration of the system of divorce, raising the marriage age for females to sixteen, and other reforms, including opportunities for the higher education of girls (*Egyptian Gazette,* July 2, 1923).

Again in 1926, a commission was established to formulate a family law after the ideas of Mohammad Abdu. The final draft was so strongly opposed by a number of Al-Azhar scholars that it was temporarily shelved. Three years later the draft was revived and with many of its key provisions omitted (limits on polygamy, making all a wife's marriage contract stipulations valid, and certain provisions entitling an injured wife to divorce) passed as Law No. 25 of 1929. The primary reforms concerned the conditions under which *talaq* divorce could be pronounced, some of the conditions under which a wife could ask for divorce, discretionary custody extension for children (to 9 for boys and 11 for girls), and stipulations about a divorced woman's maintenance (to not more than one year).

The Ministry of Social Affairs attempted to revive the anti-polygamy measures of the 1926 committee again in 1945 and failed. On the fourth try to revive the idea after the Revolution in 1953, the Ministry, according to one source, felt that conditions had changed and divorce and polygamy were no longer major problems in Egyptian society (Abu Zahra n.d.: 13). In 1960 at a conference of the National Unions the idea was yet again discussed but dropped when President Nasser commented that such matters were social and religious and should be handled by guidance rather than through laws (Abu Zahra n.d.).

Still, enough sentiment supported the reform of personal-status laws for the government again to form a committee composed mainly of male conservatives to review the laws. In 1966 the committee came out with its proposals which, to no one's surprise, avoided most of the hoped-for reforms except the proposal to abolish the *bayt al-taa,* the requirement that a woman who left her husband could be forced to return to his house (al-Nowaihi 1979: 44). Criticisms of the inadequacy of the reforms by Egyptian intellectuals were abruptly cut off by the 1967 war and not resumed until the early seventies.

An attempt by the then Minister of Social Affairs, Dr. Aisha Rateb, to revive the issue in March of 1974 similarly failed because of opposition from Al-Azhar. When she submitted her draft proposal to the Parliament, about a hundred students demonstrated and promised more serious consequences should the measures be passed. It was clear that the reforms would never be enacted without a skillful presentation that could neutralize the opposition.

And indeed more than a year later in February of 1976 it appeared that impeccable backing for the reforms had finally been assembled. A committee of the Academy of Islamic Research headed by the powerful Sheikh of Al-Azhar endorsed a new draft which was submitted to the Ministry of Justice. The draft, a watered-down version of earlier proposals, not only had the strong backing of Al-Azhar but was widely believed also to have the support of Mme. Sadat. With such formidable support, the *New York Times* on March 7, 1976 announced that the draft was "certain to be enacted." But yet again, by the time the bill was submitted to the People's Assembly in August of 1976, enough opposition was mobilized to frustrate the hopes of the reformers.

It is well to consider for a moment the issues on which the opposition base their resistance. Some argue that legal provisions are flexible enough as they are and only require more just and full use. Others resist any attempt to tamper with what are seen as divinely inspired laws. The third group simply finds no social problem that needs correcting. One writer representing this last group, for example, produced statistics to show that "divorce is not the direct producer of homeless children and vagabonds" (Abu Zahra n.d.: 30). He argued that since the negative effects of divorce are minimal, there is no need for reform.

The advocates of divorce reforms see a much broader range of problems requiring solution. They argue that without the sense of security that comes from stronger rights for women in marriage, polygamy, and divorce, tensions may be created within the household that lead to undesirable effects. In addition to the strains on the marriage relation, they cite the negative consequences of women resorting to more childbearing in order to secure the affections of their husbands. The most vocal of the organizations advocating this last position was the non-governmental Cairo Family Planning Association that numbered among its members some of the foremost progressive reformers in the tradition of the early feminist activists.

The Cairo Family Planning Association held a seminar on the legal status of women in February 1978. At the seminar, the late Dr. Mohammad Al-Nowaihi presented a paper[4] in which he argued that *ijtihad,* the right for a scholar to strive to form his own opinion, had been effectively shut in the "dark" ages making it impossible to form opinions suitable for modern times. Were *ijtihad* reopened, as called for by reformers of this and the last century, the disjunctions in the law could be repaired within the legitimizing framework of the sharia.

Subsequently, and stemming from the discussions of the seminar, the Cairo Family Planning Association initiated a project to draft their own comprehensive family code that they hoped to see adopted by the People's Assembly. Specifically, the provisions called for explicit statements of the rights and obligations of husbands and wives rather than leaving these matters to interpretation by judges, raising the minimum marriage age, giving women the unrestricted right to work, and requiring that a man advise his wife before marrying again and permitting the second marriage only after a judge finds that there is justifiable reason and a sufficient financial ability to maintain both wives. If the second marriage is objectionable to the first wife, she can obtain a divorce with indemnity. Divorce at the request of either party was to take effect by the sentence of the judge and only when all the steps at reconciliation had been taken and failed.

Girls were to remain in the custody of their mothers until marriage and boys until the age of 14 when their opinions should be considered. The welfare of the children in all cases should be considered paramount.

The women who proposed these reforms systematically embarked on a program to draft a code and recruit public and government figures to promote their acceptance. Their plans, however, stalled in the early months of 1979. According to a member of the group, the publicity surrounding the contemplated reforms aroused such opposition in conservative circles that the government backed away even from seriously considering them. Most were surprised, therefore, when President Sadat himself stepped in to initiate action on the question of reforms.

In March 1978, a month after the C.F.P.A.'s seminar, President Sadat called on the government to issue a law on personal status that would ensure the security and protection of Egyptian women before the end of the parliamentary session that year. In the absence of any action by the People's Assembly, the President decided to take steps on his own. Previously, Dr. Amal Osman, the Minister of Social Affairs, working quietly with her predecessor, asked the Al-Azhar sheikhs to indicate their objections to earlier reform drafts and eventually obtained their approval of a new draft. On June 20, 1979, while the People's Assembly was in recess, President Sadat, using the new draft bill, issued a Republican decree amending some of the articles of the personal-status laws for Muslims (Law No. 25 of 1929). He based his initiative on the constitutional authorization for a president to issue decrees that would become effective subject to the approval of the People's Assembly. Two days later a telecast symposium attended by the Grand Sheikh of Al-Azhar, the Minister of Waqfs and the Grand Mufti gave an indispensable stamp of the religious hierarchy's support for the measures.[5] In the symposium, the participants noted the need for modifications and clarifications in the previous laws to bring them more closely in line with the intent of the sharia.

With this kind of support and backing, the opposition was never able to mobilize its forces sufficiently and at their first meeting after the recess, on July 2, 1979, the Assembly voted overwhelmingly in favor of the amendments. The 33 women members of Parliament agreed among themselves not to comment during the debate for fear of arousing the opposition of the Sheikhs of Al-Azhar, without whose strong backing the measure could not be passed.

One member of Parliament commented that the subject of whether or not women should act as an opposition block had been discussed before. It was generally agreed that with "appropriate" issues like cleanliness campaigns it was safe for them to do so, but that with more controversial issues it was better that they vote individually or in governorate level blocs to avoid coalescing opposition to them as a group.

Though many of the women had reservations about certain parts, the bill (see Chapter 12 for more details) had to be passed or rejected as a whole, and they were afraid if they debated the issue they might undermine the limited gains the bill would bring. For the women, the greatest gains of the bill were the options of the judge to extend the period when a mother would have custody of her children and the financial disincentives to marital breakup. Most would have preferred also to see reforms requiring judicial adjudication of all divorce proceedings. Those still opposing the measures included the fundamentalist groups and one of their popular sheikhs, Kishk, who was particularly critical of giving women the right to work. There was also a lingering number from the *Ulama* who opposed the measures. The leader of this Al-Azhar opposition was Moussa Lashin, vice-dean of the university who expressed his thoughts on the personal-status laws in two articles in the weekly *Shaeb* magazine. He was reportedly later demoted for the part he played in opposing the measures.

With such a sensitive issue it could be expected that opposition would continue to be voiced. Some of the most resistant were the judges who were forced to alter the basis on which they had ruled in the past. *Al-Ahram*'s main story on March 2, 1982, for example, reported the case of a judge in an Aswan court who rejected the divorce petition of a wife based on her disapproval of the second marriage of her husband. Even though the new laws gave her this option, the court ruled that this ground for divorce was inconsistent with both Islamic laws and the constitution and referred the pertinent article in the personal-status law to the higher constitutional court for its abolishment.

The very difficulty of passing these reforms and the resistance they aroused even after their passage attests to the basic differences within Islamic circles in Egypt. In general, however, all these circles share the belief that any changes must at least be consistent with sharia law by bringing legal principles back to a purer and more authentic Islam; where they disagree is in the definition of what is pure and authentic. Many progressives still feel the reforms have not gone far enough to limit the prerogative of the husband to divorce his wife easily or take other wives. But they are generally pleased that a start has been made to bring the law more closely in line with contemporary conditions. In the next chapter we will examine what the specific provisions of the reforms reflect of changing family patterns.

Those in opposition to the reforms were not a monolithic group.

Some, as we noted, came from the Al-Azhar religious establishment. Others with less access to public forums to demonstrate their opposition came from Islamic fundamentalist groups that are in principle wary of any modifications in the sharia, especially those modifications coming from the "progressive" elements in society.

Fundamentalists

Much has been written recently on the politics of resurgent Islam in Egypt. Since the assassination of President Sadat in the fall of 1981 by the hand of Islamic fundamentalists, the topic has gained world-wide attention. Here we are more interested in the social aspects of the movement and its relation to family organization.

Though the specifics of the fundamentalist ideology differ according to the group which articulates it, in general one can say that fundamentalists believe that the answers to the problems of modern life can be found within the guide lines of religious teaching. For the most part they are disillusioned with the "-isms" — socialism, nationalism, modified capitalism — that have not solved their country's problems. They are searching for a formula that inspires them and gives them some hope against the ever-increasing difficulties of living in Egyptian society.

The appeal of Islam and its convenience as a base from which to stir the emotions of many is not difficult to observe. It sets out a plan for the moral life, reminds people five times a day of their obligations to its tenets, and provides the organizational structure of meeting places, spokesmen, and messages that give a sense of connectedness to individuals. More important in Egypt, Islam's claim of indigenous status makes it seem more authentic than other recent political ideologies. More than other religious philosophies, it has frankly political implications.

Egyptians usually trace the beginnings of the current movement to the period shortly after the devastating defeat suffered at the hands of the Israelis in June of 1967. The defeat had such a demoralizing effect on people, the explanation goes, that they began to question why they seemed to have been totally abandoned by the divine authority. The answer, they concluded, lay in the general moral collapse of Egyptian officials and ordinary people.

Some noted in particular the emphasis during the Nasser period on secular as opposed to religious issues, especially after the Muslim Brotherhood was officially abolished two years after the Revolution. Those who thought this way reasoned that the only hope for a better future lay in a revival of a moral religious way of life interpreted as closely as possible according to the teachings of the Prophet. The turn to a more rigid fundamentalism was not so much a return to an older way of life as it was to a new emphasis on use of the religious frame to interpret life events and a willingness to submit to the rigors of behaving according to its precepts.

From one of the few systematic studies of the movement, in this case a study of a militant group, the *Taqfir w Higra,* we learn something about the typical profile of some of the most extreme of the fundamentalists. They are young (early 20s), rural or small town background, middle or lower-middle class, upwardly mobile, from a normally cohesive family, with high achievement motivation and often coming from a science or engineering education (S. Ibrahim 1980: 30). In their generation they were significantly above the average. At the time of the study, those interviewed were incarcerated as result of their organization's participation in the kidnapping and assassination of the Minister of Waqfs. Before this event half of them had been living in the cities by themselves or with roommates rather than in their parental homes. (S. Ibrahim 1980: 28).

The fact that the students were somewhat at loose ends (most had lived in small communities as teens), away from parental controls, may have been a contributory factor in the extremity of their position. In many cases the fundamentalist peer group served as a reference point by which the morally sure-of-themselves students became alienated from their center-of-the-road bourgeois parents. It is interesting in this respect to note two of the findings of the study. The researchers commented that they never heard anything at all about the interests of the individual; it was always the interests of the *umma* (the community of the faithful) that was considered important (S. Ibrahim 1980: 17). Second, the respondents conceded social differentiation as a part of the Muslim social order but found acceptable only a differentiation based on a man's labor (S. Ibrahim 1980: 18). For a socially mobile group in a class-conscious society this conception must have seemed requisite to their own future acceptance.

Those who paid at least some lip service to the fundamentalist principles were of course much more broadly based than the extreme militant groups. A large number of young Egyptians were swept up with the greater religiosity of the times, committing themselves to, if nothing else, the outward symbols of religious observation rather than actively working toward shaping a new form of society. It is true to say, however, that the majority of their numbers were coming, as with the militants, from the lower-middle and middle classes,[9] particularly from among those droves of young people who were the first generation in their families to obtain long-term university education. These were the classes and the individuals whose hopes for a better life were aroused by their educational opportunities but who were increasingly seeing the possibilities for suitable jobs with sufficient incomes closed to them. Large-scale acceptance of outward symbols of commitment to Islamic practices made the active elements in the movement appear even greater than they actually were. Observers tended, for example, to gauge the strength of the movement by a head count of those wearing the modern Islamic costume for women (*zey Islami*), and as the headcount increased dramatically over the years in the major cities the movement seemed to take on ominous proportions.

The use of the so-called Islamic costume exemplifies several facets of the Islamic movement that are central; in particular, the various levels and depths of participation and the way customary symbols were used and rearranged into a complex new style with new meanings. Fundamentally, wearing the costume was, among other things, an attempt to infuse new meaning into sex-role differentiation in a middle-class society where widespread education and employment of women were rapidly breaking down the strict segregation of gender roles. It was a reminder of the special sexual roles of women as childbearers, as the central core of households, and as the recipients of the supportive and protective attentions of men.

The significant Islamic features of women's dress are that the figure will be modestly covered and there will be no elements designed actively to draw attention to the woman. Though the Koran is not always clear on what modesty entails, it has generally been held by the orthodox that part or all of the arms should be covered, the neck, all of the hair, from neck to knee, and perhaps more of the body down to wrist and ankle. In recent years before the Islamic resurgence, use of such patterns had been mainly confined to rural and urban lower classes. The educated classes considered such dress backward and traditional and recognized its use as based more on custom than religion. The fundamentalists were interested in reviving these traditional symbols without compromising their status in society by using symbols that could be confused with lower-class standing. In reality they used the same modesty symbols as the lower classes but rearranged them into a new costume that could be easily distinguished from those socially "inferior" classes.

There are several versions of the Islamic costume, some of which are motivated less by religion and more by fashion. Older women, for example, find longer dresses and hair-covering turbans more comfortable and flattering and if asked will answer that while inspired by what they consider the precepts of their religion to dress modestly, they dress in this way mainly because it has become fashionable in their circles to do so. Such a modified style, though reaching to the ankles and the wrists, is characterized often by its closer fit. To purists of the fundamentalist movement it is too revealing of the figure. The "standard fundamentalist" version flows from shoulder to ankle, usually in one somber color, concealing the outlines of the figure as completely as possible. The head covering surrounds the face like a nun's cowl and falls loosely to the shoulder. A subsidized version of this style is sold by fundamentalist organizations for 8£E ($12), making it very economical.

University girls who assume this costume almost certainly do so out of religious conviction since it is a big change from the everyday "foreign" dress styles of the rest of the middle class and is publicly recognized as being associated with a fundamentalist perspective. Some girls say that as one becomes purer in heart — more dedicated to following a strict Islamic life — one should move to ever greater levels of concealment, to wearing gloves, for example, and a face veil with or without eye holes that are covered by glasses. Others believe this is an extreme interpretation of the admittedly ambiguous Koranic injunctions about dress for women.[7] It is important to note that there is no consistent pattern to Islamic dress, though it is clearly distinguishable on the street from customary traditional costumes and from other forms of middle-class garb. However, except in extreme cases it is very difficult to gauge the level of an individual's religious or political commitment from observing the dress.

In the following example a young married woman is talking about the experiences of the women in her family. The speaker herself wears simple "Western" clothes; her graduate student sister, S., wears the form-fitting Islamic dress out of a serious religious conviction. The father, who happens to be a Sheikh of Al-Azhar, permits his daughters to make their own choices about dress. Since Al-Azhar is often at odds with the fundamentalists, he would not be particularly interested in seeing his daughters join the movement. In this case it is a personal religious conviction that motivates S.

> Dress is partly the experiences and background of the person and the environment in which she makes her choices. My mother remembers her own mother veiling and is therefore desirous of escaping from this oppression. It was her generation's way of liberating themselves. I am five years older than my sister, S., and it is enough to make us feel differently about dress. As a high school and university student I was keen on wearing modern styles — times were hard then, and it was a treat to have nice modern clothes like the rest of the world. Now the times are different — many more want to wear Islamic dress. I agree it is good for women to do as our religion says and cover themselves modestly, but I still think of it as a step backward. For S. and her friends, even though they insist it is out of religious conviction, it is

easy to take up Islamic dress because more are doing so now. Anyway they see it as a free choice they can make. They have no recollection of the veiling that went before. Because they choose it, it is not oppressive.

Frequently girls say their mothers are more opposed to them wearing Islamic dress than are their fathers. They explain this reaction by saying, as the young woman above, that their middle-class mothers see it as a step backward to a more oppressive time for women, and their fathers see it as showing a willingness on the girl's part to be chaste, modest, and all the things that attract good husbands and preserve the reputation of the family.

Girls of even younger age have been turning to some vestige of religious conservatism. What is said to have started as a style in the conservative Islamic university of Al-Azhar (and as of February 13, 1981 was made required dress there) has spread to other universities and down into secondary and younger grades. In the latter, the principle visible evidence is the very high incidence of scarves now worn with the pant-suit school uniforms. Here again government officials in occasional school jurisdictions have made the use of scarves mandatory.

One young twelve-year-old explained her feelings about wearing Islamic dress. She was astonishingly conversant with Koranic verses to back her theological arguments about this and other issues:

> When I first get my period I will begin wearing Islamic dress because it is what God wants. He places angels on both shoulders of a person — one which watches all the good deeds one does and one which watches all the bad. At the day of judgment the list of these deeds will be tabulated to determine whether one goes to Paradise or not. If I were not to wear Islamic dress it would be one serious mark against me. My sister [seventeen years old] does not wear it, and for sure she will be punished eventually by God. It worries my father, but he says we must decide for ourselves or we will not be sincere in our faith. He is pleased when I say I want to wear Islamic dress. I learned most of what I know about religious matters from my father rather than in school. My mother has started wearing Islamic dress and she prays constantly, but we never have much time to talk to her because she works and is busy all the time.

Individual Egyptians who are espousing greater religious conservatism through dress and other means are finding that in many ways the Islamic dress helps solve some of the problems they face in large urban areas like Cairo. These may seem insignificant when compared with the political implications of Islamic fundamentalism, but they may be extremely significant when a person chooses to adopt the new modes of behavior. The following is a "progressive" Muslim speaking and trying to rationalize in her own mind why people she knows are so attracted to either the movement or the vestiges of the movement:

> There are many reasons Islamic dress is attractive to young girls now. In the first place it is cheap, and there is no need for a whole wardrobe of matching clothes and accessories. The hair is hidden so they avoid the high cost and time that it takes to go to the hairdresser. We're all hit by inflation these days and students in particular have a hard time making ends meet. Also when they commute long distances to university by public transportation, they indicate to others their untouchableness, maybe avoiding some of the indignities that the rest of us suffer. One of the most important reasons for wearing Islamic dress is that girls nowadays are caught between two systems for getting married: by arrangement, which many educated girls reject, and by falling in love, which is difficult to do because the movements of boys and girls are so carefully regulated. A girl wearing Islamic dress announces herself to be one of the moral types men like to marry and maybe attracts a man's attention on campus as a result. If she stands talking to a man or has tea with him, everyone assumes because of her outfit that it is an innocent encounter. People laugh and say that one can't guarantee what is under the dress but in general it may have certain advantages.

We have concentrated our analysis of the social aspects of fundamentalism on wearing of Islamic dress. This is because space prevents a full explication of the social ramifications of the movement and because wearing of the Islamic dress indicates in a broad way some of the dynamics of who joins, at what level, and for what reasons.

The contemporary social movement of Islam protects the gender role differences of women by encouraging, among other means, self-imposed normative restrictions—Islamic "nice-girl" constructs—similar to those we saw in Chapter 9. Students have also been vocal in calling for other ways of protecting the physical presence of women: by calling for sex-separated places for prayer at the university, separate seating in classrooms, and separate accommodation on public transportation. The movement, in effect, reaffirms that women's primary responsibility is in the home.

Most adherents of fundamentalism, however, would not ask a young woman to turn back the pages to the time when the decent Muslim "nice girl" remained confined to the household proper and only went out when she was "born, married, and died."[8] The large majority of the young women involved peripherally or intensively in fundamentalist movements are obtaining or have obtained educational degrees, and many are employed. The way women explain this is to say that modern conditions require better preparation for motherhood and may even require that a woman prepare herself to work if necessary to help her family. In other words, the expanded role of motherhood is not rejected as long as the activity the woman engages in is subservient to the fulfillment of her maternal and housewifely roles. The emphasis on the appropriate Islamic "public dress," in a way, symbolizes acceptance of the fact that women will and must go out in public in today's Egypt.

The hue and cry has been great with regard to Islamic dress, with critics and proponents lining up in their respective corners. Where other sensitive issues are often ignored by the press, Islamic dress has captured an unusual amount of attention with the liberal internationally oriented writers almost always critical of its use. "Whether to veil or unveil" is the subject of a column in *Al-Ahram* on January 14, 1980. The columnist quotes a prominent sheikh who concludes that these matters cannot be legislated, that it is a woman's honorable intentions that count. Another article in *Al-Gomhuria* criticizing the clothing of Egyptian girls in garments similar to their grandmothers' stimulated so many negative responses that the columnist was forced to write again justifying his claim that women wear clothing suitable to modern conditions (reported in *Egyptian Gazette,* March 26, 1980). On the other side, Shaheen in *Al-Akhbar* (December 14, 1980) criticized the "monkey-like imitation of our youngsters, both boys and girls of all that comes from the West. . . ." He goes on to say that Egyptians should carefully consider what they adopt. "The tight jeans adapted to the daughter of Uncle Sam will never suit an Egyptian girl. They expose more than they hide" (reported in the *Egyptian Gazette,* December 15, 1980). El Ghazali returns with an attack on the fundamentalists: "As it turns out, the ugly costume they have come up with has nothing to do with Islam in any case; it is a relic of pre-Islamic ignorance. . . . Apart from being utterly silly in its own right . . . it gives rise to equally silly and needless controversy at home and invites ridicule from thoughtless writers around the world" (*Egyptian Gazette,* February 3, 1981).

Even though activist Muslims became increasingly polarized into progressive and fundamentalist camps in recent years, both included within their vision of a better society images of a more stable, cohesive family with women occupying a central and protected role. Each worked toward this goal in its own way, the progressives through legal reforms in personal-status laws that gave women a more secure place in their homes and with their children. The fundamentalists on their side reemphasized the special role of women and reasserted their commitment to the family as a basic unit of Islamic society.

12

New Conditions

"Your nearby neighbor rather than your far-away brother"
— Arab proverb

IN RECENT YEARS, a number of new circumstances have affected most Egyptians in indirect if not direct ways. Their significance lies in the extent to which they have measurably changed the environment in which contemporary families must operate. The five examined here — the population explosion, urbanization, internal and external migration, the spread of educational opportunities, and certain economic changes — are so interrelated that their impacts can scarcely be separated. Necessarily these external changes challenge traditional values, strengthening some, allowing others to atrophy, causing the modification of implications of others, sometimes even requiring that people dip down into the recesses of their conceptual frames for an application that has suddenly become appropriate. There has, however, been no overwhelming shift to another cultural "grammar" even when people, through the media, have been subjected to large doses of alien views.

POPULATION EXPLOSION

In April, 1980 the Egyptian population passed the 42 million mark, an increase of 1.2 million in just one year. With an annual rate of population increase standing at 2.31 percent between 1966 and 1976, 43 percent of Egyptians are now under the age of 15 (CAPMAS). If the increase con-

235

tinues at such rates there will be a population of 66 million by the year 2000, with perhaps up to 15 million living in Cairo alone (against 5.5 million in 1980). The accelerated pace of the population growth and its implications are perhaps demonstrated most forcefully by the rapidly diminishing man-to-land statistics. In 1805 with a population of only 3 million and an equivalent number of feddans of arable land, each Egyptian was supported by one feddan. With 40 million people and 6 million cultivated feddans the number has how dwindled to one-seventh of a feddan per individual Egyptian (from *Al-Akhbar,* reported in the *Egyptian Gazette,* October 15, 1980). Projections into the future show this ratio decreasing at an even more alarming rate.

URBANIZATION AND MIGRATION

As a result of the land squeeze — a decreasing capacity for so many to live off so little land — and the attraction of city living, rural populations accelerated their migrations to the city in the 70s. The pretest results of a National Center for Social and Criminological Research urban survey conducted in 1979 reported that 70 percent of urban household heads were born in rural areas and migrated to cities during their life times. A National Planning Institute conference on migration in 1979 identified the chief cause of migration as the economic gap between cities and rural areas: the location of major industries, relatively better services and public utilities in cities, the slowdown in land-reclamation projects, and the surpluses of farm labor.

Egypt is urbanizing both absolutely and relatively. All cities have increased in population, but secondary and tertiary cities have demonstrated the greatest growth rate. Between 1966 and 1976 the total population grew at a rate of 2.1 percent while the urban population grew at a rate of 3 percent. Between 1947 and 1976 the urban population, as a ratio of the total population, rose from 32.6 percent to 43.9 percent. The population of Greater Cairo alone rose to 20 percent of the total population by 1980. (All figures from the Central Agency for Public Mobilization and Statistics, or CAPMAS.)

Migration from the rural to urban areas has attracted primarily two kinds of Egyptians: the rural poor, migrating to earn better incomes in the city and to escape the drudgery of agricultural labor, and the newly educated whose diplomas fit them better for jobs that are more available in the cities. The irony for the poor is that they have difficulty competing for better paid manual labor in sectors such as the construction industries, while in rural areas in various parts of Egypt agricultural wages have soared. CAPMAS estimates that 100,000, or about 1 in 80, work in Cairo in what the government considers the "parasitic" job of street vending.

Migration out of Egypt[1] has also witnessed two kinds of emigrant: those who go temporarily in search of work (usually to the Arab countries of the Gulf, Saudi Arabia, Libya, and Algeria) and those who seek permanent migration (usually to Australia, Britain, France, or the United States). Though both groups seek better incomes and opportunities the first includes people from all walks of life — the educated and uneducated, the manually skilled and the unskilled, farmers and urbanites, teachers and technicians — while the second is often referred to as the "brain drain" because of the mostly trained talent that is lost to Egyptian development.

In 1979, for example, the newspapers reported that 1300 Egyptians in the previous six years had not returned after postgraduate studies abroad, and in 1979 alone one-third of the 820 awarded Ph.D.s did not come back. The reports concluded that Egyptians in these categories did not return because of the high rents and low salaries at home and the difficulty in getting posts appropriate to their qualifications.

Though reliable statistics are difficult to find, in one People's Assembly debate, a member estimated that migration to earn income had jumped from 100,000 in 1965 to two million in 1978. On the positive side of temporary migration are the foreign currency sums Egypt earns and the relief of pressures from the labor market at home where many are still un- or under-employed. The National Democratic Party reported that Egyptians working abroad had transferred 2,000 million pounds to Egypt during that fiscal year. On the negative side are the inflationary effects of new high incomes on domestic prices, the examples of conspicuous consumption, and the staggering increases of local wages in sectors affected by the migration.[2]

By 1983 there were indications that migration for work both within the country and to foreign countries was slowing. People were quick to point out the reasons why. It was becoming harder to find jobs in the oil-rich countries because of reduced oil revenues and the desire of those countries to hire less politically sensitive workers from outside the Arab world. Second, the costs to workers to arrange contracts abroad were rising to sometimes 1,000 £E or more. Third, better opportunities and higher pay in construction, skilled labor, and agriculture at home made migration less attractive. In Egypt itself, inflation and housing scarcities in urban areas suddenly made the prospects of commuting daily to work from villages or making a living in the countryside economically feasible.

A young married couple, both doctors, face the problem of combining home life and busy professional schedules with cheerful confidence.

THE SPREAD OF EDUCATIONAL OPPORTUNITIES

Though universal compulsory education laws have been in existence since 1923, serious efforts to provide sufficient facilities at the elementary school level were not undertaken until 1956. In 1962 formal fees for education were abolished, and in 1981 the government extended compulsory education to nine years of a Basic Education program. Though the authorities encouraged attendance for this longer period by raising the minimum work age from 12 to 15 years (amendment of Law No. 9 of 1959), until now they have not enforced compulsory education. An incentive to continue schooling has been the program instituted by President Nasser of guaranteed jobs upon completion of a university degree. Impressive gains have been made in school enrollments since the Revolution of 1952. In a National Center for Social and Criminological Research pretest for urban and rural surveys carried out in 1979, preliminary results showed an increase in the educational level of urban household heads over their fathers and of children over the household heads. In rural areas, household heads showed only a slight increase over their fathers while children showed a considerable increase over the household heads.

Nevertheless there is much ground yet to cover before the goal of universal education is reached in Egypt. According to 1976 census figures 56.5 percent of the population age 10 and above remain illiterate. Women's illiteracy ratio of those age 10 and above is 71 percent compared to a men's ratio of 43.2 percent. Nevertheless in the 1978–79 school year, 83 percent of six year-olds were enrolled in first grade and 68 percent of the relevant age group were enrolled in the six years of elementary school. Though the initial enrollments have grown rapidly, drop-out rates are still high, enrollments after elementary level drop off quickly and, because of the high birth rates, the absolute numbers of children out of school continue to climb. In 1975–76, 2.5 million children of primary age were not enrolled in school; by 1978–79, about 3 million were out of school, and by the year 2000 the number is projected to rise to 4.6 million or 86 percent more than 1976.[3]

In this transitional period when prolonged education is still a relatively scarce commodity, it plays an important social and economic role in Egypt. To a considerable extent it permits access to the opportunities that determine the level and distribution of individual income while qualifying people to reach valued social class statuses. Prolonged education serves as the most significant marker of the division between the lower and middle social classes, more significant even than such economic factors as income levels. The sizable growth in the middle class in recent decades has come about largely through the vehicle education provides for social mobility in Egypt.

One member of the People's Assembly said privately in 1981, "There are three things which we can't talk about in the Assembly and stay in office: family planning, modifying the Islamic laws and changing the education system. The first because our constituents think it is private, the second because it is religious, and the third because they all want their children to get an education and are afraid that changes will restrict their access to the more highly approved academic forms of education that give them social mobility."

The wider access of all children to schooling has led to rapid gains for women in entry to the professional fields considered, because of their intrinsic status value, to be most respectable for their sex. As early as 1960 it was discovered that urban women's labor force participation rates in non-agricultural economic activities rose dramatically in proportion to the prolongation of their educational experience, from 8.9 percent for illiterates and 2.9 percent for primary graduates, to 24.4 percent for secondary grad-

Today boys and girls of all classes spend much of their childhoods tending to the serious business of education.

uates and 70.5 percent for university graduates (Youssef 1976:202). The government's guaranteed jobs for university graduates helps by allowing women to enter certain jobs automatically without competing for entry with men.

ECONOMIC CHANGES

Initiated formally after the war of 1973 and slowly gaining momentum during the 70s, the "open door" policy was intended by President Sadat to encourage foreign capital investment in Egypt. It was part of an effort to move the Egyptian economy from its extensive reliance on public sector administration to an expanding share given over to the private sector. Proponents of the policy feel it has accomplished some of these aims while increasing the variety of goods (mostly imported) in the market and generally raising incomes.

An urban pretest conducted by the National Center for Social and Criminological Research in the spring of 1979 discovered that 60 percent of the scientifically selected sample did not favor the open door policy while the remaining 40 percent did. Critics claim that the policy has caused inflationary spirals, flooded the markets with largely luxury goods, and encouraged conspicuous consumption that has exacerbated socioeconomic distinctions in the society. They claim that foreign investors with their own profit motives in mind establish industries with little positive impact on unemployment and other development goals.

One of the issues opposition political parties from the right, left, and center are reported to be united over is what they see as the failures of the open door policy.

The government estimated the inflation rate for 1980 to stand at 16 percent, a drop from a high 25 percent in the previous year, according to the Minister of Finance, Fuad Hussain, in 1980. At the household level the enormous increases in prices that occurred starting in the middle and late 70s have not been compensated by comparable wage increases. In 1977 government announcements of reduction in subsidies for some essential goods touched off serious riots in Cairo.

A survey, as yet unpublished but thought by foreign development agencies to be reliable, reports that among urban households about 65 percent in 1979 had monthly expenditures of £E 100 or less (or were spending less than £E 3 a day). Urban households, relying, as they do, much more heavily on monetary exchanges, would in fact be expected to have greater monthly expenditures than rural families. This survey concludes that though income distribution curves do not appear to have changed significantly overall between 1974 and 1979 there is some evidence that there is increased concentration of wealth at the top and relative changes in the economic positions of certain households.

Another study of household expenditures[4] stimulated a newspaper editor to conclude that 66.8 percent of families were spending in round terms £E 1 ($1.40—there are 100 piasters to a pound) a day for all their necessities. The editorial continued: "What can really be purchased within this frugal budget? A kilo of beans cost approximately 35 piasters, the cheapest meat costs a pound a kilo and even a humble so-called luxury, a packet of cigarettes, costs 30 piasters. And then what about clothing and rent for a growing family?" (*Egyptian Gazette,* May 4, 1979).

Some of the hardest hit by the inflationary spiral were middle-class bureaucrats. Not only had they expended large amounts of resources obtaining their own training, only to be rewarded with poorly paying government jobs, but they had expectations that their own children would receive costly university training as well. It is costly in terms of wages lost, the lengthened period of dependency, and the expense of appropriate clothing, transportation, tutoring, and educational supplies borne by parents. These costs are significant to poor families.

In 1980 the minimum monthly wage in the public sector for the most minimally qualified employee was raised to £E 20. A year later in 1981 the starting salary of a university graduate entering government service was raised from £E 32 to £E 38. Cost of living allowances for government employees in 1981 were raised to £E 4 for a single person, £E 6 for a married man, £E 8 for a married couple with one child and so on up to a maximum allowance of £E 10 a month. A year earlier, married women were given a cost of living allowance of £E 3.

At the same time young graduates who elected to enter the private sector earned up to £E 200 a month and skilled technicians, plumbers and carpenters were easily earning £E 100 and more. The 1979 National Center for Social and Criminological Research pretest showed that of urban household heads about half reported higher incomes than their parents; children reported that about one-fourth had higher incomes than the household heads and the rest were about equally divided between those having the same and those having less income. In rural areas almost all reported the same as their parents' incomes while some of the children reported higher incomes and the rest lower incomes than the household heads.

The government was eager to cut down on the superfluity of government employees and in previous years had deliberately delayed the appointment of graduates to encourage them to seek work elsewhere. In June of 1981, for example, the Manpower Office announced that before the end of the year the 25,091 applicants for government jobs out of the total 56,471 graduates of June 1978 and January 1979 would be appointed—that is, two and a half to three years after their graduation.

Together these developments in the areas of changing population distributions and densities, economic and labor market imbalances, and new prerequisite educational attainments to achieve social goals created in the space of a few decades a very different ecological environment in which families had to function. Some of the most significant consequences in terms of family organization were the new physical and spatial constraints on family living, the competing sources for moral and other training of children, and the need to make new and difficult decisions about family resource generation and allocation.

CONSEQUENCES AND RESPONSES

Physical and Social Constraints of Urban Living

The whole complex of factors — of living densities, urban anonymity, separation from relatives, spatial limitations — makes it difficult in an urban environment for people to realize the ideals of behavior they might otherwise aspire to if conditions were more flexible.

The Potency of Family Name and Obligation

Egyptian peasants who migrate to cities recognize that there is a greater potency to family name and family obligations in rural areas than urban ones. Extended family as a balanced set of *wagib* support obligations is effective in the rural areas because kin work, play, and socialize together in physical proximity as a natural part of daily life. Kin develop an economic interdependence and a system of broad social controls that encourage members to seek their satisfactions within the group.

A lower-class rural migrant in urban Bulaq was asked why she inquired about the family name of a newcomer from her own village whom she was meeting for the first time: "We ask about family because in our own villages we know all the families. Once we know what family a person comes from then we know everything about them or at least whether the family has a good reputation or not. A single family can have rich and poor members but that is not so important as reputation."

When asked if she used the same identification process for city dwellers, she replied that there would be no reason to do so since families come from all over Egypt and it would be impossible to be familiar with all their reputations. "In the city we are more likely to ask where she lives because we know what the good areas are or look to see how she is dressed or how she behaves. But those things are not so sure as family is in the village." If it is remembered that the whole set of *wagib* relations needs to exist in its entirety for a potential balance of rights and obligations to be present for any individual, then some of the impact of migration to urban areas or abroad can be understood. Impersonality in a sense to an Egyptian means not being connected with the legal-moral relationship of obligation, even if that obligation is the weakest kind as with acquaintances or colleagues. Kin are, of course, those to whom the attachment is strongest, and though they may exist in urban areas,[5] it is rare to find the whole set of kin present or, even when present, close enough in the city to maintain effective daily relations.

Families in cities compensate for the lack of broader sets of conve
nient kin by placing greater reliance on nuclear family members and those
relatives who happen to be close at hand. In previous chapters we talked
about the practices of sisters' children marriage and sibling marriage as
adaptive in the urban environment in developing stronger emotional ties
in a more impersonal context. Where structurally under ideal conditions
one might be supposed to have warmer relations with a mother's sister one
might develop these relations with a father's sister instead in the city, sim
ply because she is available. Similarly, other people who can be co-opted
into a relationship on the more tenuous grounds that they are friend, of
fice colleague or neighbor may be upgraded to *uxt* (sister), *akh* (brother
or other relationships appropriate to their ages and the individual's needs
In this case the relationship is specifically a consequence of the sense of
impersonality and isolation people feel in the city.

The practice is more noticeable among the lower classes who have
migrated from rural areas and who, because of a precarious economic situa
tion, depend more strongly on support networks than it is among estab
lished middle-class urbanites who have long since made their adjustment
to city living. For the latter there are disadvantages to the encouragement
of a wider set of obligations than is necessary if these obligations may
require outlays from the family's fund of material and personal capital
In addition, the competition for educational achievement and status tends
to cut middle-class individuals off from others not identifiably of their
in-group. Even the middle classes, however, understand the importance of
keeping relationships activated in a social milieu where friends can be
counted on more than impersonal systems for achieving one's ends.

In this respect it is interesting to watch those who return from work
abroad. Anyone with a claim on the returnee expects a gift of some kind
It is up to the returnee to weigh the claims and judge the effectiveness of
the tie being re-established before dispensing gifts of carefully scaled value
The returnee judges also the services the person has provided to any per
son he has left behind and feels a sense of responsibility for. Gift giving
is a delicate and almost always conflict-producing activity that is remarked
upon for a long time afterward. It symbolizes how a person conceives of
his or her relationships.

Housing

Housing has become a scarce resource in urban areas in recent years
as a result of rapid population expansion, internal migration to cities, anti
quated rental laws, and insufficient attention to stimulating the housing
industry.

One compounding feature of the housing crisis is the 12,000 or so housing units that collapse yearly either because of age and poor condition or because new construction has been shoddy. Another unknown number of houses are in such substandard conditions that they would be abandoned if there were other places for their inhabitants to relocate (*Egyptian Gazette,* September 21, 1979 quoting housing experts). The government is attempting to reduce the problem by building about 675,000 flats between 1981 and 1985, amending rental laws to provide incentives to landlords to keep flats occupied, and by encouraging the private sector to become more involved in providing new housing units. In December 1979 the Minister of Reconstruction and Development, Hassaballa el Kafrawi, noted that the government was relying heavily on the six new communities being built outside of the present urban centers to house four million people by the year 2000.

Eilts (1980) estimates that the present shortage stands at around 1.6 million housing units with the additional need for about 100,000 flats a year. This figure may increase to a shortage of 3.6 million flats by the year 2000. It is reported that one half the population of Cairo is presently housed in one-room flats (*Egyptian Gazette,* September 21, 1979).

Whatever statistical estimates one accepts, urban Egyptians feel keenly the difficulty of locating housing or, if already possessing accommodations, of adjusting their housing to new needs. The topic comes up frequently in conversations that one hears everywhere, in homes, on the streets, and in offices. Cramped quarters are the rule rather than the exception. Where spacious apartments still exist they are almost always occupied by the élites of an older generation. Older people of the lower classes have long since been prevailed upon to give up larger quarters.

Middle-class housing by definition (small quarters with function-designated rooms) is difficult to subdivide among stranger families, though when this happens it almost always means the housing has sunk to lower-class standards. Only the lower classes accept the idea of sharing a toilet with strangers or are willing to convert a "salon" into sleeping quarters at night. It is often also difficult to accommodate an elderly parent (see Chapter 10 for the kinds of alternatives people now use for the care of the elderly) or a newly married couple in a middle-class apartment where the privacy of a single room is usually reserved only for parents. When children marry they have three choices: They can (1) encroach on parents' space; (2) move to the periphery of the city (and usually pay more rent than their parents); or (3) with a great deal of diligent searching and uncommonly good luck find a flat not too far from their work and their parents' home. It has become commonplace for young people to extend the period between engagement and marriage to several years while they

search for an apartment. One editorial writer, Abdul Rahman Fahmy, in
Al-Gomhuria (English translation in the *Egyptian Gazette,* February 13,
1981), urges young couples to go ahead with marriage plans even if they
have to board temporarily with in-laws because as he notes "nothing could
be worse than prolonged celibacy."

The newspapers frequently report the difficulties newlyweds experience in finding housing:

> Recent reports describe how a man and woman were picked up for
> sleeping together under a tree in the Barrages Garden: it turned out
> they were married and homeless. (*Egyptian Gazette,* February 20, 1981)

> The Cairo Court of First Instances has granted the divorce peti-
> tion of a wife who sued under the new personal-status laws. She claimed
> that her husband with whom she had contracted a marriage six years
> ago had failed to consummate the marriage. The husband claimed that
> he had not been able to find a flat . . . [and] his wife had asked him
> to live in her family's house but he had refused. (*Egyptian Gazette,*
> February 19, 1980)

Bringing home a newly married spouse to the parents' house is not
a new experience in the collective Egyptian consciousness. In general
outlines it is the same as the common rural custom of a man bringing his
wife to live in or near his parental home to consolidate political, economic,
and blood ties. The difference in the city, however, when the move is
generated by a combination of housing shortages and other factors related
to urban living is that the parental home selected is dictated by where there
is room or where the couple can find the support services they need. This
may mean a move to either bride or bridegroom's family. Each has its advantages and disadvantages:

> Samir and Muna had no choice but to move in with her family when
> they married. Samir's family lived in a small apartment, and several
> of his sisters and brothers were still living at home at the time, while
> Muna's parents were alone in a large spacious flat. Muna's family, mid-
> dle class but not pinched for funds, generously insisted upon provid-
> ing free lodging and meals for the couple who were both employed
> in low-paying government jobs. When their first child was born Samir
> was a devoted father, but he soon felt the competition from his parents-
> in-law for the baby's affections. Muna's parents were delighted with

the baby and assumed almost full-time care of it while Muna and Samir were away at work. Gradually Samir began spending more and more time away from home, secretly having an affair with a woman he met through his work. He blamed his neglect of his family on his feeling of impotence in the face of what he considered the takeover of his life by his parents-in-law.

Forcing family members of different generations to reside together in close physical proximity is, on the one hand, a way to consolidate ties and mutual services and, on the other, it is a way to aggravate tensions. Again, the newspapers provide extreme examples:

> The old man brought in to the General Hospital . . . had severe burns caused by an unknown chemical. He told the police that his wife, daughter, and son-in-law had thrown the chemical at him in an attempt to kill him. Investigations however revealed that the housing problem was at the back of the tragedy. Police discovered the man had . . . burnt himself . . . hoping to get rid of his daughter and her husband who shared his small home. . . . "Eight years ago they . . . moved into our house till they could find a dwelling. . . . My wife supported them. That is why I tried to get rid of the three of them." (*Egyptian Gazette*, June 30, 1980)

> A court has turned down an appeal by a man to evict his mother from their flat because he intends to marry. . . . The mother told the court she had lived in the flat for 15 years after her divorce and had asked her son to sign the lease believing that in that way he would be better able to defend her interests. The court ordered the landlord to draw up a new lease to be signed by the mother. (*Egyptian Gazette*, March 24, 1980)

The shortage of housing space in some cases has meant that the possession of housing has become a prime asset. One well-to-do family with a not-so-attractive daughter circulated word to prospective bridegrooms that she already possessed a nice flat. The bridegroom who reached for the bait quietly transferred into his sister's name the flat he had bought in anticipation of his marriage, thus giving a boost to her marriage aspirations. A television serial treatment of the housing shortage similarly portrayed housing as a prime asset. A family recognizes how much they can gain by renting their current apartment furnished and ends by discovering that the difficulties involved in finding a new apartment cause so many upheavals and moral dilemmas that they give up the attempt (see the plot synopsis in Chapter 4).

Families are now tending to organize themselves around whatever housing is available rather than organizing housing primarily around family needs. For the lower classes this means lowering the expectations to more crowded conditions than one would like or moving in with anyone whose space one can impinge on.[6] In the middle classes it means taking whatever flat one can find even though it is inconveniently located. If there is a question of owning housing property then people live in whatever arrangement is convenient.

Muhammad Bey lives in a building that he shares in ownership with three sisters. To all intents and purposes he has become the patriarch of this building's families. He owns a spacious flat on one floor and another which he rents on the top floor. He lives alone in his flat except for his mother who joined him after his wife died. His three sisters over the years have brought their husbands to live in the flats they own.

Some of the children are now grown and at the university while others are still young and around the house a good part of the time. One sister and her husband are professors at the local university; another works, as does Muhammad, in government employment. The third sister is a housewife; much of the care of the children in all households has devolved on her over the years while the children's parents were off at work.

The families compensate her by running errands for her and occasionally giving her gifts. If one household has guests, the others send up a dish or two of food; if there are special events they celebrate them together. There is a continuous movement between flats for socializing, for help with small tasks, and for the children and grandchildren to make regular visits to the old woman.

It was an accident, of course, that the property in the family of Muhammad Bey was divided among more women than men, and therefore the families centered their lives predominantly around the women's kin. The sisters' husbands remain somewhat aloof from the daily goings and comings that take place between households. There is a palpably different feel to a building where brothers have brought their brides to live than a building where sisters have brought their husbands. Sisters tend to build bonds of cooperation and closeness in a more egalitarian atmosphere. The case that follows illustrates a brother-dominated residential arrangement. In such households, the cooperative links are weakened by the lack of blood relationship between the women. In the following case, the authoritarian nature of the family is accentuated by its transitional socioeconomic status; the older couple still maintains a patriarchal control.

Ibrahim and his four sons own a shop in the native bazaar. Their profits have gone into a five-floor apartment building. As each son married he brought home his bride and was alotted an apartment by seniority, the oldest to the lowest floors and the youngest to the higher apartments. Their wives wait on the mother-in-law in degree to which they were most recently married; as they become occupied with their own children, their duties become fewer. The one wife who after several years of marriage produced no children feels the absence keenly. Children are just one way that the women compete with one another. There is a large grill work door that blocks the collective entrance-way of the building. It is kept locked at all times and the key remains with the mother-in-law. If one of the wives wishes to go out she has to obtain permission from her mother-in-law. This is said to be a safety practice to protect the women of the household when the men are away, but it is unusually drastic in what is normally a peaceful neighborhood.

A proverb, applicable to the difficulties in households which revolve around a particular type of kin arrangement, cautions: "If you have a woman (relative) in a household, go in; but if you only have a man (relative) in the household, stay out."

The significant point is that ownership of critical housing property in urban areas encourages organization around any combination of relatives who happen to inherit rights in housing property. This is quite different from rural agricultural property that encourages organization primarily around male kin work groups. Urban property ownership strengthens a bilateral interpretation of kinship relations, putting less stress on differentiating a separate quality to relations with those from the mother's or father's side. Housing scarcities reduce the chances that choice of residence will be a direct consequence of pure volition. This does not mean that people lose their schedule of preferences, rather that they lose their ability to play them out fully.

MEDIA

The rapid expansion of the electrical grid throughout rural Egypt and an increasing number of people living in urban areas has put media resources at the disposal of much larger numbers of Egyptians in recent years. Television is the medium with by far the most impact in all segments of the population. Access is not confined to set owners alone, although the ease with which sets can be purchased through installment buying makes them broadly available in even the most impoverished households. Sets are extensively found in coffee houses — the favorite haunts of lower-class men — where, for a few piasters paid out for tea, a patron can spend an evening of viewing.

What increased media coverage inevitably brings is an outside arbiter of social values and a broadening of vicarious experience. One mother summing up the differences between now and when she was young remarked: "The naiveté of both city and village girls was considerable in those days. Girls were warned to keep away from men and told how to behave, but few had any real knowledge of the outside world or what it was they were being protected from. Today if they don't get this understanding from going out in public more, they learn it from television serials where all the consequences of immoral behavior are shown before their eyes."

All media sources consciously take a didactic approach in discussing social problems. It is rare to see several sides of a social issue debated in the same presentation, though the contradictions in the contemporary context may be pointed out. The director of one of the television channels frankly admitted that issues are not debated, that instead a "correct" solution to the social problem is presented. The "correct" view in television serials, where family issues are most commonly aired, is usually based on middle- or upper-middle class value structures. According to the director this is, in part, a deliberate effort to educate the "uncultured" viewers to a more acceptable awareness of what is "right" in the modern world. The director commented with some dismay that "cultural" programs aimed at raising the standards of peasants and other "culturally deprived" groups were not very popular with these groups.

While serials are immensely popular with almost all groups, many educated viewers state a preference for foreign films and serials. The foreign shows are usually presented in a foreign language and subtitled in Arabic, requiring that the viewer, if not fluent in the language, be reasonably literate in Arabic to understand them. Foreign programs are of course not directed at Egyptian social issues, but Egyptians nevertheless are adept at drawing their own conclusions about the issues being discussed. In the immensely popular *Dallas* series, for example, some Egyptians concluded that the program was attempting to show the overriding importance of family loyalty and the pragmatic nature of extended family relations. The main issue of *Dallas* for many was how to keep such a large and contentious family together, and they saw as only natural the devisive role of the unrelated wives of the sons of the family.

In appropriate places in the text above, plot synopses have appeared that give an idea of how subjects are treated. Typically the "good" and the "bad" characters are made easily recognizable in order to convey the social message. Chance more than effort usually produces the "happy ending." In general the most common topics of serials with social import are:

Marriage: Should the choice of spouse be that of a parent or the child? Normally the plot resolves itself in favor of the child's decision, though parents are usually pictured as well-meaning. Only when a child flagrantly disobeys a parent does the plot tend to portray the parent's choice as the correct one.

Status conflicts: Should people marry others who are of vastly differing levels of wealth, education, age, or family status? Usually the television says no.

Conflicts in women's roles: Should widowed women give up their own prospects for a happy future to care for dependent children? Should women work or stay at home? Programs sometimes appear to vacillate on these issues but never at the expense of women's roles as mothers. The parent-child bond is always portrayed as immutable.

Relationships between elderly parents and their children: What are the responsibilities of grown children to their parents? The "good" child is usually portrayed as fulfilling his or her responsibilities by caring for the elderly parents.

Consequences of immoral actions: Cheating, intriguing, killing, and lapses in moral behavior all eventually bring negative consequences to their perpetrators.

Urban-rural differences: Recently a few serials are turning from picturing village life in terms of vengeful family feuds over land, water, and killings to picturing the countryside as idyllic in its peaceful beauty and "true" values. The plots in these serials usually revolve around a love affair between urban and rural individuals where the statuses of the lovers are not equal because of different opportunities they have been afforded in their different upbringings. The message usually concerns "true" values and where they are to be found.

Films in theaters are viewed by a more restricted audience than television, primarily by young urban men of lower-, lower-middle, or middle-class level. Eventually many films reach a larger audience on television. A large portion of Egyptian films can be classed as purely for entertainment, commenting on social issues mainly through situation comedy but offering little guidance on "correct" solutions. The better quality films by reputable directors tend to comment as much on political as social issues. When they take up social issues, according to the director of the film archives, some are so sophisticatedly symbolic that their social messages are lost on the bulk of the audience. Some of the most effective, *I Want a Solution, No Condolences for Women, The Sin,* all starring Faten Hamama, have brought to the attention of film viewers the difficulties faced by women wishing divorces, widows, and those suffering sexual abuse.

Newspapers have a smaller audience than television, but for the educated audiences they cater to, they provide daily comment on social questions, often with commentators debating each other from different sides of issues. A number of examples have already been cited in the text, but it may be worthwhile to give an example from the weekly, *Hawaa,* a woman's magazine that specializes in social commentary. This serialized installment of a novel by the liberal writer, Ihsan Abdul Koddus, is a comment both on generational differences and on the uncritical acceptance of Western mores. The mother has asked to hear the story of her daughter's professor at the university (the installment is excerpted here with bracketed sections filling in some of what is left out):

> It is not Dr. Bassumi's story but the frame of mind of university girls that matters. They've come to prefer the complete man. It's now synonymous with an old man. Girls today are madly in love with old men. At least an old man can afford to marry. [She raves about the perfection of her forty-five-year-old professor who has not yet married, while her mother warns:] "Listen, my daughter. A man has no natural inclination for marriage. He doesn't want marriage, but he seeks a woman. If he finds a woman he will have nothing to do with marriage . . . But a woman seeks marriage by nature. She has what is called the maternal instinct, and in order that she may be a mother, society imposes marriage on her."
>
> "You confine the meaning of marriage to the sexual relationship between man and woman," the daughter objected. "Sex is no longer of any value in civilized countries. The new generation does not fear sex as you do."
>
> Shouting, the mother said: "The countries you call civilized have gone to the extent of relieving a woman of her responsibility as a mother. She only gives birth and hands over her offspring to the government to rear and bring up. There society has relieved a woman of the status of wife and cancelled the term 'spinster' as a stigma. Nothing of that sort has happened in our society."
>
> [The daughter rises to her feet and says:] "The tragedy is that mothers are living in one world and their daughters in another." Following her with pitiful eyes the mother said: "May God protect you from that world!" (translation from the *Egyptian Gazette,* May 3, 1979)

The image of a university girl asking for unlicensed sex is extreme, as is her claim that all students desire to marry old men. Koddus leaves her little opportunity to defend this point of view in comparison with the mother who is permitted to expound at length on the meaning of marriage and the "correct" relationship between men and women. Koddus is well known for his writings on women and for his use of dialog between characters to present different sides of social issues. As in the excerpt above he usually leaves little doubt as to which side he supports.

The widespread access to media sources in contemporary Egypt is still a recent enough novelty to stimulate considerable discussion among viewers of programs like serials, where identification with actors in complex plots is possible. One need only sit with viewers a short while to feel the involvement — they comment on the morality of the characters and feel disappointed when a player does not respond correctly according to the role (a daughter does not recognize and rebuffs a long-lost parent) or is not punished appropriately. There is enough respect, however, for the broadcast or printed view to lend moral weight to the outcomes of plots.

The models that television provides, often contrary to those used by the lower classes to organize their lives, are in many cases beyond their resources to imitate. That the values presented are in most cases doggedly middle-class, however, has the result in the long run that people are led gently to acceptance of new realities and new expectations: children should have choices in whom they marry, modern dress is not necessarily a flagrant sexual display, women need to be educated, and their employment can be carried out gracefully without jeopardizing their other roles. In other words, the media, particularly television, have played a role in expanding and modifying the concept of appropriateness — what a "nice girl" can do and still remain a "nice girl." The media have contributed significantly to moving the concept of "nice girl" from one imposed by outside protectors to one that is largely internalized and self-imposed.

In more general terms, the media have also served the function of preparing the way for intergenerational social-class mobility. Children progressing up the educational ladder, and their parents, see at first hand on their television screens what is involved in the middle-class life style. Some[7] argue that the numbers of rural migrants to urban Egypt have served to countrify centers like Cairo. While this is undoubtedly true, one would also have to balance this assertion against the present impact of television's exposure in the countryside that prepares migrants for city life before they come and, once they are in the city, for life in other social classes. Eventually one might predict the homogenization of Egyptian society that would reduce the surface color and variety that has and still does give it so much excitement.

RESOURCE GENERATION AND ALLOCATION DECISIONS

With the new economic realities — inflationary effects that are often not matched by wage increases, rising expectations, greater availability of consumer goods, imbalances and disruptions in the labor market, the importance of prolonged training periods for children, and increasing numbers of heads of households absent from home for work or other reasons — deciding how to accomplish all of a family's goals within the limits of the resources available has become a more formidable task. In broad outlines the way many families have responded is by finding new ways to generate income, by diversifying their risks, consolidating their capital investments, rescheduling their time, redefining what is appropriate to various role positions and investing more in the longer-term goal of children's training.

Consolidating Capital Investments

Mustafa Amin in *Al-Akhbar* comments: "It is absolutely difficult for any young university graduate to raise the money needed for buying an engagement present or for paying the dowery. An engagement present which used to cost a maximum of a hundred pounds, now costs more than £E 1,500 because of the sky rocketing price of gold. A dowery that could formerly buy the furniture of three rooms is now hardly sufficient to buy a wardrobe. Even when the money needed . . . has been found, the flat is not available" (translation in the *Egyptian Gazette,* March 6, 1980).

The costs for such essentials, including also anywhere from several hundred pounds in lower-class neighborhoods to several thousand pounds in other neighborhoods simply as "key money" to open negotiations for the rental of flats, are well beyond the pocketbooks of most young people. More than ever they depend upon relatives to help them amass these sums of money to marry, to get started in their careers, and to subsist in the early years until they have sufficient incomes themselves. Almost as much as rural family-organized work groups, the facts of urban economic life encourage family members to pool their energies and resources. With what are, in terms compared with wages, immense costs for marriage, it becomes all the more necessary for some families to insist upon some form of successive rights of children to marry, so that the family can focus its resources on one child at a time and avoid controversy. Similarly there is encouragement to pool resources by living together, by contributing income to a common pot, and by exchanging services that save money.

Diversifying Risks

With more alternatives to choose from in Egypt now, it is common to find families distributing their efforts and resources in a variety of directions.

> Ahmed is an administrator in one of the ministries of Cairo. His father is a respected traditional leader in their village in the Delta, not far from a large provincial town. In recent years the father's traditional functions as mediator and advisor in local problems have been largely stripped away as formal functionaries appointed by the government have assumed them. When Ahmed was a boy his father reviewed the potentialities of his sons and deliberately set about training them for the futures he expected of them. Four brothers were sent to the local religious school run by a sheikh. After a short time Ahmed and one other brother switched to a modern school and continued up the ladder until they received their university degrees and entered government service in Cairo. A third brother dropped out of the religious school after he was literate and went to work in the business of a relative in the nearby town. The fourth brother continued on through the religious school and Al-Azhar University until he himself became a religious sheikh. A fifth brother was deliberately kept at home to assume responsibility for farming the family land.

Diversification may mean not only diversifying the resources that are allotted to the long-term goals of families and their individual members but diversifying the way resources are obtained. This may involve diversification over time as, for example, when a man decides to go abroad and earn large sums of money for a period of years at the expense of absence from his family and then returns to settle into his old more poorly paid work in Egypt. Or a college graduate may decide to take a lower-status job — such as taxi driving — for a period of time to earn better income before he settles into work appropriate for his qualifications. He may also diversify simultaneously by holding, for example, an accounting job in the public sector that pays poorly but gives him his sense of worth during the day and driving a taxi at night, where on a good night he may earn about one-half the monthly salary of his government job.

Training Children for Adulthood

Resources are scarce enough in most Egyptian households to make the decisions about the extent of general education or other preparatory training for children difficult ones. Even though it is now pretty much an assumption of the middle classes that children will experience long periods of education, prolonged education is still unusual enough to be a valued asset in Egyptian society: by 1976, out of those aged ten and above only 3.2 percent of males and 1.2 percent of females had obtained university or higher institute degrees. In many urban households, education (or other training) has become the critical prerequisite for the other desired goals of adult life, a way to earn a secure income at an appropriate status-level position and to attract an appropriate spouse. (See the cases of Moneim and Nabila and Nowal in Chapter 8.)

Egyptian parents usually view education in terms of how it opens up or places obstacles in the way of a child's future opportunities. A farm family may see education as totally irrelevant to, or even interfering with (if a child becomes "too good for manual labor") the child's future life as a farmer. Another farm family may see education as a vehicle for a child's escape from manual labor. A family may consider it adding to or subtracting from a daughter's attributes for marriage. What are the options that education at different levels provides?

According to governmental criteria, satisfactory passage of sixth-grade Arabic exams give a child what is regarded as basic literacy. Basic literacy and numeracy is generally recognized by most parents as having broad utility; it is also a prerequisite for entry into public sector industrial jobs and certain technical training courses offered by the Ministries of Industry and Manpower and Vocational Training. Completion of the three years of intermediate school reinforces literacy and permits entry into higher-level academic or technical training streams. It, like secondary school completion, permits other program entry but does not in itself prepare students in any significant way for direct open labor market entry.[8] A university diploma, as does a diploma from a technical secondary school, guarantees a job in the government public sector and gives a better edge in private sector employment. As far as qualifying for employment, therefore, there are two major qualitatively significant educational levels: elemen-

Children of the lower classes typify in their dress the mix of indigenous and Western influences affecting contemporary society.

tary, providing functional literacy, and university, permitting a guaranteed job and entry into the valued professions.

Children more than ever depend on the support of parents to provide the resources, conditions conducive to study, and the restraint to forego the work and income children might provide. In many urban households the emphasis on education has created a distribution of tasks organized around the dictates of the educational process. Both parents and children focus their home activity on the study tasks of children, parents frequently feeling they must "study" with children.

In households where children are not involved in schooling, work tasks revolve around the work of adults, a boy perhaps helping his father in peddling vegetables and a girl in caring for younger children or helping in the housework. In these households where adult skills are learned by imitation, tasks are given over gradually from one generation to the next. At holidays, although school children assume some household chores, these are viewed as peripheral to the more important work of school. Parents support this view with their solicitous talk about children needing "to rest up" for the next arduous school year. Since children are, in effect, trained by outside institutions rather than as apprentices to their parents, they lose the closeness that comes from working together on identifiably identical goals. The valued training becomes the outside skill rather than the skill the parent imparts.

Parents view education for boys as related primarily to their occupational futures (all other factors being equal; see Rugh 1981b). It is neither new nor a phenomenon confined to the lower classes for parents to view boys' education in terms of the occupational opportunities it opens. Until recently, of those who sent children to private schools, girls went to French schools to become "cultured" and boys went to English schools to prepare for business and political life.

The case is somewhat different for girls. Although increasingly parents from all walks of life are coming to see the utility of education for girls, as yet enrollments of girls have not matched those of boys. The female percentage of total elementary school enrollments has remained fairly stable (between 33 and 39.6 percent) over the fifty years between 1930 and 1979. These figures make it all the more remarkable that, according to a speech of the Minister of Social Affairs at a conference on women in 1980, 138,000 young women are enrolled in universities, or 46.7 percent of all university students (reported in the *Egyptian Gazette,* June 8, 1980). The lower enrollment rates of girls are, to a certain extent, a result of the different views on how best to prepare a girl for her future. In the following cases, parents of different views feel very sure of what they want for their daughters.

> Gamiila is a bright, energetic girl of about fifteen, dressed in the traditional *galabiya* and head scarf but more independent and forceful than many other girls of her age and class. She actively seeks handwork that she can do at home to earn money and is prompt in returning her orders and collecting new ones. She was one of the brightest children in the local Bulaq elementary school, achieving one of the highest scores in her sixth grade passing exam. That same year her elder brother who had repeated the sixth year took the exam with her and failed. Their father arranged for him to start work as a garage mechanic. Gamiila was anxious to continue her studies, but her conservative father, who came originally from Upper Egypt, refused, saying that it was inappropriate for a girl to study for a longer duration than her brother. He felt Gamiila should stay home and learn housekeeping skills while she waited to marry.

> Fuad, who lives in an Upper Egyptian village very close to Aswan, is a Nubian. Traditionally Nubians have been known for their protectiveness toward their women and their reticence about letting women out of their homes to go to school or to work. Fuad dreamt of having a son who would care for him in his old age, but his hopes were never realized. Instead two daughters were born, the youngest with a handicap that meant it was necessary for her to stay at home. Fuad pinned his hopes on his eldest daughter Fatma, whom he encouraged through all the stages of her education. Several times she failed critical exams and had to repeat them, but Fuad patiently supported her. His hopes rested in her ability to obtain a high enough degree to make her eligible for a government job. The status of a "professional" job would be sufficient to compensate for him having permitted a woman of his household to work. A position lower than that of government employee was out of the question as far as Fuad was concerned since it would give the appearance that Fatma was working out of financial duress.

In the first case, the father felt his daughter could prepare for her future as well outside the formal educational system. In the second, the father felt that nothing less than the highest degree would prepare his daughter for a secure future. In the back of both parents' minds the future for a girl means marriage; both are considering how to enhance the girl's preparation for that event, the first by providing the skills she needs as a housewife, the second by making his daughter, as an income earner, a more attractive choice as wife.

Among those lower classes where education is chosen rather than assumed, girls are beginning to profit from the growing desire of parents to give them an employable skill that is not manual labor. In two lower-class samples,[9] the ratio of girls enrolled at the intermediate level was higher than that of boys, a reverse of what is true for other educational levels and other higher-class neighborhoods. Interviews with the parents in one sample indicated that at about the age of puberty parents make critical decisions about their children's futures. Boys have reached the age when their physical capacities make it worthwhile to withdraw them from school to earn income or to become apprentices to skilled craftsmen. The study shows[10] that adequate or more than adequate resources in the lower-class family were not the necessary ingredient to keeping children in schools. In fact the more affluent lower-class families had the lowest rates of enrollment of appropriate age group children. This appears to be a result of the better opportunities these families can afford their children outside the formal educational system: career opportunities for boys and the prospect of financially secure husbands for the girls.

In the specific case of intermediate school girls, lower-class parents appear to evidence the contradictory views of the parents in the two cases above. Although all parents care most strongly about the marriage chances of their daughers, some see the best preparation as one where the girl stays at home to learn beside her mother, protected from questionable behavior, and others see the best preparation as staying as long as possible in school to gain the prerequisites for a job of satisfactory status. Each group of parents sees their own view as enhancing the marriageability of the girl. Similarly, girls of élite families earlier received educations only through the end of secondary school, but as Hussein (1953) notes, now élite parent no longer feel the security of their properties after land reform, and so feel compelled to send daughters to university to increase their chances of marrying well.

Generating Family Income

Inflationary spirals have put pressures on Egyptian families to find new ways of earning income. At the same time new opportunities to earn income have opened up in an expanded private sector and in the possibility to migrate for work either outside or within the country. Adequate income comes more and more to depend upon personal initiative.

It is mostly men who are called upon to solve the problem of insufficient income. They spend longer hours at work and in committee meetings (for which in the government they are paid extra), take a second job, or seek better work with more fringe benefits. Many are under pressure to take greater advantage of the opportunities at their disposal, especially when their jobs put them at the juncture between a legitimate and a potentially questionable activity. One who dispenses a needed document or service, for example, can accumulate large sums by giving clients "special attention." This is clearly an illegal activity, but other grey areas such as private tutoring where a parent comes to feel the child will not pass without the service is not so clearly categorized. It is not unusual for teachers to earn more then £E 1000, or more than their annual salary, in the few months before major exams.

Recent rapid changes in wage scales in some sectors and not in others have caused major upheavals in the social structure. A recent film *Attention Please* depicts somewhat extremely but nevertheless vividly what is happening.

At the start of the film, a congenial garbage collector, Antar, with cart and donkey collects the refuse of the central family in the drama, a family that includes Galal and his sisters. He asks Galal's father for the hand of his attractive daughter whom Antar mistakes for a servant girl. The father refuses because Antar is only a garbage collector even though Antar explains that he will be taking over a whole garbage district after his father dies and will be earning £E 600 a month. Galal, who is a professor at the university, becomes happily engaged to a girl named Aida and the story revolves around the preparation for their marriage. In some detail the plot goes into the difficulties and expense of marriage in contemporary Egypt. The main focus of the story, however, concerns the couple's quest for housing. For years they search for an apartment. The one building in which there is an apartment that suits the taste of the bride turns out to be owned by the garbage collector, Antar, who in the meantime has become rich from the sale of his recycled garbage and other somewhat shady investments. Antar takes them to visit his expensive villa, wife and four children, fancy car, and his garbage processing business. Antar insists that Galal pay £E 5000 "key money" to obtain the apartment, but Galal refuses on principle because key money is illegal. Between episodes of the apartment drama Galal goes to the publisher of his five scholarly books and finds that he has earned only about £E 200 from their sales. The publisher, however, offers him a large sum of money to write pornography for the general public. He sticks to his principles again and refuses.

Eventually Galal borrows and scrapes together enough money to give Antar a down payment on the key money because Galal finds he will never get an apartment without it. Antar invites Galal and Aida to a night club and gives the entire down payment to a belly dancer; Galal gets drunk. Aida and Galal argue over principles and practicality. In the dénouement Aida decides (and her family concurs) in favor of marrying the garbage collector who can provide her with the luxuries she craves. Galal is dazed, and in the last scene, while lecturing to his class, stops and mumbles, "Reality is Antar," then staggers out.

The inequities are accentuated in this drama by choosing the extremes of status positions—a garbage collector and a professor. Real-life stories, however, often come close to imitating drama.

A middle-class family reported that two of the previous guard-janitors (usually considered the object of sympathy because of their poor circumstances) in their building had become very well-off from tips and extra payments for services to people in the building. One guard-janitor moved away to establish his own business, and as the outraged woman telling the story complained, "sent his business card to me last week to see if I could find him a secretary." The other guard-janitor little by little enlarged the flat on the roof where he and his family lived until it became a luxury flat that he could rent for a large sum of money. The other flat owners did not notice until it was too late, and they could not legally evict the occupants.

This case illustrates the imaginative ways that exist to earn income in contemporary Egypt and the alacrity with which some people take up the quest. As has happened historically before, the slack in incomes is also increasingly being taken up the paid work of women but not without a great deal of debate about the proper role of women in society.

Women's Roles

Recent changes in Egypt have affected women's roles in at least two potentially important ways: in households where husbands have migrated for work, women have sometimes been asked to assume the role of heads of household, and in resource-starved households of all kinds they have increasingly felt the pressure to contribute more substantially to family income.

One study (Khattab and El-Daeif 1982) of village households where a husband had migrated for work suggests some of the changes that come about. Frequently there was a change in household living arrangements, with the wife leaving her mother-in-law's house to return to her own mother's house or, if there were sufficient funds, into an independent house of her own where she could escape the domination of her mother-in-law. The husband and wife were often brought closer together by the greater need to share in decision making and by the husband's recognition of the wife's capabilities to deal with problems in his absence. Mothers who felt they needed to assume more of the discipline of children often expressed anxiety over their ability to accomplish these duties successfully. In terms of the interim finances of the household, as women waited for paychecks to arrive, the value of the contribution they made to the family income became significant. And often their management of the large sums from abroad allowed a more effective use of money for the long-term needs of the family. This study like others of its kind is unable to comment on the long-term effects of what are usually rather short-term migrations in search of additional income. One suspects that the change which has the most potential for permanent impact is the move to an independent household and the break from communal commodity distribution controlled by an older generation. That women would attempt such a break as soon as they are able fits well with the expectations about where their best interests lie (see Chapter 7). But whether it will be a pattern that many women follow seems dependent to a large degree on the extent to which a fairly large and independent income can be obtained.

In periods of inflationary pressure, women are increasingly called upon to take up the slack in incomes. In the NCSCR pretest for an urban survey, 20 percent of the households reported that wives were working in 1979. Until recently in the lower classes women preferred when possible to earn income through incidental work rather than regular employment. Incidental work — raising chickens or pigeons, selling produce from their villages of origin, or doing piecework sewing — is considered part of their housekeeping duties. It does not interfere with housework, does not leave a woman open to criticisms of neighbors about her moral behavior, and does not reflect negatively on a man's ability to support his family. High family status in lower-class populations is still usually associated with the financial resources to permit women to remain unemployed at home.

In 1976, the view was still being expressed strongly in Bulaq that women should remain at home and not seek employment however dire their family's circumstances. Those few who did work outside their homes tried to hide that fact from their neighbors and where possible from other relatives, sometimes even from their husbands. By 1980 and 1981 (see Rugh 1981a), many more women were working openly outside their homes and often at what they had considered before to be morally compromising work such as cleaning in homes. The changes could be attributed to a number of causes above and beyond inflationary pressures and the example of consumer spending brought back from the Gulf, though these were clearly motivating factors. There was also the sharp rise in wages for maids resulting from the increasing numbers of women from other classes joining the work force and needing the services. The higher wages—sometimes higher than those paid to university graduates entering government service —began to compensate for the other disadvantages, even bringing a status of its own that an unskilled woman could bring so much money from regular work. At the same time, lower-class women were watching their middle-class sisters in real life or on television extolling the virtues of work as a way to provide more benefits for the family, and a few were even encouraging their own daughters to prepare themselves through education for a career. The change did not come over night, nor is it complete. The role of the working woman is almost directly antithetical to the traditional concept of a woman's role in Egypt. Lower-class working women, still in the minority, tend to be defensive about their work. There is evidence that they attempt to compensate for criticism by being more circumspect in their dress and demeanor and by justifying their work as an extension of their mother roles (B. Ibrahim 1980).

The overall pattern of participation of women in the non-agricultural labor force has been uneven in Egypt. Historically women have tended to gravitate to certain fields[11] and to participate in these fields in relation to the general economic conditions of the time. Now, in selected fields like government service where tenure can be lost if a woman drops out, it is not as easy to move in and out of the work force. Since 1937 there has been an overall decline[12] in the economic activity rate (those age six and over who are in the labor force) for the whole population with a turnaround and upswing only since 1972 that has not yet matched 1937 proportions. The women's rates in 1937, 1970, and 1976 followed the same pattern of decline and recovery but with somewhat greater exaggeration than the figures for men[13] reflecting what is particularly true for the employment of women in Egypt, that their passage into or out of the work force depends to a large extent on how men are faring in the work force, the availability of jobs, and the ability of men to earn sufficient income for the household.

When the labor market is flooded it is easy to resurrect cultural norms

that discourage women from working. In the 80s with the government bureaucracies overloaded with employees in many branches and with scarcities in the general labor force of certain technical skills, there is evidence
that attempts are being made selectively to encourage women to enter some
new fields and withdraw from others. For example, in the last few years
women are being welcomed into three- and five-year commercial, agricultural, and industrial technical schools. In 1978–79 out of 493,000 students
in these schools 37 percent were girls. Of that number 53 percent were
enrolled in commercial, 10 percent in agriculture, and 11 percent in industrial schools (figures supplied by the Ministry of Education).

Unlike the lower classes where employment of women is only now
gaining grudging acceptance as an activity that individuals may engage
in even when they are not totally impoverished, the middle classes have
accepted women's employment as a fact of life, if not always an approved
one. One of the significant debates going on in Egypt now revolves around
the roles of women as housewives and workers. There is significance in
the fact that the debate usually concerns women government employees —
that is, women in fields with a superfluity of workers. A widely reported
study by the National Center for Social Research concluded:

> People who encourage women to work do so for the wrong reasons —
> not because they want women to develop their personalities or to help
> them lead economically independent lives but because they fear a re-
> duction in family income. The survey showed that low-income popula-
> tions were now more in favor of work than those of higher income
> groups, who see most of their salaries spent on keeping up appear-
> ances and employing nurses to look after their children. In the survey
> 52 percent of the wives and 54 percent of the husbands agreed that
> women should stay at home for a number of years taking care of their
> husbands and children while they received half their salaries. (para-
> phrased from the *Egyptian Gazette,* May 5, 1981)

This study shows the shifts of perception already appearing in the population. The reference to women staying home refers to proposals being initiated through government channels. One member of the Shura Council
in February 1981, for example, proposed that a newly married female government employee be compelled to stay home for five months during which
time she would receive half her salary. Proponents of the bill argued that
it would ease unemployment among males, and opponents feared that it
would lead to shortages of staff for jobs typically held by women (*Egyptian Gazette,* March 5, 1981).

A number of newspaper articles have appeared commenting on the issues as columnists (mostly men) see them. The following excerpted column, from *Al-Akhbar,* is designed to arouse the indignation of readers. It is entitled, "A Woman Genius and Her Boss."

> The reason for her grudge against the boss was that he ordered her to come to the office in the evening so as to bring her daily work schedule, adding morning and evening hours, to a total of seven. She said she could not conform to the order because of transport congestion. The columnist asked her if she would work seven hours without interruption from 8 A.M. to 3 P.M. To her this arrangement meant that she would be late home to cook food for her husband, who was accustomed to having his lunch at 2 P.M. It seems that the company must change its office hours so that the worthy husband may take his meal at the fixed time! (*Egyptian Gazette,* May 14, 1980)

To be fair to him, this columnist, Mustafa Amin, in other articles has been sharply critical of people who think they can keep women at home and solve unemployment and traffic problems and improve moral standards.

Another comment in a similar vein appeared as an editorial in the *Egyptian Gazette.* The editorial writer was complaining about inefficiencies in the government bureaucracy and noted that department chiefs are almost always men:

> These men are forever complaining, with a great deal of justification that they cannot get their women staff to stop talking, let alone to work. Women, they say, view time spent in the office as a break from home routine to be spent catching up on gossip, reading their horoscopes and knitting. Sometimes they bring their preschool children along to work. The impression you get on a visit to the back room tallies very closely with the complaints of the manager at the desk. . . . This system in the long run serves neither home nor state. Women are exhausted by the mere effort of going out to work while trying to cope at home. Men do less than their share, that is to say, make almost no effort to help at home yet are dissatisfied to find their wives dispirited by a double work day. . . . The authorities, mostly men, begin to spread the idea that women shouldn't work at all. (*Egyptian Gazette,* February 29, 1980)

Studies in 1979 by a joint committee of those involved with manpower problems of Egypt, the Ministry of Manpower, CAPMAS and others looking into the questions of absenteeism, apathy, and malingering among government employees, discovered that 75 percent of men who do not report for work are absent because they have second jobs while the same percentage of women fail to report for work because of personal reasons. Absenteeism among unmarried women is less frequent than among married women who have more responsibilities at home.

The most balanced view comes from the female Minister of Social Affairs who said at a conference on women and development at Al-Azhar University in June of 1980 that the issue is not now whether a woman should go to work or stay home but rather how she can be helped to coordinate her duties toward her husband and children with her working responsibilities. Governmental attempts to legislate benefits for women have in fact been extensive and in some cases may even by their costliness have deterred women's employment in the private sector.

The late 70s and early 80s saw several reforms in the legislation concerning women's employment. Law 47 (concerning the civil service) and Law 48 (concerning the private sector) both from 1978 had identical provisions granting benefits to women. Article 70 states that a woman employee is entitled each time she bears a child to up to a maximum of two years leave without pay for purposes of taking care of her child. During her working career she may exercise this privilege three times. She has a choice of having the employing agency continue her social insurance benefits or pay her 25 percent of her salary. Article 71, subsection 2, gives a woman employee a three-month leave after delivery, a right that can be exercised three times during her career. Article 72 says an employer can permit a woman worker to work half the official hours with half pay. Law 91 of 1959, still in large part in effect, states that women are forbidden to work from 8 P.M. to 7 A.M. except in cases determined by the government. Other regulations include time off for nursing babies and provision of day care centers in enterprises hiring 100 or more women. At one time the public authorities considered operating buses exclusively for women passengers because of complaints about transport difficulties of working women but in the end instituted only special buses for women university students. Another recent benefit established in late 1981 by the Ministry of Social Affairs includes a system of domestic service centers to prepare foods, launder, iron, and provide house cleaning services on an hourly basis at reasonable prices.

An editorial commented that a Member of Parliament's proposal that working women be eligible for retirement on full pension at the age of forty, if they had completed fifteen years service, "would guarantee, if passed, that women would ultimately be phased out of almost all pensionable employment" (*Egyptian Gazette,* February 15, 1980).

All this discussion reflects, besides economic realities, a present ambivalence about the employment of women. If there is agreement at all, it seems to be that, if accommodation must take place, it must be in the role of women as workers rather than women as mothers. Some of the flavor of the argument comes out in the plots of two television serials shown in 1979 and 1980:

A young illiterate woman, Zeinab, brought up in the traditional mold of learning housekeeping skills from her mother, married her neighbor who had not yet finished his studies at the university.[14] While her husband studied with his colleagues, Zeinab performed the household tasks, serving him and his friends food and drink when their studying for exams brought them to her house. Increasingly Zeinab's inability to converse about anything substantive irritated her husband, and her anxious willingness to serve his every need only demonstrated further how little of significance she could find to do. His impression was compounded by comparison with his intelligent women colleagues. Their marriage began to deteriorate, culminating finally in the husband's travel abroad to do further graduate work.

Zeinab meanwhile became pregnant but before she had a chance to inform her husband, received news from overseas that he had divorced her. She bore a boy and began to think over the advice she had been given before her marriage had disintegrated—that she could improve herself by learning to read and write. She began to study elementary texts and soon began to pass one exam after another until she was eventually able to enter the university. All the while she continued to raise her son successfully with the help of supportive relatives, and earned income by sewing for neighbors.

When she graduated from the university she took a more substantial job outside her home. In the final episodes her son befriends a man at a sporting club who eventually discovers that he is the father, and his ex-wife has now become the kind of woman he had earlier wished for.

The transformation of Zeinab is accompanied by the symbols of change Egyptians recognize. She is first clad in *galabiya* and has her hair covered. In the end she is dressed in modern clothes with hair uncovered and styled in the modern fashion.

Fawziyya was a successful student in the journalism faculty of the university, in love with a young student in the same department and a protégé of the department head. Upon graduation, her parents sought to arrange a marriage for her with a successful small businessman whom her father, a struggling civil servant, felt would give her a secure future financially. She refused this marriage at first, hoping to marry the student whom she loved. The young man, however, was the son of a prominent man who, when he heard of his son's choice, refused on the grounds that Fawziyya was not from a prominent enough family. In disappointment at the weakness of her suitor, who was unwilling to contradict his father's wishes, Fawziyya finally decided to marry her own father's choice, provided that he agree to let her work after their marriage. It was clear that the match was not a love one from Fawziyya's side, though her husband from the start did everything he could to make her happy.

Fawziyya singlemindedly concentrated her attentions on building her career as a reporter at a newspaper where she worked long and irregular hours. Her husband often came home to an empty house and had to fend for himself at mealtimes. One of his female customers, recognizing his loneliness, brought him things to eat and came frequently to talk with him in his shop.

Meanwhile to Fawziyya's dismay she discovered she was pregnant, and despite her efforts to abort the child, produced a daughter. Both her husband and parents urged her to stay home to care for her child, but Fawziyya was becoming ever more successful in her career and refused. Her mother and husband were left with the care of the child. One day when Fawziyya had remained at work and forgotten the child's birthday, the little girl burnt herself badly by pulling a birthday candle over on herself as the father went to open the door for the grandparents.

All through this period Fawziyya's career was blossoming; through a stroke of luck she was recruited for a film which soon made her a well-known celebrity. Her husband had by this time sent her out of his house and she had moved into a luxurious apartment of her own. As she became more famous, however, visions of her daughter growing up without her flooded her mind.

In the final episode of her story, after a series of further disasters including rejection by her own parents and being caught in an act of international smuggling which her employers had involved her in without her knowledge, she must choose between a man who promises a further career for her and a husband whose only condition is that she no longer work but who promises her a life with her daughter. She chooses the daughter.

Though the messages of these two plots seem contradictory — one encouraging and the other discouraging women from work (Fawziyya is even symbolically "done in" by her work as she is caught in the act of smuggling) — a closer look reveals a single theme: motherhood comes first and should always remain dominant over other roles. Zeinab used her employment to support her son and herself (that is, to support her role of motherhood) while Fawziyya escaped that role by her employment. Her happiness is expected to return once she chooses her daughter, her maternal role.

These serials illustrate the perspective most families have retained in recent decades even as more and more women have become employed — that woman's role as worker must remain subservient to her role as mother and wife. Women are expected to carry on their household duties as before by themselves, or by finding substitute services from among kin, hired helpers, or in a last resort public agencies. This is one good reason for living as close as possible to relatives, (even in the same dwelling as a mother, or aunt, or some other willing helper) or of marrying maternal relatives and strengthening female exchanges that include vital babysitting services. But as one young girl astutely asked her working mother: "If I go to grandmother's house when you are busy at work, whose house will my children go to when I work?" Although this generation relies heavily on parents to provide such services, as more women work there are fewer women around willing to provide that help.

Men rarely assume household tasks in any kind of meaningful way. As one well-educated upper-middle-class husband put it, his wife could work if she wanted to but only if it did not interfere with her duties at home. He expected her to get up in the morning before him and prepare his breakfast; be home early so his food was ready when he returned from work. He provided full support for her and felt anything she earned should be spent as she chose on extra clothes, jewelry, holidays. This basic attitude is also found among more hard-pressed families — that women's household roles should not be jeopardized by employment, and men should appear at least to be contributing the lion's share to family income while women's incomes are used for lower-class "luxuries" like private doctors, tutoring, household appliances, etc. Such a division makes it difficult to say categorically that women derive a greater status in the household from their financial contributions, since men have a vested interest in preserving the appearance that they provide the bulk of the income. Nevertheless, women themselves often express a feeling of greater security in their economic independence.

Women who work, in effect, have two jobs — one at home and one outside. For this reason, like women in other countries, they tend to take jobs which are not too demanding and consequently are not usually well paid. At a conference on women and management held at American University of Cairo, discussants noted the limited numbers of women who sought managerial jobs, laying the blame on the fact that because of their home responsibilities women do not have the energies to assume extra re-

sponsibilities at work. Guaranteed jobs after obtaining a university degree
have, since Nasser established them, served to secure middle-class women
employment in the relaxed non-demanding, non-competitive government
work that fits in well with homemaking responsibilities. The jobs are financially satisfactory only as second incomes.

To put it in other terms, most women do not involve their egos heavily in careers or in the financial support of their families as long as a man
is present. They feel that their roles as housewives and mothers are more
valued to their sense of self than their income-earning abilities. To put work
outside the home in proper perspective and assuage their guilt, women often
"explain" work in terms of their family roles: "My children are all grown
up now and away from home, so rather than sit home all alone, I work."
"When my children were young, I used to work to give them the extras
our income couldn't afford, nice clothes so they wouldn't feel ashamed
at school and money for holidays at the sea." "If I didn't work my children
would have to stay home from school. This way I can open opportunities
for them so they will never have to work with their hands and scrape for
money as my husband and I do."

In short, being a good mother for many women nowadays in times
of inflation and rising expectations, means expanding the definition of
mother roles[15] to include helping to increase the financial resources available for bringing up children. In some cases a woman's contribution may
even be pivotal in intergenerational social mobility if it helps to keep children in school. It does not mean that woman's new role as worker over-
whelms her role as mother. Just the opposite is true; she usually works
to be a good mother.

Institutionalizing Protection of Women's Rights

It makes sense at this point to go back and finish what was started
in earlier pages. Islamic sharia law was first shown as a foundation supporting a fairly stable form of family life in Egypt. Second, attempts to
modify the sharia were seen as central to the "progressive" Muslims' move
to correct abuses in family life, resulting from outdated or ambiguous provisions of the law (Chapter 11). Now, with the background of the present
chapter, it becomes clearer what rights were being secured for women and
how the new conditions in Egyptian society make some remedies better
than others.

A brief review of the new provisions adopted in 1979 will show that
the changes were directed primarily at guaranteeing and specifying the eco-

nomic rights of women within the household. Secondarily, but not going as far as some women leaders wished, regulations covered the rights of women in divorce and in the custody of children. In both cases, the crux of the regulations supported a more secure position for women within their households. The changes were *not* directed at realizing the same or equal rights with men in either the domestic or the public domain. The complementarity of male and female roles still remained intact.

The provisions concerned with women's economic rights achieved their goals usually by specifying more clearly what those rights were. The man's obligation to support his wife was reconfirmed, but, in a substitution paragraph for Article 1 of Law No. 25 of 1920, support was given clear definition as food, clothing, lodging, costs of medical treatment, and other customary items. Women were entitled to support as long as they were legitimately married, in sickness as in health no matter what their financial condition or religion. A woman forfeits her support if she disobeys her husband or refuses to return to her home when requested by her husband to do so (though she can appeal this condition to a court). Support should not be stopped, however, if a woman goes out of her home for necessities or for lawful work without her husband's permission, unless in the last case she abuses the privilege to the detriment of her family.

A woman, divorced by her husband, who does not want to be divorced and gave no cause for divorce was given a longer period of alimony (minimum two years) in addition to the allowance for the waiting period before her remarriage. Child support was specifically made the obligation of the father until the girl married or the boy reached fifteen, or until both were able to support themselves. One of the most significant of the new provisions was the clause granting the divorced wife with custody of a child the right to occupy the rented marital home (unless another suitable place was prepared) until the end of the custody period. In the present context of housing shortages, this provision was considered a strong economic deterrent to divorce and an additional economic asset to the woman. The only new provision that favored men slightly over older provisions was the stipulation that alimony payment size be evaluated in terms of a husband's ability to pay (but not less than what the woman must have for necessities) rather than as a function of the standard the woman is used to.

Women made some headway in strengthening their rights in divorce and child custody. A woman was required to be informed immediately if her husband wished to divorce her (her divorce was not effective until her knowledge of it), or if he wished to marry an additional wife. In the last case she was given the new right to ask for a divorce within a period of a year after the new marriage if she had not given her consent to the marriage.

Stiff penalties were incorporated in the new provisions to insure that men met all the requirements of the law in these and in their other obligations. Other provisions set the procedures for attempts to reconcile spouses with marital differences, but the law said if the differences remained, and the woman asked for a divorce, it would be granted with the wife forfeiting her financial rights either totally or in part and even paying compensation to the husband if grounds existed to do so.

The new provisions also extended the period when women had the right to custody of their children, from the discretionary seven to nine years to ten years for boys and from nine to eleven to twelve years for girls unless a judge decided it was in the best interests of the children to remain longer with the mother, in which case he could extend the period to fifteen years for boys and for a girl until she marries. The new provisions, in effect, still recognize the relationships to a child of custody or care (*hidana*), guardianship (*wilaya*) and support (*nafaga*), but have extended the period when it is felt that children need the kind of supportive care a mother gives. A father is still held responsible for the financial, legal, educational, moral, and religious guidance of the child, but the new provisions seem to recognize the extent to which outside institutions such as schools have made his continuous presence not quite as essential as before.

The new stress on the question of custody is further emphasized with a designated succession order list of female relatives who have rights to custody if the mother is unable to fulfill her function. The order favors the mother's mother, the father's mother, and then other relatives, always giving first preference to the maternal relatives before paternal ones. Nowhere is a male assigned this kind of care. The provisions also specify the rights of both parents and of grandparents to visitation of the child.

The new amendments to the laws, in effect, are designed to relieve some of the anxieties of Muslim women over the question of divorce, by strengthening their rights in the home and giving them added rights to request divorce themselves, giving them a greater sense of economic security, and by giving them more control over their children in the event of divorce. To a limited extent the amendments were a victory of the "progressive" elements in the society over their opponents, but the full victory may be short-lived. By 1982, conservative elements were launching attacks in the People's Assembly to repeal the amendments.

Seen over time and cumulatively, the reforms in personal-status laws reflect a gradual shift in the gravity of family life from a preponderance of the legal weight in favor of the husband's position to an increasing consolidation of the woman's position as central in the family. If we take this shift to represent where the valued social arenas lie — ones considered worthy of sustaining the battle until a strong foothold is gained — then

Egyptian women's choice of family is in some ways comparable to American women's choice of public life as the place where consolidation of interests is worth the price. Each is central to the value systems of its culture.

In this chapter we have tried to show how new conditions arising out of historic trends make it difficult to carry out customary behaviors in the same way. When the old behavior does not produce a satisfactory result, people can modify it, scrambling in an effort to protect the deep structural, cultural value it represents. The rearrangements of contemporary behavior are thus underlaid by much the same sets of generating principles that shaped past responses. It is only the surface behaviors that assume a new form.

13

Conclusions

"Your wealth brings you respect — while your son brings you delight"
— Arab proverb

As a cultural relativist sees it, every society develops a unique set of shared understandings, modes of action it considers appropriate, and a specific world view. Seen together as a system, these parts mesh with reasonable internal consistency. By predigesting the way external events should be viewed, by excluding conflicting ways of reacting, each culture reserves for its members the potential to act directly, without the hesitation that unlimited choice would require. To begin to understand what motivates people's behavior, one needs to look not only at individual needs but the rationales and the desired ends the society sets for its members. People seek the social rewards that accompany accepted behavior. They feel guilty when they behave in a way that is socially unacceptable.

When new behaviors become necessary they carefully work them into the old rationales in order not to upset the basic tenets of the society. In this way each cultural system has its own logic, and the behavior of its members can only be understood in terms of the standards set by that culture. Similarly, while cultures can be compared, there is no single measure of efficacy or value that without bias qualitatively or quantitatively sums up the advantages of one cultural system over another. Each behavioral act is so inextricably bound to its context and to its indigenous rationale that to extract it from this context would distort its very meaning and purpose. This fact is often ignored when people of one culture look at another culture.

Westerners, for example, tend to view Egyptian culture from an out-

275

Public housing, provided for Bulaq residents as part of urban renewal, breaks down some of the formerly close-knit neighborhood groupings while at the same time affording generally more healthful surroundings in which to raise children.

sider perspective which has its own priorities and views. As all peoples, Westerners tend to regard their own social values as fundamental truths to be applied uncritically to societies everywhere. Fundamental "truth" for Americans is associated with such values as individualism, equal rights and opportunities and the chance to realize individual goals. Far less important in American social ideology are the "truths" many Egyptians value — corporateness, the complementarity of social roles, and the ethic of sacrifice to group goals. Each of these societies is built on fundamentally different premises, and each rejects, as secondary, those values that conflict with its own essential views.

The importance of culture-specific norms and the extent to which a culture can ignore paths extraneous to its central focus is revealed in a recent book by Gilligan (1982) on Western psychological theory and woman's development. There she points out how Western analysts have posited maturation stages in terms of gradual achievement of separation from others, justified by an ethic of individual rights and equal respect. Gilligan says that this development cycle that the West accepts as a norm is one based primarily on the ways males conceive of growth and maturity. In her studies she finds that women define mature growth differently, as learning to balance the claims of the other and the self in a responsible, compassionate way. The inability of women to achieve the separateness of the "male" perceived maturational track has often caused them, in the context of Western society, to be labelled "immature" and "incomplete" in their psychological development. They have difficulty reconciling their "natural" desires for relationships of intimacy and caring with the need for separation, defined by the Western analysts as maturity (Gilligan 1982: 164–65).

Westerners, in their singular focus on the individual and his/her rights, have come to overlook the paths of development that lead to other ends. If a theory conforms to patterns a society comes to value, there is little incentive to seek alternative models of development even when large segments of the population feel the conflict of alternative desires. Feelings are ignored in the face of what people would like to see happen.

Gilligan's alternative track to psychological development — the unremarked "woman's" track in Western society — is strikingly similar to the standard track in Egyptian society with its greater emphasis on responsibility to others and caring, especially within the social subunit of the family. Consider for the moment the implications for women's position in society and their sense of self-esteem when the dominant mode of accepted development is also the mode most naturally followed by women. Consider also the implications for women's status, however that term is defined, when a society places social group first and considers the arena of women's activities, the family, the primary unit of social value. Some of these implications are discussed below.

A Westerner looking superficially at Egyptian society may be disturbed by the Egyptian's sense of hierarchy, the separation of sex roles and a seeming submersion of the Egyptian personality by "unproductive" group ends. There is much illustrative material in the cases of this book that might give rise to such an uncritical observation. It would be a mistake, however, to assume that the social costs are calculated in the same way by Egyptians, or that, compared with alternative social costs, they are not bearable. Some abnormally extreme cases have been given in this book deliberately to show where the stresses and strains of Egyptian family life lie. Uneventful everyday life demonstrates one form of reality; abnormal events depict others. Sometimes, for example, the extreme cases show the penalties of rebuffing the system or show where people, when pressed, feel their obligations and allegiances lie. Such contingency reactions lie dormant in the subconscious of people until such times as they are activated by emergencies.

By the same token, an Egyptian might accuse American society of domination by those objectives our society has given highest value — separation and equality of position and role — values that do not rank particularly high on the Egyptian scale of values. As evidence, this Egyptian would note the emphasis on values of public performance, occupational achievement and self-realization. In addition the Egyptian might point out that the "masculine" (by Gilligan's analysis) values are so engrained in American society that even women distort their "natural inclinations" toward relationships of intimacy and caring in order to achieve esteem through the culturally approved channel of public individual achievement. The Egyptian would see in American society a lack of social connection, a de-emphasis on family life, and minimal time spent by both males and females in demonstrating the affection they feel for one another, and regard this as a heavy and possibly even unacceptable social cost.

In large measure individual satisfaction and the events that should lead to that state of mind are culturally defined. Independence is a valued end in Western society; it carries social penalties in Egypt. Self-realization is considered a basic need in the West; it may be considered selfishness in Egypt. The Westerner may not be willing to sacrifice much self-interest for closeness with another person; the Egyptian may give up his right to equality and independence for connection and feel the sacrifice worthwhile.

American and Egyptian cultures are not separate stages of a single development. They are, rather, separate cultural entities, headed along separate paths with fundamentally differing perspectives and organizing principles. Major among these differences is the attitude toward membership in a group — what we have termed here the "corporate" experience of the Egyptian and the "collective" experience of the American. With their fierce loyalties to group and the extensive obligations that membership entails, Egyptians reserve their best efforts for the intimate family gathering, seeing at various times other groups as foes or friends as they hinder or help the progress of their own group. Americans also function in groups of various kinds, but the "collective" American approach never fully merges individuals into the group. Because of the greater impersonality in the relations of individuals to the group, Americans can organize loosely on a broader scale, without the fear of the larger group allegiance interfering with more intimate groups. The intimate groups do not in any case absorb the individual's attentions fully.

What holds principles like the Egyptian "corporateness" in place over so long a period is a fundamental proof of success and, negatively, a lack of direct assault by devastatingly more successful ideologies. The climate in Egypt has been favorable for such a maintenance of family structures for the historical, economic, and political reasons we have outlined in the text. Foreign occupiers were more interested in modifying those aspects of social life that allowed them greater control over criminal, civil, and commercial jurisdictions, leaving the matter of family organization and controls largely to the private disposition of local communities. At the same time, after the throes of the Islamic invasion were over, indigenous family practices either overlapped with the rulers' preferences during the Ottoman period or served as a storehouse for what was authentically national and different from the customs of the foreigners in power during the British period. In both cases among the masses of the people the core principles of family as the Egyptians saw them remained intact. Now in contemporary Egypt with the advent of technological and communications revolutions the challenge of other-culture "imperialism" is stronger but still not necessarily devastating to indigenous perspectives.

Islam can be credited with contributing a strong share to the strengthening of family institutions through its detailed guidance on family organization and by the sheer weight of the impeachable legal and moral authority it lends to compliance with that guidance. The reluctance to modify Islamic law may lie not so much in a "backwardness" that reformers claim but in a realization that for general purposes the laws serve to stabilize a society that has many economic and political reasons for instability. For example, one could argue that giving women and men equal rights in personal-status law reduces their dependence upon one another, consequently reducing their very need for marriage and family life. With family so overpowering other institutions of social integration, a weakened family institution may appear to some to portend a reduction in general social control. One can, of course, argue the other side, that laws not in tune with social realities lead to conflict. In many ways, Islamic personal-status laws come closest to providing a written charter for what most people of the culture envision as the ideal way to carry out family life.

With the majority of Egyptians engaged in agriculture until recently, family practices had centuries of a relatively stable subsistence base to grind any rough edges into finely-tuned relation with the soil. In recent decades, and especially in urban areas, family practices and assumptions have faced new challenges. Overall, the general understandings appear to have sustained the onslaught well even while the scramble of supporting behaviors reacting to new realities sometimes have seemed contradictory and random. The purpose of this book has been to show that what we observe is usually not contradictory or random but rather manifestations of a coherent social system organized by deeper cultural rules that we can infer. These deeper rules can and still do provide a set of generating principles that mediate successfully between people and their eco-environments. And they still offer a uniquely Egyptian frame through which people can order their perceptions about their world.

Culture may not be set immutably in some formative period, as Geertz suggests, but it is also not so unstable that a society can be transformed in the space of a few decades. There is much that stays solid and stable in the way people of a culture perceive the world. If one wants to penetrate this essence—this uniqueness of a culture—one must look for the core deep structure principles that are basic to all its culturally determined behavior.

THE IMPLICATIONS OF CORPORATENESS

Corporateness is just one of the cultural premises that carry organizational weight in Egyptian life, and family as we observe it is only one manifestation of its organizational potential. Family, when defined in the dynamic sense, is itself a subset of generating principles that assign values and implications to the behaviors that facilitate or obstruct the realization of the greater good—the greater good in the limited corporate sense requiring that individuals realize themselves through immersion in the group. As a cultural premise, corporateness, and its subset of family principles, sets up a tension for Egyptians to shape their behaviors in a way that avoids direct conflict with its precepts. The closer behavior comes to its ideals the more society rewards the performance. This exercise does not necessarily preclude self-actualizing behavior. It is consistent, for example, for a person who subscribes to the corporate view to compete with or defer to other members of a household attempting to enhance their shares of the resources as long as that activity does not interfere in the long run with the solidarity of the family.

It is also appropriate to try to enhance the security of one's position within the group. We have seen these behaviors in young people competing for resources for marriage or education, and in women, bolstering their legal rights in marriage and divorce. The household is, after all, the source of greatest security. In the same way it is consistent for individuals to compete with others outside the group in the public domain for a larger share of economic and political power to enhance the status of their group.

Both activities recognize the primacy of group: in the first case, as the arena within which to realize one's needs and, in the second, as the institution to which one devotes one's utmost energies. It is in the way of conceptualizing the activity as enhancing group or one's ties to group that makes this world view different from a view like the collective one that stresses the need for an individual to realize an independent identity, separate from but perhaps helped along by the group. Egyptians see their happiness as resting in the realization of certain corporate activities: in marriage, in having children, in experiencing a satisfying family life, in exerting efforts to strengthen and coalesce their family ties. By the very act of believing that family, however it is defined, is the most significant institution of the society, it becomes so.

Corporateness has other social implications that can be discovered by reviewing some of the points made in earlier chapters. Though family is the central theme of this study, providing the classic example, corporateness is a cultural premise with broad social implications relevant in one way or another to the experience of any group with which people feel an identity, whether for temporary purposes or long-term association. The points below use the term "group" to indicate the diffuse applications of corporateness, except when specific examples of family are presented.

First, group—most often family—becomes the bottom line for most kinds of social and economic organization. There is little use in talking about how an isolated individual copes in his socioeconomic environment since so much depends on the back-up support he commands. Part of what makes families so cohesive is the relatively rigid complementarity of roles that in degree are financially supportive, nurturing, legalistic, and affective and which under normal circumstances may not be substituted one for another: a father cannot in theory be mother to a child or vice versa. Similarly people are arrayed within networks of rights owed and obligations due that are complete and balanced only when viewed across a full complex of kin. Because of age, sex, and kind of tie two people in kin relation rarely if ever see themselves in directly equivalent relationship to one another even though theoretically each and every person should have equivalently balanced sets of rights when viewed from the perspective of the whole. What may seem a contradiction, but is not, is the case where family hierarchies of age, sex, and relationship may at times be virtually suspended within the intimate family circle in the awareness that each individual person and each special role has a value to the whole that is equally indispensable. Considering all these factors it is not difficult to see why most individuals feel "whole" only when immersed in a complete complement of kin. Only then do they command all the rights due them and all the respect and appreciation due their position. The central institution of marriage brings into play many of these potentials of family as an organizing apparatus: demonstrating support, drawing lines of cleavage and cohesion, overtly marking roles and their implied obligations, and reorganizing priorital relationships.

Second, people feel a strong sense of who stands in a relation of outsider or insider, however they may momentarily define these categories. The zero-sum game, attributed to Egyptian social behavior, is based to a large extent on the sliding perception of who stands outside and who inside the group in any attempt to garner resources. Kin of varying degrees of distance can at different times fall in or outside the circle of alliance depending upon the activity at hand. In a dispute over inheritance, for example, divisions may occur between kin at the most elemental level. On a broader level, members of friendship circles or school buddies may go to great lengths to help secure good positions for each other because of the affective ties they have developed for one another.

There is a tension in Egyptian society between the need to cooperate to attain one's group's ends on the one side and on the other the need to consolidate gains at the expense of others. In an economy which up until now has shown limited growth, it is understandable why life seems overall a zero-sum game; when others get ahead, there are not so many opportunities left for one's own group.

The villain for the individual Egyptian is almost always perceived as an outside aggressor rather than the Egyptian himself, his failings, or the failings of someone of his committed inner circle. This allows projection of problems on outside others rather than on introspective self-doubts or vital group members. The greater good requires that these kinds of deceptions be sustained by everyone concerned lest the solidarity of group be threatened. To combat the outside threat people seek to consolidate groups which can either strengthen life's chances or spread life's burdens. Limited and versatile groupings like the family are effective tools under these circumstances.

Third, confidence between people is based on trust which in turn is more likely to occur where structural relationships of group exist. The stronger the overlay of ties, jural and affective, the more confidence a person invests in another person. The jural ties of kinship are strongest, even without affective ties, for there is a strong moral obligation for kin to come to the aid of other kin, even when there have been no effective relationships between them over a long period of time. The stranger with no structural ties is at best neutral and at worst hostile simply because he is an outsider. The most dangerous (or the most suspected of being dangerous) is the stranger who has intimate ties with the household but no structural ties of blood relationship to guarantee loyalty to a victim — the stranger sister-in-law, daughter-in-law, other wife, mother-in-law, step-mother. One way to avoid this condition is to bring relatives into these positions whenever possible.

Some people claim that because there is an increase in the number and intensity of non-kin relationships today that kinship ties are not as significant any more. A more likely argument is that in recent decades more of the necessities of life are concentrated in the hands of strangers, and as a result people are required to cultivate the friendships of non-kin to obtain what they desire. Cultivating friends to the point of intimacy where their help can be relied upon takes considerable time and effort. Kin, by contrast, can be relied upon by the very nature of their structural ties, requiring little preparation or persuasion to keep operational. The confidence people possess with regard to kin in other words allows them to exert effort in improving their life's chances elsewhere with strangers. Kin are not therefore unimportant in the contemporary world; their connection is simply more reliable.

Fourth, the measure of greater good tends to relate to group advantage or disadvantage. What is good for the group should also be good for the individual member and vice versa since it is assumed that the interests of both are overlapping. A member should modify plans for the future if asked to do so by the group. The good or bad behavior of the individual reflects on the group and is not isolated in the offender. It may cause serious sanctions to befall other members as for example when the family reputation is compromised and it becomes difficult for others to marry the candidates they would like. The effect is that moral compulsion is strengthened when the individual must think not only of the consequences of his actions to himself but also to his group members.

Fifth, a large share of social control rests internally in the hands of the group. There is a felt collective responsibility to protect the moral behavior of members and punish lapses in their behavior. We have observed this fact in the protective control exerted over young women and, in extreme cases of rural Egypt, the murder of young girls who have been thought to commit, or have had committed upon them, moral improprieties. Only by publicly wiping out the blot can the group be restored to its original purity. Since an immoral action that is publicly known has more negative repercussions than one not publicly known, the group may help the individual conceal an indiscretion. By doing so, the group avoids the necessity of imposing public sanctions. In conflicts of its members with outsiders not involving sexual breaches the integrity of group is maintained by supporting its members, right or wrong, and when possible, by avenging harms done to them.

Sixth, the group controls the significant sanctions of the society, both positive and negative: marriage, disapproval, and banishment. Without the support of group, individuals are impotent in Egyptian society and cannot expect to enjoy what are considered to be the good things of life. Without group support it is difficult for individuals to marry and lead a happy life with the full intercourse between generations that is considered essential. We have shown how institutionalized orphans have difficulty finding marriage partners, not only because of the social stigma generalized to them by the possibility of illegitimate sexual relations between their parents, but also because of the restricted life a person without relatives is thought to lead. In extreme cases of disapproval—for conversion to a different religion or marriage to a spouse the parents reject—families can refuse to see their children altogether for short-or-long-term periods. The full significance of these sanctions is only grasped if it is realized how much of the greater good is seen by Egyptians as resting in marriage and family life. Families retain strong control over these benefits for future generations.

Seventh, the safety nets of the society are provided by the primary group much more than by impersonal public or private institutions. A bride abused by her husband or an angry wife will often return to the parental home; kin networks or societies of close friends supply cash when it is needed; the elderly are cared for by their children, the orphaned are usually absorbed into the households of kin; women kin count on each other for solace in crisis and help with household tasks on a routine basis. The devil-possessed seek solace accompanied by their kin in group dances or religious ceremonies.

Eighth, individual initiative is rewarded primarily as it enhances the prospects of the status of group. Without great effort outside the group, one can be an appreciated group member by dutifully fulfilling obligations of roles and relationships within the group. This is clear in television serials where good and bad events befall the heroes and heroines and they are judged not so much by their effort to overcome events as by their intentions toward others and their unfailing fulfillment of their expected roles. With luck and a good character good again befalls the heroes and heroines in the end. This emphasis upon the quality of group relations tends to focus most people's attention and efforts toward domestic roles as opposed to public and professional roles. The latter tend in any case to be accessible to a large extent as a result of the ascribed nature of opportunity and resource levels. Even when by dint of strong initiative, a person moves from lower- to middle-class status and obtains a government job, his/her advancement thereafter depends upon specified step increases unrelated to individual initiative. Work for most of those in the middle and lower classes is engaged in primarily to support family goals and not to reach specifically personal goals.

Ninth, status and respect come primarily through group membership. Status and respect form two scales by which people are measured. The major difference is that the first is primarily ascribed in Egyptian society while the second can be achieved. A person can rank positively on either one of the scales without ranking positively on the other. For the most part status is ascribed through birth in a particular family. Only secondarily is status and its companion, respect, achieved by other means still related to family: for a woman, indirectly through her husband's status position, by bearing children, by successfully satisfying her role as mother and wife; for a man, by his capacity to provide the economic and political resources his family needs and by the kind of family he builds around him.

There are important implications to these sources of status and respect because they indicate the fields where crucial investments of time and energy are most highly rewarded and those where investment brings fewer rewards. For example, a woman of high ascribed social status is usually deferred to by a man of inferior social status. The same woman may defer to a man of equal status because of their sex differences. She overcomes her sex disadvantage when she occupies a higher socioeconomic status. While there is only limited possibility to affect status levels, in some areas of leeway women hold an advantage over men: They can try to raise their level by marrying a man of higher status. (A woman never wholly loses her original status of birth but usually out of respect for her husband she will be accorded a status — or respect — similar to his.) The Arab adage, "If you come from a bad family, marry into a good one," encourages this option. This is one of those adages that seems contradictory to other adages urging the marriage of equals. By viewing both from a deep-structure perspective, the consistency is revealed. One adage says in effect that one's own group will reflect the glory of a marriage up while another is directed at assuring the inner harmony of group. Both are by this perspective pro-group adages.

Similarly, while employability may help a woman marry more advantageously, depending on what class she comes from originally, employment does not necessarily enhance her status in itself or the respect of people toward her. Women's employment is too commonplace a practice among the middle classes, holding little intrinsic value of its own, and it is regarded as a matter of necessity to be avoided, if possible, among the lower classes. A woman is more likely to enhance the respect people feel for her by being a good mother and wife, just as the man gains his respect from being a good provider. This is not to say that she does not feel a greater sense of personal economic security or that she cannot conceptualize her role of worker as somehow enhancing her mother role and in that way gain satisfaction from employment. It says society rewards women in their roles as wives and mothers more than in their roles as workers.

It is for this reason that increases in figures of women's work force participation do not accurately predict a higher status for women in Egyptian society. Employment may be a measure of status in societies that see woman's emancipation predicated on her ability to compete equally with men in the work force but it is not necessarily a measure of status in societies which do not invest the same kind of value in employment.

The man gains respect and status from increasing his economic or political position, mainly, as was noted above, for what it means for the enhanced possibilities of his family and not so much for his achievements in themselves. Where women and men are able to improve the status and respect positions they occupy as individuals, it is largely a result of either their ability to enhance the status of the group itself or their ability to enhance their own position within that group.

The greatest hope for long-term enhancement of status similarly comes through a group process—the realization of children's potentials through the resources a family can bring to bear to make that possible.

Tenth, because family is a central institution in Egyptian society, family roles as opposed to public roles are the most valued social roles. People exert their main efforts toward achieving a good family life and feel most rewarded when they succeed. Mother and wife roles are valued more than successful public roles and therefore most women feel rewarded for fulfilling these roles well. This point is worth reiterating despite its similarity to points made above. When family is the core of a society, supported as central by the majority of Egyptians as well as the most all-embracing institutions of government in statements, policies, example, and actions, the measures of status and worth are different. It is not individual initiative that counts but how well the person meets the measure of responsibility that family membership implies.

Women have an advantage, when family is central to a society, that has been overlooked by those focusing on authority patterns. They are the central figures in the central institution of the society; they control the organization of the domestic domain and financial dispersals a good part if not all of the day, they are potent forces in the communication between households, they control those things that are most valued by the men— sex, honor, children, a happy well-organized household. They have the central directive of making a family more than the legalistic requirements of *wagib* relations by asserting their "natural" role in developing affective ties. At the same time they can sometimes be over-worked, physically abused, suffer from restricted rights and denied free movement in public spaces. This does not take away from the fact that they occupy valued, respected, and rewarded roles in society.

Men may retain the reins of power legally and theoretically in the household, but in reality, from the perspective of household action, their functions may be considered peripheral; they are out of the home much of the time to support the operations of family and reduced by role expectations to greater expression of jural as opposed to affective relations with other household members. Men, theoretically, possess a disproportionately larger share of authority, but if anything this authority may set them farther off from the centers where effective actions of family take place. Men in their households are much like members of a board of directors, ultimately responsible, but invested with a control that depends upon information the administrators selectively assemble for them to know. Women's arts of persuasion, indirect as they may be, may in the end prove more powerful. Legalistic or authority aspects of relations, while basic, are not in the end what people are seeking in the way of quality family relations.

Clearly families differ with regard to how they organize personnel and resources. However, if we give weight to the informal networks of organization that, because of personalized requirements of confidence, have added force in Egypt, it is not surprising to find Egyptian women frequently exerting a dominating influence in their households. In a sense they can afford to dominate when they are so sure of the boundaries of their spheres of influence. It is a domination that, while real, is nonetheless conscious of the cultural understanding that women's and men's roles are different and should not be confused. Women do not in any real way encroach upon men's perogatives and vice versa. In practical terms, this distinction is what makes for self-confidence in one's role as long as that social role itself is not questioned.[1] It makes also for an appreciation by both sexes of how much they depend on one another to meet the needs they cannot accomplish for themselves.

If one were to draw a tentative conclusion about the effect of contemporary life upon the urban family in Egypt, one would have to note the declining centrality of male-controlled spheres of activity in the household. Gone is the need for the head of household to organize women and children in the daily work group by exerting his authority over their activities a good part of the day. If the urban woman works outside the home she moves off to a work group controlled by another manager, or if she stays home she organizes her own activities. In both cases, she escapes the central control of her husband. Not usually living now with or near a host of other females (related to her affinally through her husband) who naturally assume a share of duties in the household, a city woman controls some leverage with her husband in seeking to set up the conjugal household near her parents' home where her relatives can help out if she goes to work or simply gets overwhelmed by household chores. It must be remembered that wife's relatives, according to theory, bring in help while husband's relatives demand help of the couple. Urban children now are much more likely to be brought up with the help of maternal rather than paternal relatives. Pragmatic residence choices, a greater value invested in women's exchanges, and the articulated desire of some in the lower classes to marry mother's sister's children are all evidence of this trend toward consolidation of female ties as a solution to the difficulties of urban living. Along with the declining control of men over their women's activities and the increasing household concern over how to solve the problem of nurturing children (the burdens of housework are increasing for even the stay-at-home lower-class women whose children must not be allowed to focus their attentions on school work instead of helping out at home) comes a deepening of the core of household around women. What serves to restrain a more blatant control by women is their anxiety about men's privileges in divorce and their knowledge that without marriage their status is diminished.

Women today hold the key to alleviating many urban household problems, whether they exercise this potential or not. To all intents and purposes, men's input into the family remains a fairly stable constant, while more and more women are asked to make the extra contribution that counts: in added income, in bringing in the exchange help of other women, in creating the kind of warm stable home people want. The new gains women have made in control of custody of children in divorce testifies to the recognition that if one parent must be chosen the mother is the overwhelming favorite to take over the parenting role. The public discussion now about whether women should work, or whether as a worker she should command a specially protected position, indicates the real dilemmas families face in attempting to realize the quality of life they want. The reinforcement of women's roles by the Islamic fundamentalist movement comes down hard in support of women's household functions but is not ready to exorcize their public roles as students and workers. The dilemma is that women are often needed in both kinds of roles simultaneously.

In general the shift in the gravity of family has in urban areas moved to a strengthening of woman's position in the family, and this, in essence, means a strengthening of woman's absolute power if one considers the family as the significant institution of the society. Writers have claimed that with urbanization and development, women's position has weakened as a result of their greater isolation from kin group, the more rigidly segregated roles of the sexes, and the sometimes reduced role they command in family production. We must be cognizant of the very significant — in some cases determining effect of economic factors in channelling behavior in a society, but we must not neglect the resiliency of culture to restructure behavior, where there is leeway, in molds that suit deeply cherished values. People, including women, have also the capacity to redress their positions if they feel them intolerable and aim toward securing for themselves a larger share of what the society defines as the greater good. In Egypt most women achieve these aims through consolidating their position in the family.

Family in Egypt is seen here as stable and constant when viewed as a set of behavior-generating principles. Its manifestations are viewed as fleeting and transient when observed as the superficial behavioral outcomes of the set of principles. As a set of principles, family provides a useful instrument with which Egyptians can manipulate life's chances and respond to the requirements of contemporary life. The Arabic definitions of family express this dynamic sense of function that includes closeness, economic support, residing together, interdependence and connectedness in the emotional as well as the legal sense. The changes in present-day Egypt have brought at least as many pressures to consolidate family as they have to relax family ties, though not always through the same channels or for the same reasons as in the past. Realizing basic social goals through identity with family remains a primary value in Egyptian society, one worth protecting and one that, perhaps as well as ever, still works effectively in the contemporary world.

"To forfeit one's family is to forfeit one's dignity" — Arab proverb

Notes

Chapter 1 — Influences

1. In a speech on October 2, 1980, President Sadat said: "I am proud to be the head of the society of the Egyptian family, which I have called for. I am proud to have this title over any other position, whether in the presidency, the leadership of the party, or anything else. My position as head of the Egyptian family takes precedence. . . . The source of my happiness is that we were able to establish the Egyptian family with its institutions, values, solidity, mobility, goodness, and the love that prevails in it."

2. Lami El-Moteei, in *Al-Akhbar*'s opinion page (translation from the *Egyptian Gazette,* January 30, 1981), relates the Egyptian traits of homogeneity, moderation, solidarity, and a spirit of compromise to the country's dependence on the Nile, its temperate and relatively stable climate, and its geographical location at the crossroads of three continents.

3. Muhammad Shaalan, "Egyptian Identity, Stability and Change," n.d., mimeographed.

4. The Coptic Church disputes this number, putting the numbers of Christians as high as 10 to 16 percent.

5. Wakin (1963) claims that the Arabic language became dominant in the tenth century, while Hanna (1963) feels the change did not come about until the seventeenth century.

6. Al-Nowaihi, in a 1979 article in the *Middle East Review,* disputes the use of sharia to mean Islamic law or family law. Technically Islamic law is *al-fiqh* (jurisprudence) which is only a part of sharia.

Chapter 3 — Family as Social Group

1. A *moulid* is a birthday anniversary celebration of a Sufi saint.

2. Springborg (1975) has a more detailed discussion about how friendship, academic, and kinship groups are manipulated by political élites in Egypt.

3. There is a logic to this when it is made clear that bureaucratic organization in Egypt is more efficiently dealt with through personal contact than impersonal routes. It should

be noted, however, that these kinds of influence are exerted most frequently in the higher positions of bureaucracy. The mainstream personnel structures are governed primarily by rules of longevity in the system and certificate achievement.

4. In fact one might say that the characteristics of impersonal treatment, equity, individual responsibility, etc., keywords of Western bureaucracy, have been absorbed in many cases by the more personalized attributes of family institutions. It is not surprising that when M. Berger (1957) measured Egyptian bureaucracies against some of these Western criteria he found them wanting.

5. See also S. Ibrahim (1978), who states: "Social scientists . . . have increasingly come to the realization that other societal institutions must provide a 'democratic infrastructure' for the political system if democracy is to succeed. The family, in particular, is cited as pivotal in this regard. Individuals socialized in an authoritarian type of family are not expected to enhance democratic practices in the political sphere of the society at large" (p. 59).

Chapter 5 — Roles

1. A child named "Muhammad Abbas Ahmed" is the son of Abbas and the grandson of Ahmed in the traditional system.

2. The difference in age between husband and wife, with men averaging a little more than ten years older than women in the Bulaq sample (Rugh 1978), contributes to the earlier mortality rate of husbands.

3. Strictly speaking, in the case of the boy child returning to his maternal grandmother, same-sex closeness is not involved. However, people tend to see this return as consistent, because the link is initiated by two females.

4. Translation in the *Egyptian Gazette,* January 30, 1981.

5. Translation from the *Egyptian Gazette,* June 8, 1981.

6. I am indebted to Safia Mohsen for some of these insights on American and Egyptian mother-daughter relations.

7. This is not a wholly reliable assumption since crimes of violence are much more typical of males than females. Female tensions tend to manifest themselves in more covert ways—in sickness, devil possession, superstitions, and "nervousness."

8. See Ramzia El-Gharib (1972) for more on the changes in family life in Egypt.

9. An attempt to obtain the full study failed, so it was impossible to determine any particulars on numbers involved or methods used. Still, the newspaper account was considered worth including to suggest the trend and the ideology that supports a new way of organizing family life.

Chapter 6 — Ties

1. One parent describing her sources of income said: "I would rather eat bread and tomatoes [cheap items] from the little money my son gives me than ask my married daughters for anything."

2. One could argue that there are generalized jural obligations to show kindness to parents and to help anyone who needs help. As a result, these acts are technically obliga-

tions. However, most people would agree that neither was strictly required of the individual and, therefore, both the acts can be considered favors.

Chapter 8 — Marriage: Practice

1. Um Fuad lives the life style of the lower social classes, but through her persistence, two sons have completed fairly extended periods of education (intermediate school in the case of the clerk and university in the case of her engineer son working in Libya). The two educated sons have thus broken into the middle class.

2. Translation from the *Egyptian Gazette,* December 12, 1978.

3. It may not be the happiest solution, however. In an article entitled "Five arrested for kidnap, rape" (*Egyptian Gazette*, March 28, 1980), a young girl explained how she ran away from her family in Alexandria when they tried to force her to marry a relative she disliked. She was attacked in the Cairo suburb of Maadi while seeking the protection of one of her aunts.

4. I was surprised at the number of university graduates who insisted upon the accuracy of this view of genetics. Another stated that if you want to determine the father of the child you only have to take blood from both father and child and they will match.

5. Both husband's and wife's responses were recorded because the two may be related to each other in different ways. If, as sometimes happens, they are related four different ways as a couple, we have taken the terms of reference they use themselves to claim the relationship. These couples are the heads of households and generally not those who are very recently contracting marriage.

6. The numbers involved are so small that they suggest the truth of the generalization rather than confirming it in any final way.

7. Again each marriage partner is counted as one in order to express the fact that two preferences are involved.

8. Economic cooperation is still an important function of family in the city, but it is manifest in other ways (see Chapter 12).

9. This reduces, of course, some of the advantage of brother's children marriage when children grow up in different households. Then, marriage to each other requires somewhat greater rearrangements in their lives.

Chapter 10 — Disruption

1. The *Egyptian Gazette,* March 27, 1980, reports a case where schizophrenia was not considered grounds for divorce. A second appeal by the wife on the grounds of her husband's impotence and their unconsummated marriage was also refused when the court ruled that three months was too short a time to consider the husband's health hopeless.

2. Reported in the *Egyptian Gazette,* May 2, 1980.

3. They cite as evidence a twenty-five year low in marriages in 1967, the year of the Arab-Israeli War, to 225,000 marriages (or 7.3 percent of the population) and a drop in divorces to 57,000 (or 1.8 percent of the population). They point out a similar low (9.9 percent

of 383,000) in 1977 and attribute this last decrease to the high cost of marriage and divorce in recent years.

4. The study was published in 1975 by the National Center for Social and Criminological Research with Dr. Adel Azer as principal investigator.

Chapter 11 — Religion

1. Writing about Lebanon, Khuri (1975) sees the tensions in family life of Christians and Muslims arising in the opposite direction — among Christians between husband and wife and, among Muslims, between parent and child. My perception is that the tensions Khuri mentions are secondary ones. If a Christian marriage is not going well it is true there can be serious strains, particularly because the alternative of divorce does not exist. But in the happily married household the primary concern of parents is to keep children protected and within the Christian fold. With Muslims, the tensions that exist between parent and child do so secondarily as a result of the tensions that arise in the marital relation. Each parent tries to line up the support of the children.

2. Observers are usually keen to analyze whether the possessed person is deceitfully using possession to gain a desired end or whether it is a genuine affliction. This is perhaps the difference between a conscious and unconscious use of possession.

3. See Safran (1958) for more details of the debate over the new laws. From public statements it appears that not all Christians were opposed to the legislation and not all Muslims in favor.

4. *Changing the Law on Personal Status in Egypt within a Liberal Interpretation of the Shari'a* later appeared in the Summer 1979 issue of the *Middle East Review*.

5. Springborg (1981) sees this public support as the *quid pro quo* exacted by Sadat from the religious establishment for his active support of their interests.

6. Fadwa el-Guindi, who nas been interviewing women university students involved in the Islamic movement, feels that members are not distinguished by particular class affiliation. While it is true that members may be found from all classes, I would tend to agree with those like S. Ibrahim (1980) who argue that the circumstances of lower-middle and middle-class families are more likely to propel members into the movement.

7. Several women have told me that dress of the fundamentalist style is specifically required by the Koran, but when I asked for the authoritative passages they only came up with the ambiguously worded phrases that are familiar. Some added their own interpretations that were much more concrete. The most commonly quoted Koranic verses regarding dress are Sura 24: 31: "And say to the believing women that they should lower their gaze and guard their modesty; that they should not display their beauty and ornaments except what must ordinarily appear thereof; that they should draw their veils over their bosoms and not display their beauty except to" (then follows a list of persons whom they are forbidden to marry), and Sura 33: 59: "O Prophet, Tell thy wives and daughters and the believing women that they should cast their outer garments over their persons [when abroad]; that is most convenient that they should be known [as such] and not molested and God is Oft-Forgiving Most Merciful."

8. One fundamentalist critic of the personal-status reforms, Sheikh Kishk, in an interview used precisely this phrase to express his objections to giving women the right to employment.

Chapter 12 — New Conditions

1. CAPMAS reports that for the first time (the previous census was 1966) the 1976 census picked up a considerable percentage (3.7 percent) of Egyptian citizens abroad.

2. People's Assembly member, Ali Hilali, for example, noted that construction workers' wages rose by 400 percent between 1971 and 1976 and by 600 percent in one year alone, between 1978 and 1979.

3. *Rapid Contract AID, The Effects of Population Factors on Social and Economic Development,* n.d.

4. Dr. Kawsar Mustafa at a symposium of Egyptian economists reported in May of 1979 that 11.8 percent of families spent less than £E 150 a year (£E = $1.40); 55 percent spent between £E 400 and £E 1000; 2.3 percent between £E 1000 and £E 2000 and 0.4 percent more than £E 2000.

5. Nadim (1977), studying an area in the Darb il Ahmar section of Cairo, reported that 38 out of 117 inhabitants have no other relatives living in the area while the remainder have from one to twelve relatives living there. Rugh (1978) found that out of 174 lower-class households, thirty-one already had relatives other than a spouse and children living in the same building but not in the same household, ten had no relatives near besides spouse and/ or unmarried children; only one lived alone with no relatives near at all. The remaining families reported relatives somewhere in Cairo but not immediately close at hand.

6. In Rugh 1978, of 175 lower-class households studied, twenty-five different household patterns were present including the most common husband, wife and children pattern to an assortment of in-law arrangements, sibling arrangements, and nuclear families with an additional live-in kin member.

7. Abu-Lughod (1969) comments that men are more likely to acculturate to modern urban life than women who tend to remain localized within their urban communities "recreating the physical and social accoutrements of village life" (p. 172). Again this effect may be reduced by the experience of television viewing.

8. Clatanoff (1979). Indirectly, however, the point level of the secondary finishing exam determines the university faculties a student is eligible to enter and therefore strongly encourages him or her to select a field with the highest grade/status appeal.

9. One sample of 617 children living at home in Bulaq (see Rugh (1981b) showed that out of those six years of age and older (437), 172 attended elementary school and 38 attended intermediate school. Another 107 children never went to school and of these, 64 percent were girls. In elementary school the sex ratio was 52 percent boys to 48 percent girls, while in intermediate school the ratio reversed with the girls sustaining a higher ratio (53 percent) to boys (43 percent). The general enrollment figures for another lower-class educational district, South Cairo, shows a similar higher ratio for girls (56 percent) at the intermediate level (AID Report, *Survey on Basic Education in Egypt,* 1979).

10. Rugh (1981b) shows the relationship of the participation rates of school age children (six to fifteen years) to the economic level of the family. Poor families had a participation rate of 61 percent; self-sufficient ones had a rate of 76 percent, and those of a good economic level had a rate of 42 percent.

11. Youssef (1971) points out that in 1960 women occupied 16 percent of the positions in the service industries, 2 percent in factory work, 5.5 percent of the positions in trade and sales and 4.5 percent in the nonprofessional white collar positions. She compares these low figures with the fact that one out of four professional positions were occupied by women, mainly in teaching and nursing.

12. The economic activity rates for the over-all work force are: 37 percent in 1937, 26 percent in 1970, 27 percent in 1972, and 31.5 percent in 1976. Population Census 1937, 1970, 1972, and 1976 and Labor Force Sample Surveys, CAPMAS, from Arab Republic of Egypt, *Economic Management in a Period of Transition* VI May 8, 1978, *Statistical Annex,* World Bank, p. 5.

13. Women's economic activity rates were 7.9 percent for 1937, 3.5 percent for 1970 and 9.2 percent for 1976. Men's rates were 65.1, 49.5 and 52.9 percent respectively, Population Census, *ibid.*

14. Though it is perhaps more common for an educated man to marry an educated woman, there are some who feel that a woman of lesser education is more tractable, less independent, and more willing to focus her energies on serving her husband's needs. Zeinab's characterization in the early part of the drama reflects this perception.

15. The redefinition of mother roles was first brought to my attention by B. Ibrahim in her research on Egyptian women industrial workers. She also makes the important analytical distinction between identity and roles.

Chapter 13 — Conclusions

1. Very few ever publicly question the role of women as it stands in Egyptian society. In fact most public discussion centers around how to better preserve the primacy of women's roles as mothers and wives. The most outstanding exception is Dr. Nawal El-Saadawi whose writings urge a sexual revolution that would free men and women from their gender-determined roles.

Bibliography

Abu-Lughod, J. 1961. "Migrant Adjustment to City Life: The Egyptian Case." *American Journal of Sociology* 67 (July):22–32.

──────. 1969. "Varieties of Urban Experience: Contrast, Coexistence and Coalescence in Cairo." In *Middle Eastern Cities,* ed. Lapidus. Berkeley and Los Angeles: University of California Press.

Abu-Lughod, J., and L. Amin. 1961. "Egyptian Marriage Advertisements: Microcosm of a Changing Society." *Marriage and Family Living* (May 1961):127–36.

Abu Zahra, M. n.d. "Family Planning and Birth Control." Paper presented at the Second Conference of the Al-Azhar Academy of Islamic Research.

──────. 1955. "Family Law." In *Law in the Middle East,* ed. Khadduri and Liebesny: 132–78. Washington: Middle East Institute.

Ali, A. Yusef. 1968. *The Holy Quran: Text, Translation and Commentary.* Beirut: Dar el Arabia.

Anderson, J. N. D. 1968. "Law Reform in Egypt 1850–1950." In *Political and Social Change in Modern Egypt,* ed. P. M. Holt: 209–30. London: Oxford University Press.

──────. 1971. "The Role of Personal Statutes in Social Development in Islamic Countries." *Comparative Studies in Society and History* 13, no. 1:16–31.

──────. 1976. *Law Reform in the Muslim World.* London: Athlone Press, University of London.

Atiya, N. 1982. *Khul-Khaal: Five Egyptian Women Tell Their Stories.* Syracuse: Syracuse University Press.

Azer, A. 1979. "Law as an Instrument for Social Change: An Illustration from Population Policy." In *Law and Social Change in Contemporary Egypt,"* ed. Nelson and Koch. Cairo Papers in Social Science, vol. 2, monograph 4. Cairo: American University in Cairo Press.

El-Bayoumi, S. 1976. "Sex Role Differentiation and Illness Behavior in an Egyptian Nile Delta Community." Paper presented at the MESA meeting.

Berger, M. 1957. *Bureaucracy and Society in Modern Egypt: A Study of the Higher Civil Service.* Princeton: Princeton University Press.

Boctor, W. G. 1981. "The River of Time: Time and Human Relationships in Egyptian Business." Lecture delivered at the University of Southern California Business Seminar on Egypt, April 10.

Chomsky, N. 1965. *Aspects of the Theory of Syntax.* Cambridge, Mass.: MIT Press.

Clatanoff, W. B. 1979. "Manpower Projection for Planning Education and Training," U.S. AID Report.

Duvignaud, J. 1970. *Change at Shebika: Report from a North African Village.* New York: Pantheon.

Eilts, H. F. 1980. "Egypt—Some Economic Issues of the Eighties." *Leviathan* 3, no. 1.

Fakhouri, H. 1972. *Kafr el Elow: An Egyptian Village in Transition.* New York: Holt, Rinehart and Winston.

Fernea, R. 1973. *Nubians in Egypt.* Austin: University of Texas Press.

Fox, G. L. 1977. "'Nice Girl': Social Control of Women Through a Value Construct." *Signs* 2, no. 4:805-17.

Geertz, C. 1968. *Islam Observed.* Chicago: University of Chicago Press.

El-Gharib, R. 1972. "The Family in Egypt, Analytical and Psychological Study." in *Education and Modernization in Egypt,* ed. Kotb. Cairo: Ain Shams University.

Gilligan, C. 1982. *In a Different Voice: Psychological Theory and Women's Development.* Cambridge, Mass.: Harvard University Press.

Hall, E. T. 1959. *The Silent Language.* New York: Fawcett World Library.

Hanna, S. 1963. *Who are the Copts?* 3rd ed. Cairo: Costa Tsouma.

Hill, E. 1979. *Mahkama! Studies in the Egyptian Legal System, Courts and Crimes, Law and Society.* London: Ithaca Press.

Hussein, A. 1953. "The Role of Women in Social Reform in Egypt." *Middle East Journal* 7, no. 4 (Autumn):440-50.

Ibrahim, B. 1980. "Social Change and the Industrial Experience: Women as Production Workers in Urban Egypt." Department of Sociology, Indiana University.

Ibrahim, S. 1978. "The Socio-Economic Requisites of Democracy." In *Democracy in Egypt,* ed. Dessouki. Cairo Papers in Social Science, vol. 1, monograph 2. Cairo: American University in Cairo Press.

———. 1980. "Anatomy of Egypt's Militant Islamic Groups—Methodological Note and Preliminary Findings." MESA Conference paper, Washington, November 6-9.

Itzkowitz, N. 1972. *Ottoman Empire and Islamic Tradition.* Chicago: University of Chicago Press.

Khattab, H., and S. El-Daeif. 1982. "Impact of Male Labor Migration on the Structure of the Family and the Roles of Women." The Population Council: West Asia and North Africa.

Khuri, F. 1975. *From Village to Suburb: Order and Change in Greater Beirut.* Chicago: University of Chicago Press.

Lane, E. W. 1954 (orig. 1860). *Manners and Customs of the Modern Egyptians.* London: Dent and Sons.

El-Messiri, S. 1978. "Self-Images of Traditional Urban Women in Cairo." In *Women in the Muslim World,* ed. Beck and Keddie. Cambridge, Mass.: Harvard University Press.

Nadim, N. 1977. "Family Relationships in a Harah in Cairo." In *Arab Society in Transition,* ed. Ibrahim and Hopkins, 107–20. Cairo: American University in Cairo Press.

Al-Nowaihi, M. 1979. "Changing the Law on Personal Status in Egypt within a Liberal Interpretation of the Shari'a." *Middle East Review,* Summer.

Nyrop, R. F. 1976. *Area Handbook for Egypt.* Washington, D.C.: American University, Foreign Area Studies.

Pergrouhi, N. 1959. "Adjustment in the Family and Patterns of Family Living." *Journal of Social Issues* 15, no. 3:37–8.

Rapid Contract AID. n.d. *The Effects of Population Factors on Social and Economic Development.*

Rugh, A. 1978. "Religious Community and Social Control in a Low Income Area of Cairo." Ph.D. diss. Washington, D.C., American University.

———. 1979. *Coping with Poverty in a Cairo Community.* Cairo Papers in Social Science, Monograph 1. Cairo: American University in Cairo Press.

———. 1981a."Conceptual Considerations in Development Programs for Women: Women and Work in Bulaq." *Proceedings of the Middle East Institute of Ain Shams University on Rural Women and Development.* Cairo.

———. 1981b. "Participation and Relevance in Basic Education: Lower Class Parents' Strategies in Educating Their Children." Helwan University Conference on Basic Education.

———. 1982. "Orphanages and Homes for the Aged: Contradiction or Affirmation in a Family-Based Society." *International Journal of the Sociology of the Family* 11, no. 2 (July–December).

El-Saadawi, N. 1980. *The Hidden Face of Eve: Women in the Arab World.* London: Zed Press.

Safran, N. 1958. "The Abolition of the Shari'a Courts in Egypt." *The Muslim World* 48 (January and April).

Said, A. A. 1979. "Precept and Practice of Human Rights in Islam." *Universal Human Rights* 1, no. 1 (January–March):64–79.

Sharkawi, A. R. 1962 (orig. 1954). *Egyptian Earth.* London: Heinemann.

Springborg, R. 1975. "Patterns of Association in the Egyptian Political Elite." In *Political Elites in the Middle East,* ed. Lenczowski, 83–108. Washington: American Institute for Public Policy Research.

———. 1981. "The Politics of Resurgent Islam in Egypt, Syria and Iraq." *The Politics of Islamic Reassertion,* ed. Ayoob. London: Croom, Helm.

Stino, L. 1976. "The Working Wife: Attitudes, Perceptions, Role Expectations of Five Male Cairenes." American University in Cairo, Master's thesis no. 329.

Wakin, E. 1963. *A Lonely Minority.* New York: William Morrow.

Wikan, U. 1980. *Life Among the Poor in Cairo.* London: Tavistock.

World Bank. 1978. "Economic Management in a Period of Transition VI May," *Statistical Annex,* Arab Republic of Egypt.

Youssef, N. 1971. "Social Structure and the Female Labor Force: The Case of Women Workers in Muslim Middle Eastern Countries," *Demography 8,* no. 4:427–39.

————. 1972. "Differential Labor Force Participation of Women in Latin America and Middle Eastern Countries: The Influence of Family Characteristics." *Social Forces* 51:135–53.

————. 1976–77. "Education and Female Modernism in the Muslim World." *Journal of International Affairs* 30, no. 2.

Zaalouk, M. 1975. "The Social Structure of Divorce Adjudication in Egypt." American University in Cairo, Master's thesis no. 303.

Index